ALIAS O. HENRY

THE MACMILLAN COMPANY
NEW YORK · CHICAGO
DALLAS · ATLANTA · SAN FRANCISCO
LONDON · MANILA

BRETT-MACMILLAN LTD.
TORONTO

ALIAS
O. HENRY

A Biography of William Sidney Porter

by

GERALD LANGFORD

New York
THE MACMILLAN COMPANY
1957

Library of Congress catalog card number: 57-8270

ACKNOWLEDGMENT

For permission to quote from publications under copyright, thanks are due to the following:

Doubleday & Company, Inc., for quotations from stories and letters in *The Complete Works of O. Henry* (copyright 1899, 1901, 1902, 1903, 1904, 1905, 1906, 1907, 1908, 1909, 1910, 1911, 1953, by Doubleday & Company, Inc.); for quotations from *O. Henry Biography*, by C. Alphonso Smith (copyright 1916 by Doubleday, Page & Company); for quotations from *Letters to Lithopolis*, by Mabel Wagnalls (copyright 1922 by Doubleday, Page & Company); for quotations from *O. Henry Encore*, by Mary Sunlocks Harrell (copyright 1939 by Mary Sunlocks Harrell);

Harper & Brothers for quotations from *Postscripts*, by Florence Stratton (copyright 1923 by Harper & Brothers), and for a quotation from *Expression in America*, by Ludwig Lewisohn (copyright 1932 by Harper & Brothers);

E. P. Dutton & Co., Inc., for quotations from *The Quiet Lodger of Irving Place*, by William Wash Williams (copyright 1936 by E. P. Dutton & Co., Inc.); also E. P. Dutton & Co., Inc., and J. M. Dent & Sons Ltd., for a quotation from *The Confident Years*, by Van Wyck Brooks (copyright 1952 by Van Wyck Brooks);

Appleton-Century-Crofts, Inc., for a quotation from *Understanding Fiction*, by Cleanth Brooks, Jr., and Robert Penn Warren (copyright 1943 by F. S. Crofts & Co., Inc.), and for a quotation from *American Fiction*, by Arthur Hobson Quinn (copyright 1936 by Appleton-Century-Crofts, Inc.); also for permission to reproduce a photograph of Sara Coleman Porter from *The Caliph of Bagdad*, by Robert H. Davis and Arthur B. Maurice (copyright 1931 by D. Appleton and Company);

Alfred A. Knopf, Inc., for a quotation from *Prejudices: Second Series*, by H. L. Mencken (copyright 1920 by Alfred A. Knopf, Inc.);

Duke University Press for quotations from a group of O. Henry letters published in the *South Atlantic Quarterly*, January, 1939;

v

ACKNOWLEDGMENT

University of Pennsylvania Press for quotations from *O. Henry: The Man and His Work*, by E. Hudson Long (copyright 1949 by University of Pennsylvania Press);

Mrs. Frances G. Maltby for quotations from her book *The Dimity Sweetheart* (copyright 1930 by The Dietz Press).

TO BUBBA AND NANCY

CONTENTS

ILLUSTRATIONS

FOREWORD

It is not easy, even today, to be dispassionate about a personality as appealing as that of the elusive man known as O. Henry: "a likable, extremely modest man," as Art Young once commented, "with a natural courtesy and a beautiful wit." [1] Those who knew him and who have written about him in the past have found it difficult to intrude, even retrospectively, upon the privacy of a man who held his closest friends at a certain distance and who had one of his characters (a struggling young writer) remark: "I see the game now. You can't write with ink, and you can't write with your own heart's blood, but you can write with the heart's blood of someone else. You have to be a cad before you can be an artist." [2] Specifically, of course, O. Henry was a man with a secret—a prison record. But there was more than that behind the mask he wore, a mask which only once, toward the end of his life, did he remove even partially.

With so little known about him, an O. Henry legend grew up even before his death, and this legend has never in the past been examined critically. Thus, although half a dozen books and hundreds of magazine articles have been written about the man and his work, the information which can be assembled from all these publications is disappointingly incomplete. In particular there has been no realistic treatment of either of O. Henry's two marriages, nor any adequate examination of the evidence in the embezzlement trial. Of the wealth of biographical material which C. Alphonso Smith assembled for his authorized biography in 1916, a very considerable portion was not used by Smith himself and has not been used by any subsequent writer, although the entire collection has for many years been available in the public library of Greensboro, North Carolina. There are various other unpublished materials too, some of which have been used inadequately, some not at all. From these materials emerges a personality no less appealing but considerably more complex than the one shown in the official portrait painted by Smith and successively touched up by others during the past forty years.

Told even in broad outlines, as it has been, O. Henry's life has seemed colorful enough to justify his own remark when he was asked why he did not read more fiction than he did in later life. "It is all tame as compared with the romance of my own life," Smith quotes him as replying.[3] From a human-interest standpoint, no justification is required for telling the man's life in sufficient detail at last. But, some mid-century readers may inquire fastidiously, is the life of O. Henry really worth examining as literary biography? Surely O. Henry's vogue is long past, such readers will insist, and a reconsideration is hardly warranted for what they will call his dated and ephemeral work, addressed as he himself said it was "to the man who sits smoking with his Sabbath-slippered feet on another chair, and to the woman who snatches the paper for a moment while boiling greens or a narcotized baby leaves her free. With these I love to sit upon the ground and tell sad stories of the death of kings." [4]

The fact that such an attitude is to be expected from certain quarters is one main reason for the present undertaking. Not, of course, that there is any real danger of O. Henry's being forgotten. Whether some of us like it or not, the fact which ought to be clear by now, half a century after his death, is that O. Henry is here to stay. He has survived two decades of ludicrous overpraise and three decades more of deprecation and neglect in critical circles. People still read O. Henry, and there is good reason why they should continue to do so. It is true that there is hardly a single one of his stories which is not to some degree marred by sentimentality or farfetched coincidence or triviality of conception. Yet in spite of all the charges which can so easily be adduced against his work, what we have to do with in O. Henry is a kind of minor classic. One hastens to emphasize the word *minor*, and to qualify the pronouncement in other ways. O. Henry, one inevitably feels, is a rather disreputable figure in the company to which such a classification admits him. Nevertheless, the time has surely come to cease blaming him for the sins of his formula-bound imitators. The time has come to grant him the niche to which he is entitled among the permanent figures in American literature. In the words of Carl Van Doren, "no writer in the language seems clever immediately after one has been reading O. Henry." [5] And as one of his severest early critics conceded about his stories: "Nowhere else is there anything else just like them. In his best work . . . he is unique." [6]

In the decade following his death no other writer's stories, except Kipling's, sold more widely and were more highly esteemed than O. Henry's. By 1920 close to five million volumes of his stories had been sold in the United States,[7] with an indeterminate additional number in England, where a set of complete works had been brought out in 1916. The authorized biography in 1916, written by the well known scholar and critic C. Alphonso Smith, was based on the conviction that "O. Henry's work remains the most solid fact to be reckoned with in the history of twentieth-century American literature." [8] As even the dissenting critic F. L. Pattee observed in the following year, O. Henry was the leading literary success of the generation, and in fact was "already crowned, it would seem, as an American classic. . . . He has been given a place beside the masters. . . . Success like his means imitators, a literary school, a standard of measurement." [9]

Nor was his vogue confined to the United States. By 1923 translations had been made into French, Spanish, German, Swedish, Dano-Norwegian, and Japanese.[10] Hugh Walpole, in a discussion of recent American writing in the London *Daily Mail* in 1922, contended that American literature—dependent on England up through the work of Mark Twain and Henry James—had truly come of age with O. Henry, who "is the father of this new American literature." [11] By 1927 Russian readers were, according to one investigator, "so earnestly enraptured with him that . . . they try to attach a new 'O. Henrian' philosophy to his works and build a literary school around him. . . . [Beginning writers] are enjoined to follow the methods and optimistic theories of 'the greatest American writer'—just as young Americans of today are advised to follow Chekhov." [12]

Incidentally, O. Henry's popularity in Russia has persisted, despite the abandonment of the attempt to read social protest into his work. In 1945 Alexander Ainkst wrote that "a sense of humor and irony can only be found in a strong and vigorous people who are sure of themselves and know that the future belongs to them," an attitude which helps make comprehensible another of Ainkst's statements, this time not a matter of opinion but of fact: "There have been 1,403,500 copies of his works and 94 editions published in the past twenty-five years alone."[13] According to an article in the *Russian Review* in 1953, O. Henry's stories continue to be republished in Russia. "One may speculate on the motivation of the Communist Party in continuing to sanction his publication. But it is clear that, despite years of constant indoctrination, Russian readers still like to seek release in a good yarn."[14]

A graphic idea of the aliveness of O. Henry in other foreign parts is furnished by a few statistics. The stories have, of course, been industriously pirated all over the world, but even the list of authorized foreign reprintings in the last two decades is impressive. Asian rights (for such languages as Amharic, Marathi, and Thai) were granted in 1954; British rights in 1940, 1945, and 1948; Burmese rights in 1954 and 1955; French rights in 1955; German rights in 1950, 1952, and 1954; Hebrew rights in 1953; Italian rights in 1945; Japanese rights in 1952; Norwegian rights in 1946; Persian rights in 1945; Serbo-Croatian rights in 1944; Spanish rights in 1945 (Peru), 1954 (Mexico), and 1954 (Spain); Ukrainian rights in 1952. Individual stories have been authorized for school textbook publication in England and Germany (in 1940 and 1930 respectively), and French book-club rights were granted in 1955.[15]

In the United States, however, the tide had clearly turned by 1920, when H. L. Mencken spoke out about "such cheesemongers as [Richard Harding] Davis, with his servant-girl romanticism, and O. Henry, with his smoke-room and variety-show smartness. . . . In the whole canon of O. Henry's work you will not find a single recognizable human character; his people are unanimously marionettes; he makes Mexican brigands, Texas cowmen and New York cracksmen talk the same highly ornate Broadwayese."[16] Since the early 1930's O. Henry has been conspicuous for his neglect in critical circles. In 1931, on the appearance of the adulatory memoir *The Caliph of Bagdad*, by Robert H. Davis in collaboration with Arthur B. Maurice, a review by John Chamberlain contained the statement: "Clearly he [O. Henry] must be reckoned a milestone in the history of American taste, but he will hardly last as anything more than an entertainer, and when his slang, his running contemporaneity, are merely part of the archives, it is questionable that many of his stories will even provide a good laugh." [17] In the following year Ludwig Lewisohn found a bit more to be said for O. Henry, whom he bracketed with Bierce, Crane, London, Norris, and David Graham Phillips: writers whose work, though full of shortcomings and even puerilities, had about it "a light of energy, of creative honesty, of freshness of at least intention, that was new and has not wholly faded yet." O. Henry's importance, according to Lewisohn, lies in his subject matter. Instead of writing about battlefields or economic forces or wolves in the frozen north, O. Henry "scrutinized the actual scene of life in its common manifestations, and so he penetrated to the permanently significant." Abominable as his influence has been—in the direction of cheap smartness and ingenuity rather than true creativeness—nevertheless "he saw and for the first time he rendered New York. . . . A perished, amusing moment is somehow captured and held fast." [18]

In 1936 Arthur Hobson Quinn also tried to take a balanced view. "It is amazing," he wrote, "when we reread his volumes now, to think how seriously he was taken at the time of his death." He granted, however, that O. Henry at times rises above his general level by virtue of "his deep sympathy for the underdog, for youth striving for a taste of joy before the humdrum of existence settles down, for the loyalty of true love, illumined by sacrifice." Of the 250 stories, Quinn found about a dozen that seemed to him "first-rate," and another dozen that were "creditable"; the rest he placed on the level of the Sunday supplement.[19]

During the 1940's and 1950's critics have all but ignored O. Henry. In the first of the two decades appeared a doctoral dissertation in the form of a brief biographical study,[20] a learned article on the embezzlement trial,[21] a mere paragraph of dismissal in the imposing scholarly work *A Literary History of the United States,* written by a panel of leading specialists in the field, and finally a derogatory analysis of the story "The Furnished Room" in a critical anthology, *Understanding Fiction,* edited by Cleanth Brooks and Robert Penn Warren. It is possible, Brooks and Warren concede, to make use of a surprise ending in a good story, but only if the surprise develops logically and meaningfully out of the preceding action. In "The Furnished Room," they feel, O. Henry has simply withheld a piece of information (the fact of the girl's suicide) in an attempt to make the fact seem meaningful when he surprises us with it at the end of the story. The only meaning which the story actually has is the threadbare and sentimental proposition that the bonds of true love are not to be broken even by the sordidness and brutality of the big city. By way of contrast, Maupassant's "The Necklace" contains a surprise ending which throws a sudden clear light on the character of the heroine: the false jewels become symbolic, not merely ironic. In short:

Readers who feel that the end of this story ["The Furnished Room"] is a shabby trick will be able to point out other symptoms of cheapness; the general thinness of characterization, the cluttered and sometimes mawkish description, the wheedling tone taken by the author, and the obvious play for emotional sympathy in such writing as the following: "Oh, God! whence that odor, and since when have odors had a voice to call?" In other words, we can readily surmise that the trickery involved in the surprise ending may be an attempt to compensate for defects within the body of the story itself.[22]

This is penetrating criticism, which surely is valid as far as it goes. But it seems no more the final word on O. Henry than was the overpraise of Stephen Leacock, for example, to whom the same story showed O. Henry "at his best as a master of that supreme pathos that springs, with but little adventitious aid of time or circumstance, from the fundamental things of life itself." [23] If the one critic was unable to see the stunted trees for the forest, surely the other two critics are unable to see the undeniable forest for the trees. When O. Henry is judged by his artistic accomplishment in separately considered stories, his work seems of precious little consequence. In fairness, his work must be judged in larger units than the individual story unit. Except in a purely historical context, O. Henry is not memorable as a writer of short stories. On the contrary, he is a memorable writer in spite of having produced only stories which individually are disappointing.

This truth about O. Henry is suggested in the only significant discussion written as yet in the present decade: a brief chapter in Van Wyck Brooks's *The Confident Years*. The Texas stories, Brooks observes, inevitably suggest Bret Harte, as the stories of New

Orleans suggest George Washington Cable, and those of Central America suggest Richard Harding Davis. But New York is truly O. Henry's own, because of his fresh curiosity and feeling of wonder, "which made for a literary virtue transcending his occasional cheapness and coarseness, his sometimes unbearable jocularity and meretricious effects. . . ." Brooks comments on such vivid and typical O. Henry effects as "the night-sounds in hotel corridors, the quarrel in the next room, the unloading of the coal-carts in the morning . . . , the old brownstone dwellings where the steps swarmed on summer nights with 'stoopers'. . . ." Occasionally at least, Brooks concludes, O. Henry was a real artist, who, with his gift of inventiveness, managed to convey a genuine sense of the romance of New York.[24]

Perhaps Van Wyck Brooks's discussion is a straw in the wind. Perhaps at long last the time has come when O. Henry can be given his rightful place in American literature. Although his place is not so high as that of Stephen Crane, say, it is definitely higher than that of Richard Harding Davis, and probably higher than that of Jack London. But regardless of exactly how high or how low, the point which should be clear is that his place is a unique one.

Uniqueness, by definition, cannot satisfactorily be defined or explained away. But one or two of its more obvious components can be singled out. O. Henry created a city which still lives in his books, a city which is somehow both the New York of actuality and an enchanted metropolis more real and more durable than the actuality of time and place. Moreover, whatever his setting—whether New York or Texas or Central America—O. Henry's work is pervaded by humor which, despite all the successive predictions to the contrary, has lost little of its contagion. Pattee contended that O. Henry used only the traditional devices of American humor: exaggeration, incongruous comparisons, malapropisms and misquotations, irreverence, and inflated circumlocution. This is a list which includes everything but the one important thing: the fact that, whatever its devices, O. Henry's humor is very different from that of Mark Twain or Artemus Ward or Bill Nye or any of the other writers whom Pattee had in mind. O. Henry is much closer in spirit to such modern humorists as Dorothy Parker and Robert Benchley and E. B. White, all of whom are clearly indebted to his lightness of touch. Finally, in a more graphic fashion than Henry James or James Joyce or any other major figure, O. Henry is concerned with what one critic has called "the great contemporary subject: the isolation and frustration of personality." [25] His is a more total involvement with the problem, for he not only presents us with characters caught in the toils of the problem, but his work is itself the blighted, imperfect thing which the isolation and frustration of O. Henry's personality made of it.

✻   ✻   ✻

I should like here to express my indebtedness to the Research Institute of the University of Texas for granting me a leave of absence from teaching during the writing of this book, and for generously supplying funds for microfilming quantities of documentary materials. In many ways I am deeply indebted to many individuals, particularly to Dean Harry Huntt Ransom of the University of Texas for his more than generous assistance with several time-consuming problems which I unaided could not have solved. I wish to express my appreciation also to the following:

Miss Olivia Burwell, Librarian of the Greensboro Public Library, who placed at my disposal that library's large and invaluable O. Henry Collection; also Mr. Karl Prickett, President of the Greensboro Historical Museum, who gave me the use of the collection of O. Henry letters held by that institution;

Mr. Witter Bynner, who gave me helpful information about O. Henry in New York;

Professor Thomas M. Cranfill, of the University of Texas, who assisted me in gaining access to valuable materials;

Senator Lyndon B. Johnson, who secured for me access to pertinent documents in the files of the Department of Justice;

Mr. John S. Mayfield, of Bethesda, Maryland, who allowed me the use of manuscript materials in his possession;

Mr. Alexander Moffit, Librarian of the University of Texas, and Mr. Frank Schmaus, Assistant Reference Librarian, who gave me valuable assistance;

Mr. William F. Price, of Clearwater, Florida, who gave me important information about O. Henry as a bank teller in Austin;

Dr. Hyder E. Rollins, retired professor of English at Harvard

University, and Professor William A. Jackson, Director of the Houghton Library at Harvard, who allowed me the use of documents and notes collected by Professor Rollins not long after O. Henry's death;

Mr. Cecil Scott, of The Macmillan Company, who has given me much more than routine assistance in the final revision of the manuscript;

Mr. Beverly S. Sheffield, Director of the Recreation Department of the City of Austin, who allowed me to reproduce several photographs in the collection of the O. Henry Museum in Austin;

Mr. John Cook Wyllie, Librarian of the University of Virginia, and others on the staff of the library, who generously gave of their time to assist me;

Mrs. L. D. York, of Charlottesville, Virginia, who granted me permission to make use of the C. Alphonso Smith Papers on deposit in the Library of the University of Virginia.

GERALD LANGFORD

The University of Texas
Austin, Texas

CHAPTER ONE

· ⟨∿⟩ ·

William Sidney [1] Porter—laureate of "Bagdad on the Subway," the New York of Stanford White and George M. Cohan and young Theodore Dreiser—was born on September 11, 1862, in Greensboro, North Carolina, the town where two and a half years later Jefferson Davis held his last Cabinet meeting after learning that Lee had surrendered. In those days Greensboro, with a population of 2,500, was an elm-shaded village whose rural quietness was only emphasized by the occasional creaking of one of the three or four street pumps on which people depended for their water, or by the mealtime clanging of the big bell on the gallery of the two-story frame Southern Hotel. With a half-century of history behind it, the town boasted its share of ante-bellum mansions whose imposing disrepair after the war O. Henry was later to describe in such stories as "The Guardian of the Accolade." The Porter home on West Market Street, however, was not one of these mansions. It was an unpainted one-story affair with three front doors, each of which had for steps two rough slabs of granite suggestive of the plainer sort of farm homes. Even so, the house incorporated some of the oak logs from the historic old courthouse at Martinsville, site of the battle in which General Nathanael Greene turned the tide of the Revolution with his stand against Cornwallis. That is to say, the Porters were far from well-to-do people, but they were— and in the society of the time they had reason to be—proud of their family connections. As O. Henry was to write facetiously, though not entirely facetiously at that: "'Well,' said I, 'I know it [my blood] should be blue; but this is a country of mix-ups. Some of my

1

ancestors were cavaliers; but they got thick with some people on Nantucket Island, so—'"[2]

The maternal grandmother of William Sidney—or Will, as almost everyone called him—had been Abia Shirley, one of the Shirleys of Princess Anne County, Virginia, and her first husband had been William Swaim, an early editor of the Greensboro *Patriot*. On the paternal side Ruth Coffyn Worth, the Quaker grandmother who helped to rear Will, was the sister of Jonathan Worth, Governor of North Carolina from 1865 to 1868. But the man she married—Sidney Porter, agent of a Connecticut clock company—turned out to be an improvident, genial tippler; he ran a general repair shop until his death in middle age left his wife a widow at forty-three, with seven children to support by sewing and taking in boarders. It was her home in which Will was born, a fact indicative of the financial status of his parents.

Will's mother had been given every advantage by her well-to-do stepfather (coincidentally named Lyndon Swaim but apparently not related to the girl's dead father, William Swaim). She had attended both of the local schools for women, entering Edgeworth Female Seminary at the age of twelve (for one session) and graduating from Greensboro Female College in 1850 (on which occasion she wrote a commencement essay entitled "The Influence of Misfortune on the Gifted": a prophetic comment on the life of her son Will). In spite of her advantages, Mary Virginia Jane did not marry until she was twenty-five. She was "not a beauty," and —another point which might have kept the typical rustic swain at his distance—she was "quick of wit and a match for any would-be iconoclast who undertook to match repartee with her." In any event, "this most winsome woman" waited until in the end she made what must have seemed a match well worth waiting for.[3]

Dr. Algernon Sidney Porter, a notably promising young doctor, was one of the most eligible bachelors in the county. Although he had not attended medical college but had learned to practice medicine by clerking and studying in the drugstore of Dr. David P. Weir, he was reputed to know more about drugs than any other local physician, and he had even lectured on chemistry at the Edgeworth Seminary. In short, he was already considered the leading physician in Guilford County; there was, however, another side to the matter. In those days a large practice was not equivalent to a large income. Although his bride brought as dowry a home which her stepfather presented to the young couple, in less than four years—that is, before Will's birth in 1862—both the house and the deceptive air of prosperity were gone. Dr. Porter had moved his family (one son, Shirley Worth, had already been born in 1860) into the unpainted old house where his mother and his sister, Evelina, lived.

Pipe-smoking old Ruth Worth Porter well knew her son's main failing, a failing which he had inherited from his father and which he was to pass on to his son Will. Foresightedly she did not turn over to him the ownership of her home; instead, at her death, she designated her daughter as her administratrix. The legal ownership changed only when Evelina Porter deeded it to J. M. Worth on September 20, 1892,[4] so that throughout Will's boyhood he lived not under his father's roof (his mother died when he was three) but under that of his grandmother and his aunt. Old Mrs. Porter tried to help out by taking over the business side of her son's work. Although it was not customary in those far-off days for medical men to send bills to their patients (who theoretically settled up their accounts once a year), Dr. Porter's mother realistically faced their situation and began sending bills to delinquent patients. Against this unprofessional conduct there were protests, of course—one in particular from the father of two spinster sisters. Dr. Porter's visits had been only social calls, said the irate old gentleman. The presumption is that he paid his bill, though, when he got the unintimidated old woman's reply: "I want you to understand that my son Algernon don't make social calls on maiden ladies at two o'clock in the morning and they a-suffering with cramp colic."[5] When even such tactics as these did not bring in enough money for the family to live on, the doctor's mother studied medicine under her son and became a practitioner herself.

During the war the Edgeworth Seminary was used as a military hospital, and Dr. Porter was a busy man indeed. Now there was the steady stream of casualties from both Confederate and Union armies, in addition to his regular practice (which included a large share of deliberate charity work). "He was the best-hearted man I ever knew," a friend later said of him. "Rain or shine, sick or well, he would visit the poorest family in the county. He would have been a rich man if he had collected a half of what was due him." [6] With the added burden of war work, and the increase of money troubles as his family increased, it must have been about this time that Dr. Porter began to give evidence of the third trait which he inherited from his improvident, genial, tippling father. A statement by a later editor of the Greensboro *Daily Record* concerns a period not long after the one in question:

I shall never forget something that happened in my boyhood. A giant of a negro had been cut down the back in a street fight. He passed me straight for Doctor Porter's office, and yelling like a steam piano. Everybody in those days when they got hurt made for Doctor Porter's office as straight as a June shad in fly time. When I got to the little office, I'll be john-squizzled if Alg. Porter didn't have that darkey down on the floor. He was sitting on him and sewing him up and lecturing to him about the evils of intemperance all at the same time. He lectured sort of unsteadily on that theme but nobody could beat his sewing.[7]

One explanation was that Will's father began to drink on account of "exposure": perhaps a reference to the origin of the rheumatism which his son Shirley Worth later urged as the true reason—rather than drink—why he at last gave up his practice entirely. Another, likelier, suggestion was that the habit began in the local drugstore, a sort of club where men who would not go into a saloon partook so unabashedly of the druggist's decanter that Will, when he began clerking in his uncle's drugstore, lampooned the custom in a cartoon. After an exhausting day's work with the sick and the wounded, Dr. Porter might well have begun to depend on both the stimulation of alcohol and the diversion of conversation in a relaxed atmosphere. If so, it was a short-lived period of such sociability, for by the time Will was in school his father bore little resemblance to the popular, hard-working doctor of whom we are able to catch one or two glimpses.

The death of Will's mother must have had a good deal to do with what happened. She died on September 26, 1865, at the age of thirty, six months to the day after the birth of a third son, David Weir (who was to die in early childhood). "Her death," observed the *Patriot*, "is a great social loss to our community; but especially

4

to her affectionate husband and three little children. Her disease was consumption." [8] (Shirley Worth Porter later said their mother did not have tuberculosis; possibly she may have died of some complication after childbirth, but the fear of tuberculosis was to be important in Will's life.) Along with the death of his wife, Dr. Porter was confronted simultaneously with the collapse of the social order in which he had grown up and made a place for himself. Quite conceivably, without these two catastrophes his later life might have continued to be a useful if somewhat impoverished one. But the father of Will's earliest memories was a man who had already lost his grip.

The activity to which he devoted the latter part of his life began as a hobby not inappropriate for a scientifically inclined man. Like another member of the drugstore club, a jeweler who in his spare time was a would-be inventor, Dr. Porter became interested in mechanics, and the possibility of building a perpetual-motion water wheel began to absorb him. In his case, however, such work was not a mere hobby, as it was for the jeweler: it was a means of escape from the impasse that confronted him. As one of Will's schoolmates later wrote:

After he began to tinker with inventions it was only a short time until he became obsessed with the idea that he could work out the problem of perpetual motion, and from this time on he went rapidly down hill, unfortunately taking to drink, in which habit he was inclined to be solitary, not having become a bar-room loafer, but remaining most of the time in his barn with his machines and his bottle, oftentimes sleeping as much as one-half of the time. And this continued until his death. [9]

Those who have written about Will Porter's childhood have uniformly idealized it as a kind of Tom Sawyer period in his life. Like children in much worse situations than his, Will was capable of a certain amount of fun, but to confine one's attention to instances of such fun is not to learn much about the man Will was on the way to becoming. The most noteworthy point is that the mainstay of his family was his father's sister—Miss Lina, everyone called her— who ran a small private school. Although a handful of loyal old-timers attempted to remain patients of Dr. Porter's to the end, he was for all practical purposes another dependent for Miss Lina, along with his mother and his two sons. This state of affairs—which made the boy Will conspicuously different from other boys, who not only had two parents but whose fathers were respectable bread-winners—was surely the main cause of his shyness, which (according to his brother) he developed very early and which "increased to such an extent as to become at times embarrassing to both himself and his friends." [10] All of his boyhood friends later commented on Will's reticence, and one of them even felt there was something "almost effeminate" about him: [11] a quality which must have been aggravated by his relationship with his older brother. Later in life Porter told Anne Partlan, a writer friend in New York, that he and his brother "Shell" had definitely been enemies from the beginning.[12] Shell was a rough-and-tumble specimen who in his later teens went to work for a construction company and lived in work camps in the Smokies, and it is not hard to imagine what happened on the sort of occasion when, shocked by something Shell planned to do, his younger brother—touchingly devoted to his Sunday-school teacher—would threaten, "Miss Annie says that's wrong, so you know it is, and I'll tell her if you do it." [13]

Not that anyone who knew Will Porter as a boy ever stigmatized him as a real sissy. True, his best friend, Tom Tate, later idealized his boyhood with the remark that he "never did or said an unclean thing." [14] And another friend said that he was "entirely free from that primal ruffianism which characterizes most boys. . . . I never knew him to have a quarrel or a fight in his life." [15] Moreover, in school he always ranked at the head of his class; after his school years were past, according to a boarder in the home, Miss Lina always said that he had been her star pupil of all time. But there was another side to the boy too, showing that the repression caused by his home environment was less pervasive than might have been expected.

Probably the most familiar story about Will's boyhood has to do with the mischievous sketches of his aunt in her role as teacher, either executed on his slate and exhibited when she was not looking, or even more audaciously drawn left-handedly on the blackboard while with his right hand he worked an arithmetic problem. This must have been a delicate feat, not only in ambidextrousness but also in timing, for while one group of pupils was at the board

Miss Lina walked back and forth facing the rest of the class, with a switch ready for just such pranks; the drawing had to be completed and erased before she turned at one side of the room to glance toward the board and resume her march. Nor is this the only sort of extracurricular activity which we hear about. His boyhood friends later told of such escapades as an attempt to run away to sea, and Will's daring showed itself in another, quite different incident. Once—presumably when he was somewhat older—he went on a picnic with a group of both boys and girls. At the proper time, in those days of segregated swimming, the male contingent went a suitable distance up the creek, after which the girls began to lift their skirts and wade out into the cool water—only they were not so private as they supposed. Will had slipped back and concealed himself to draw a sketch of what he saw: a sketch which must have stirred up quite a bit of interest around town.[16]

On some occasions, however, the boy's spirit of fun was more devious than his more simply motivated companions seemed to realize. According to one of these companions:

> Will was a great lover of fun and mischief. When we were quite small his father, Dr. A. S. Porter, fell a victim to the delusion that he had solved the problem of perpetual motion, and finally abandoned a splendid practice and spent nearly all his time working on the machines. His mother, who was a most practical and sensible old woman, made him betake himself and his machines to the barn, and these Will and I, always being careful to wait for a time when the doctor was out, would proceed to demolish, destroying often in a few minutes that which it had taken much time and labor to construct. While, of course, I do not know the fact, I strongly suspect that the doctor's mother inspired these outrages.[17]

The unconscious cruelty of such a prank indicates a good deal more than a love of mischief. It points clearly to the boy's sense of inferiority, his divided loyalties, his vindictive satisfaction in aligning himself with the upstanding forces of respectability against his shamefully inadequate laughingstock of a father. Will's situation, that is to say, was a more complicated one than Tom Sawyer's.

Miss Lina, moreover, does not seem entirely suited to the role of Aunt Polly, in which reminiscent friends of the family tried to cast her. Her relationship with her younger nephew was of crucial

7

importance in his life, and since she served both as his parent and as his schoolteacher, her influence was greater than any single influence in the life of the average child. It was not only on her own nephew that she had a powerful influence. One of her pupils later wrote: "I feel that whatever I have accomplished in this life, is perhaps more due to her than to any other individual with the possible exception of my parents and my wife." [18] Miss Lina was clearly a force to be reckoned with.

Twenty-five years ago [wrote O. Henry] the school children used to chant their lessons. The manner of their delivery was a singsong recitative between the utterance of an Episcopal minister and the drone of a tired sawmill. I mean no disrespect. We must have lumber and sawdust.

I remember one beautiful and instructive little lyric that emanated from the physiology class. The most striking line of it was this:

"The shin bone is the long-est bone in the bod-y."

What an inestimable boon it would have been if all the corporeal and spiritual facts pertaining to man had thus been tunefully and logically inculcated in our youthful minds! [19]

In giving to her charges the necessary incentive for learning, Miss Lina was alternately typical of the day and ahead of her time. Shell Porter later reminisced about the number of peach-tree limbs and apple-tree sprouts she wore out on him. Each morning, another of her pupils was to report, she would have an ample supply of switches brought into the schoolroom. After sampling the quality of them by giving a resounding whack across her desk with one of them, she would stand the batch in the corner ready for use, and as the day progressed the chastising became "so frequent that it became monotonous." [20] On the other hand, this able woman believed in learning by doing. One of her teaching devices was to begin an original story, calling successively on each of her pupils to contribute a portion to the narrative. In the attempt not merely to pump into and back out of the children a given set of facts but also to interest them in learning, she carried on a round of activities, partly social and partly educational. In the spring she took her pupils on wild-flower hunts. She staged an annual "exhibition," to which came all the parents to see their children perform. And she read good books to them, both during the recess hour and on Friday nights, when there was always a quorum for a popcorn-popping, chestnut-roasting weekly social.

Having attended only the Edgeworth Seminary herself, Miss Lina was not adequately prepared for teaching in the upper grades. Reportedly she knew no Latin at all, and it was only during the brief period when she was assisted by a twenty-year-old niece that Latin and algebra were taught in her school. But whatever her preparation, she seems to have been a born teacher, for she got results. Gifted though her younger nephew was, Miss Lina's stimulation and guidance must have had a good deal to do with the fact that Will, as he later remarked, "did more reading between my thirteenth and nineteenth years [he was nineteen when he left Greensboro] than I have done in all the years since, and my taste was much better than it is now, for I used to read nothing but the classics. Burton's Anatomy of Melancholy and Lane's translation of The Arabian Nights were my favorites." [21]

By the time he had reached his teens, Will had progressed far beyond the dime novels of which he and Tom Tate, as the latter was to report, once had "the biggest collection I have ever seen outside of a cigar stand (and I don't think we could have been more than eight years old)." [22] The amount and kind of reading he did are attested by the number of allusions in the O. Henry stories to Chaucer, Shakespeare, Lord Chesterfield, Edmund Burke, Lamb, Hazlitt, Dickens, Tennyson, Bulwer-Lytton, and Trollope; also to Homer, Epictetus, Aurelius, Tasso, Montaigne, Tolstoi, Dumas, and Ibsen, not to mention the frequent references to the Bible.

His love of Scott [his first biographer tells us] came via an interest which he soon outgrew in *Thaddeus of Warsaw* and *The Scottish Chiefs*. He considered *Bleak House* the best of Dickens' works and *Vanity Fair* of Thackeray's. Dickens' unfinished story, *The Mystery of Edwin Drood*, occupied much of his thought at this time and he attempted more than once to complete the plot but gave it up. Of Charles Reade's masterpiece, he said later: "If you want to read philosophy well put up in fiction, read *The Cloister and the Hearth*. I never saw such a novel. There is material for dozens of short stories in that one book alone.[23]

Not only did Miss Lina educate the two Porter boys; she fed and clothed them as well. At first she used for her school one of the low-ceilinged rooms in the old Porter home, but as the enrollment grew (so that she found it necessary to call upon the assistance of her niece at one time and of her still-vigorous old mother at other times) she built a one-room school building in the yard. By the time Will was twelve years old she was able (perhaps with the assistance of her brother, the druggist) to have the disreputable old house torn down and a new, larger one built (which, in its turn, incorporated the old logs from the Martinsville courthouse).[24]

Clearly Miss Lina—as parent, as teacher, and as breadwinner—was a remarkable woman. But for a sensitive child like Will, that must have been just the trouble. She was too much of a local celebrity, and not always for the right reasons. She expressed herself, for instance, somewhat more forcefully than was customary among the mothers of Will's friends. In the schoolroom, it seems, she "never went beyond the limits of respectable Southern slang," confining herself to the sort of homespun wisdom and diction found in one of her favorite expressions: "Every tub must stand on its own bottom." [25] But there were many stories like the one brought home by Tom Tate and a certain nameless citizen on the day when, having walked out from town with Tom and Will, she went in wading with the two boys. Probably the hapless male she caught staring at her from the bank was less intrigued than aghast at the sight of that particular pair of legs on display, but Miss Lina no doubt had her vanity. "Loosing upon the unfortunate beholder a withering stream of invective, followed by a broadside of profanity, she sent him scurrying." [26] Taking into account the restraint of her former pupils and fellow townsmen, who were supplying their information after O. Henry had become a famous writer, it is safe to assume that Miss Lina had the vocabulary of the proverbial sailor.

Nor was it only a matter of words. There is the story of the fight which had been scheduled between her boys and those of a Professor Joyner, a Baptist minister who for a short time operated a rival school. News of the coming event leaked out, and when Miss Lina appeared on the scene, both sides fled. "She later pursued those who had taken refuge among the ruins of the old college, and I heard that one of the larger boys . . . attempted flight the second

10

time but that Miss Lina hurled a brickbat with such effect that she 'brought him down.' " [27]

It was (even if apocryphal) the typical sort of story which people told about Miss Lina, and in the light of such stories—along with those that were told about Dr. Porter and old Mrs. Porter—it is easy to understand Will's mixed feelings about his family. The only one toward whom he could possibly have felt unreserved loyalty was his dead mother, whose barely remembered love and tenderness always made her for him "a thing ensky'd and sainted." [28] Proud as his aunt was of his scholastic attainments and of his drawings (of which she had a large album on display in her home), she felt the heavy burden of her responsibilities, and she was never one to hold her tongue. At times, a family friend was to report, she "would get cross with him and accuse him of showing his superiority": [29] a phrase which can be recognized for the understatement it was when we come upon one of Will's own comments later in Texas. Granted that he was expressing only one side of his attitude, nevertheless he made indisputably clear what he had been feeling through all the years of his boyhood. To Mrs. Richard Hall, in whose home he lived, he spoke of his grandmother and his aunt "not affectionately. He didn't love them. They didn't understand him [he said]; they repined at having to help Shell and Will— treated them rather as nuisances; [he] said they were harsh with him." [30]

Of such sort, then, was Will Porter's boyhood. At one time his ability to draw, which had brought him to the notice of the whole town, placed within his grasp an opportunity which it must have been more than a passing disappointment to have to decline: an opportunity not only to continue his education but to escape from his uncongenial home situation. Colonel Bingham, director of the well known Bingham military school located just outside Asheville, wrote "to offer him his tuition and board in order to get the use of his talent as a cartoonist for the amusement of our boys. . . . But he could not accept my offer for lack of means to provide for his uniform and books." [31] As to whether Will ever had any schooling beyond Miss Lina's, there is some disagreement. The usual statement is that he attended only the one school. Tom Tate, though, spoke of a term or two in a graded school, and another contemporary even drew a sketch in 1919 of the graded school which, according to his memory, Will attended in 1875 or 1876.[32] The matter is of little importance, since all parties agree that the boy's schooling ended at the age of fifteen. Going to work in his uncle's drugstore, he learned—like Ikey Schoenstein in the Blue Light Drug Store in New York—to compound pills behind "its tall prescription desk— pills rolled out on its own pill-tile, divided with a spatula, rolled with the finger and thumb, dusted with calcined magnesia and delivered in little round pasteboard pill-boxes." [33] At an age when his comrades were still going to school and living as protected children, Will Porter was put to work at a man's job. He was living in the home of a charitable relative, and he had to earn his own keep. It was the kind of situation to bring an unavoidable sense of shame to a boy imbued with the family pride of the Old South.

The Greensboro of which young Porter began to take a more comprehensive view, now that he was associated in business with the adults of the town, was still in the throes of Reconstruction: an upheaval of particular interest in Greensboro because of the thirteen-year residence there of the carpetbagger Albion Winegar Tourgée, who in 1879—the year he moved North again and published his novel *A Fool's Errand*—became nationally famous. Made a judge by the Negro vote, Tourgée became the Republican boss of the state, the man who—in the words of one of Will's contemporaries—"had sought, so we were told, to introduce social equality among negroes and whites; who had wrecked the good name and financial integrity of our fair State by his unexampled extravagance when he was in control of the State legislature, and who had brought about almost a reign of terror, so that he was justly considered by all good people to be a veritable monster." [34]

The truth of the matter seems to be that Tourgée was not only an able but a well meaning man, who—as another contemporary put it—"was not popular with the other carpet-baggers nor with the prominent native scalawags—which speaks much for his honesty and independence"; and at least among the more fair-minded of the leading men of the old régime, "because he was outspoken and did not seem to court favor, he commanded a certain kind of respect." [35]

His novel is a wooden, didactic affair, but at least it leaves no doubt of the author's integrity as a man. Tourgée (like the hero of his novel) lived as "an outlaw in the land where he hoped to have made a home and which he desired faithfully to serve," [36] and in the end he came to regard himself as a fool for having attempted to implement the program of Reconstruction, a program which he pronounced inadequate because it was the result of political compromises in the North.

Over him in Greensboro hung the constant threat of being hauled from his bed by the Ku Klux Klan (there were some eight hundred members in Guilford County), but to the end he refused to compromise his principles. Somehow the Klan kept its distance as scrupulously as did the small boys like Tom Tate, to whom "he was a sort of ogre. . . . Very dark stories were whispered of his doings out in far-off Warnersville, the negro settlement out by the Methodist graveyard. He held meetings out there that we were almost prepared to say were a species of voodooism." [37] When Will was old enough to be interested in a summer visitor named Sallie Coleman (who many years later was to become his second wife), he rounded up his best friend for moral support and at midnight hiked the six miles out to Tourgée's home to gather magnolia blossoms by way of a floral offering. Why the trip had to be made at midnight, and why magnolia blossoms could not be gathered from a closer source, we are not told. Clearly the answer has to do with the popular feeling about Tourgée, and Tom Tate long remembered "the creepy sensation that I felt when we mounted the fence and started across the open field for the trees and the relief that came when we crossed that fence with the loot. We carried them back and laid them on Miss Sallie's doorstep." [38] (Perhaps this daring deed was undertaken preparatory to Will's asking Sallie if he might squire her to the Greensboro College commencement exercises. If so, his gesture did the trick, for Sallie accompanied him, and he sat—more gauche than forward—"with his arm stretched on the back of the bench. I did not think it would be nice to ask him to remove it, and my back aches right now again at thought of the rigidity of my spine through the long hours of the female evening.") [39]

With the loyalist Carolinians who defeated Reconstruction—the solid citizens bent on protecting their old way of life against the carpetbagger, the scalawag, and the newly freed Negro—Will Porter became well acquainted during his career as a druggist. All too well he came to know the type he was later to caricature in his story "A Municipal Report," but even so he remained a loyal enough Southerner to reject Tourgée's version of Carolina life; more than ten years after moving to Texas he wrote for the Houston *Post* a satirical sketch called "Vereton Villa," in which he made extravagant fun of such Northern books as *A Fool's Errand* and *Uncle Tom's Cabin*.[40]

In Clark Porter's drugstore Will was to work until he was nineteen, becoming a member of the North Carolina Pharmaceutical Association (and thereby a registered pharmacist) on August 30, 1881.[41] Here he was to continue to develop his ability as a cartoonist, which was to prove not only amusing but useful in the drugstore. When an unknown customer wanted his purchases charged, Will would draw a sketch of the man after he had left, from which his uncle had no trouble recognizing the customer. Gradually, as his sketches of local characters became more skillfully executed and more widely known around town—and especially after the reading around the pot-bellied stove of the comic drama he wrote at sixteen, lampooning the foibles of the town's leading citizens—the boy became something of a local celebrity. In the words of a contemporary, Will "held a little court of his own at the drug store. He was the delight and pride of men two and three times his age." [42] It was all the more confidently expected that he would make his mark in the art world because of his kinsman Thomas Worth, who had been on the art staff of the firm of Currier and Ives.

Will's drugstore days—like his school days—were idealized in most of the later accounts furnished by his friends, who knew and remembered the store in only one of its aspects: that of the social club where the future O. Henry furthered his education by observing human nature. There was always a chess game going in the rear room, we are told, and around the big stove gathered the judge, the colonel, the doctor, and other leading citizens to discuss affairs of state while smoking Clark Porter's cigars and drinking his whisky (usually with the assumption that such refreshments were on the house). After hours also, according to later informants, Will's life at this time was one to be remembered nostalgically. One friend, John S. Michaux, later reminisced about the summer evenings after he and his brother had finished setting type for the religious paper published by their father. They would stop by for Will, and after he had closed the store the three of them would roam around town serenading the college girls and their own respective sweethearts. (Will, who played second violin, reportedly spent an undue amount of time getting and keeping his instrument in tune.) [43] On winter nights, Tom Tate remembered, Will's father always had a good fire waiting for him when he got home from work, and the two of them would have a midnight supper of eggs, potatoes, and coffee.

Apparently Tate did not notice the jarring detail of the word *midnight*. Clark Porter (whom a later editor of the *Daily Record* remembered as having a stiff neck when he was drunk) seems to have taken his bottle and gone home comfortably early, leaving the store to be kept open until midnight by a boy still in his teens—a boy, moreover, who seemed to have inherited from his mother a tendency toward tuberculosis (if it was tuberculosis of which she died). Pale and thin, he already had a cough which was of serious concern not only to himself but also to his friend and later benefactor, Dr. James K. Hall. Will took no one, not even Tom Tate, completely into his confidence; but the long hours of confining work, the weight of responsibility in the job he was filling, and the shame of his father's irresponsibility were the things he was to remember about his life in Greensboro. Many years afterward in New York he told Anne Partlan that he had been wretched and anxious to get away, that the grind in the drugstore had been agony for him. And although Dr. Porter was said to be the best-hearted man in town (so much so that children always went out of their way to speak to him on the street), other things were said too. He was a hopeless alcoholic, of course, and in addition Mrs. Richard Hall was later to report that her Greensboro mother-in-law (the wife of Dr. James K. Hall) "assured her that Dr. Porter was an opium-eater." [44]

According to Bettie Caldwell (who as a college student boarded in Miss Lina's home in 1879–1880, when Will was seventeen), Dr. Porter's room was littered with wooden wheels and other bits and

15

pieces of gadgets which had been filed under the bed and forgotten. The old man—he seemed old to everyone, although he was only fifty-five at the time—still kept up the pretense of working on his inventions. Latterly it had been a flying machine. "It's completed," he would say, "with the single exception of . . ." and his voice would trail off. Between two people such as Will's father and his aunt there must have been constant if unspoken tension, and, according to Bettie Caldwell, the household was a silent, gloomy one. Old Mrs. Porter, who smoked her pipe "incessantly," ate with her son separately, but even so there was never any sparkle from Will, who "appeared at mealtime silent, but always courteous when questioned, and left the house after eating for the drug store and his friends among men and boys. His work, pleasure and interests were all away from home." [45] The testimony as to Will's diffidence and reserve is unanimous. Tom Tate remembered how he "would slip around to the back door of Miss Lina's if there was company in the front of the house." Shell Porter and various others spoke of how cautious he was about admitting people to his confidence, of how few intimates he had. Already as a boy he was being forced into a withdrawal, a rejection of the actualities of his situation.

On the other hand, this diffident and unhappy young man had an incongruous fondness for practical jokes. One of the stories long and hilariously remembered around the drugstore concerned the "good one" which Will pulled on the old Negro store porter, Pink Lindsay. Apparently Pink's ingenuity in managing to get his share of the store's whisky supply was never explained until Will happened to notice an inconspicuous hole bored in the top of the barrel down in the cellar, with a pair of long straws on an adjoining shelf. Without a word to anyone Will filled the straws with red pepper, and at the next opportunity he sent Pink on an errand to the cellar. After the expected interval "there was a howl that would have done credit to a Comanche Indian." Up the stairs and through the store raced the old Negro, heading for the water pump out in the street. "Will pumped water for him until he could talk, and then he pumped the truth out of him about the straws. . . . All the while Will was as sober as a judge. He never smiled, and Pink did not suspect him." [46]

On another occasion Will's victim was his later benefactor, Dr.

16

James K. Hall, who—fearful that he had diabetes—left a specimen of his urine in the store, intending to return and test it when he had time. Confronted with this opportunity, Will added to the urine a generous portion of sugar syrup. Although Dr. Hall's worst fears were more than confirmed when he ran his test, Will made no move to relieve his mind, so that, as one contemporary put it, "The old Doctor almost died of sugar in his urine before he found out that Will had doctored it." [47]

Both of these practical jokes contain the same element of cruelty to be found in the boy's earlier destruction of his father's gadgets. And yet in afteryears no element is more conspicuously absent than cruelty from the gentle personality of Will Porter. Clearly it was—at a time when the future seemed without hope—the reverse side of his shyness, a shyness so crippling that his grandmother kept wishing they could have sent him to Trinity College, because (as she said) President Braxton Craven "makes every student feel that he, Braxton Craven, is the greatest man on earth and the student himself the next greatest." [48]

In short, Will felt himself to be an alien in Greensboro. He was the talented poor boy, pitiable on account of a family situation which deprived him of the advantages and opportunities enjoyed by his less gifted comrades. His inevitable reaction was to retire within himself instead of trying to deal with a problem which seemed to have no solution. This disinclination to face reality was to be intensified by several later experiences, and was to become a lifelong handicap both in his life and in his writing.

For his immediate problem, as things turned out, a solution presented itself in his nineteenth year. On account of his "hacking cough," commented on by everyone at the time, Dr. Hall felt that the confining work in the drugstore was the worst sort of work the boy could be doing. Dr. and Mrs. Hall therefore invited Will along as their guest when, in March, 1882, they undertook the long trip to Texas, where they were going to visit their four sons in that storied land of adventure and fortune. The Halls thus became the first in a series of older friends who were, during Will's young manhood, to go far beyond the bounds of mere friendship in their protective, parental impulse to help him.

17

CHAPTER TWO

. ⟨∽∾⟩ .

In those days people just said "G.T.T." It meant "Gone to Texas," and it was sufficient explanation of what had happened to some prodigal son or why a warrant could not be served on some malefactor. In 1869, at the age of nineteen, the Hall's eldest son, Leigh (he afterward simplified it to Lee for Texans), had joined the G.T.T. ranks—not because he was in trouble but because he was the type of swashbuckling young man whom the West needed and whose services it could bountifully recompense. From a job as a country schoolteacher in Grayson County, just north of Dallas, Lee Hall moved on to the post of city marshal in Sherman, from where in very short order began to emanate colorful accounts of his dealings with the riffraff, whom he had "jumping down the trail at the toe of his boot." [1] After accumulating a further record of exploits as deputy sheriff in the trouble spot of Denison, the largest town in Grayson County, he graduated to the Texas Rangers. By 1874 Lee had made a national reputation.[2] He was to become one of the all-time heroes of an organization whose dealings with trigger-happy desperadoes made good stories as far away even as sequestered Greensboro, where they were eagerly repeated by wide-eyed Will Porter and his friends.

By the time Will found himself headed for Texas, Lee Hall had married and—at the insistence of his gently bred wife—had retired from the Rangers to assume in 1880 the management of a great ranch-empire which was being built up by the Dull brothers of Harrisburg, Pennsylvania. The younger Hall brothers (Richard and Frank and Will) had immigrated too and were all working on the ranch under Lee's supervision. Dr. and Mrs. Hall must have left

18

Greensboro in March, 1882, and trains being what they were then, the trip would have taken close to a week.

You remember [Will wrote Mrs. Hall after she had returned to Greensboro] how often you used to have the train stopped to gather verbenas when you were coming out here? . . . I can go over in my mind almost every little incident in our trip to this country. I can see the conductor walking towards me with Dr. Hall's bottle of currant wine in his hands, which he let roll away from him down the centre of the car some 300 times on the journey, and which the conductor invariably brought to me, handing it in full sight of everybody, and saying, "Here young man here's your bottle." I think he always suspected the Dr. of dropping it but when he passed along by his seat, the Dr. would survey the bottle with such an indifferent, unrecognizing look that he always settled on me as the guilty party.[3]

In Houston, one of the stopovers where the party changed trains, they visited in the station with the Cave family, whose young daughter found Will "an indifferent and somewhat awkward-looking country chap with long pants that were short of being long, making him look like a big bashful schoolboy." But the holiday mood had taken complete possession of him by this time. When Lollie Cave acknowledged the introduction by offering her hand and saying, "How do you do, Mr. Porter?", he reached—with "a merry twinkle in his eyes"—to shake hands in the mock-rustic style which he must have gathered was expected of him ("my wrist was nearly broken," Lollie remembered), and while the families visited he addressed to her a series of "teasing remarks."[4]

Cotulla, when they finally reached it, was the kind of town which O. Henry must have had in mind when he described the town of Nopal, "which seemed to have been hastily constructed of undressed lumber and flapping canvas," and where the local group that met the train "was clearly composed of citizens accustomed to and prepared for rude alarms." The last stage of the trip, the forty miles from Cotulla to the Dull ranch, was surely made in just such a conveyance as the "feather-weight buckboard, behind a pair of wild cream-colored Spanish ponies," in which Madame Bo-Peep made a similar trip.

They swept out of the little town and down the level road toward the south. Soon the road dwindled and disappeared, and they struck across a world carpeted with an endless reach of curly mesquite grass. The wheels made no sound. The tireless ponies bounded ahead at an unbroken gallop. The temperate wind, made fragrant by thousands of acres of blue and yellow wild flowers, roared gloriously in their ears . . . [until] the ponies rounded a gentle, brush-covered hill, and then swooped, like a double cream-colored cyclone, upon the Rancho de las Sombras. . . . A lordly grove of magnificent live-oaks cast an area of grateful, cool shade. . . . The house, of red brick, one story, ran low and long beneath the trees. Through its middle, dividing its six rooms in half, extended a broad, arched passageway, picturesque with flowering cactus and hanging red earthen jars.[5]

In this description O. Henry was remembering Lee Hall's home as somewhat more impressive than it actually was, although it would in actual fact have seemed a luxurious establishment by comparison with the home in which he was to be a guest—that of the young Richard Halls twenty-five miles away.

In Richard Hall's two-room house, one room was divided by a curtain to serve as kitchen and dining room; the other was a bedroom for Mrs. Hall and an infant daughter. Will, along with Richard and Mrs. Hall's brother, B. F. Hughes, slept outdoors. At this time Richard Hall, who had been educated at Guilford College in North Carolina, was trying his luck managing a sheep ranch under his brother's general supervision. He was later to become Land Commissioner of Texas, in which capacity he was to continue to befriend Will Porter in Austin. Betty Hall, a cultivated young woman who had been educated in Louisiana and Virginia, had a well chosen small library, to which were added new books every time her husband made one of his periodic trips to San Antonio. This young couple took Will into their primitive household—not only for the three months of the scheduled visit but as a permanent guest after they saw his reluctance to go back to North Carolina.

La Salle County—in which lay the greater portion of the Dull ranch, although it spread also into McMullen and Frio counties— had traditionally been a vast pasture land where ranchmen turned out their stock to graze freely. When Lee Hall began building fences, trouble began. "Dull and Hall have run their fences around us," commented a contemporary newspaper, "taking in besides small tracts, 400,000 acres, and we find the gentlemen exceptional to the general rule. . . . They have gone to each one who owned land outside their pastures and offered him more than a liberal price for his land, with the privilege of free rent for five years." [6] But the process was not generally so peaceful as this account might suggest. The fencing of this vast holding (within whose 120-mile circuit the Halls herded some 12,000 head of cattle and some 6,000 sheep) brought on a vicious fence-cutting war, which was still in full swing when Will Porter arrived. Lee Hall, as his wife later wrote, "was in constant danger. His life was threatened in many ways, and the mail was heavy with warnings, generally in the shape of crude sketches, portraying effigies with ropes around the neck, and bearing the unfailing inscription, 'Your Necktie.' We usually travelled at night, nearly always with cocked guns." [7]

For some time the sheriff of La Salle County was a tool of the cattle thieves and fence cutters. When Hall tried finally to supplant him with a former Ranger, Sheriff Tompkins threatened to keep Hall and his men away from the polls. This was Hall's chance to score a strategic victory over the outlaws. Riding without warning into town with his cowboys, he had them all sworn in as peace officers before the opposition realized what was happening. Next morning, confronted by Hall's men standing guard at each voting place, the Tompkins gang tried to take possession by force. The new peace officers opened fire, after which a properly supervised election resulted in a victory for Hall's candidate, who until his untimely death presided over a new era of law and order.

As a frequent visitor in the home of Lee Hall, Will Porter came to know and to admire the man whom he was later to use as a model for many stout-hearted Texas Rangers in his stories.[8] By contrast, his own life during his two years' stay at Richard Hall's sheep ranch was as undramatic as life in Greensboro had been, and even more uneventful. It was, however, the first truly carefree existence he had ever experienced, and he took full advantage of it. For his threatening cough his hosts must have prescribed plenty of rest (they did not need to prescribe fresh air, since his bedroom was the outdoors), and as O. Henry later recounted the experience:

On a cool canvas-covered cot in the shade of the hackberry trees Sam Galloway passed the greater part of his time. There he rolled his brown paper cigarettes, read such tedious literature as the ranch afforded, and added to his repertoire of improvisations that he played so expertly on his guitar. . . . Here he had food and lodging as good as he had ever longed for; absolute immunity from care or exertion or strife; an endless welcome.[9]

With his "unquenchable thirst for knowledge," to be remembered by Betty Hall, Will rapidly went through the supply of books which the ranch afforded—Dickens, Thackeray, Hume, Guizot, Tennyson—after which he resorted to such "tedious" idems as almanacs and mail-order catalogues while awaiting the arrival of new books from the city. His Webster's dictionary was no mere reference book; he read it by the hour. Within three months he reportedly spoke better Spanish than any other American on the ranch, having corrected with a grammar text what he learned from the "frowsy-headed Mexicans [who] would snip the fur off [the sheep] with back-action scissors"[10] during the day, and in the evening "would come up from their shacks with their guitars and sing the weirdest of heartbreaking songs."[11] According to one of his own letters at the time: "I am with Spanish like Doctor Hall's patients, still 'progressing,' and can now tell a Mexican in the highest and most grammatical Castilian to tie a horse without his thinking I mean for him to turn him loose. I would like to put my knowledge of the language into profitable use, but am undecided whether consulship to Mexico or herd sheep."[12] His new-found leisure even allowed him to work at French and German, of which—as many of his stories attest—he picked up at least a smattering.

From the "pale, anemic boy weighing scarcely a hundred pounds,"[13] Will soon developed into a reasonable facsimile of a rugged Texan, although when it came to ranch work—lassoing cattle, dipping and shearing sheep, riding constantly in search of new pasturage—Betty Hall said he remained an onlooker. Betty's brother did indeed say (with obvious overgenerosity), "In six months' time he had developed into a regular broncho-buster, and was as valuable as any man in Lee Hall's service."[14] And Mrs. Lee Hall, while remembering that Will's relationship with her husband had been "more of a social than a business nature," thought that "he acted as cowboy for a period under Captain Hall about the year 1882." [15] No regular work was expected of him, though, and he was never a real horseman, preferring to sit on the corral fence when horses were to be broken. The closest he came to actual ranch work was on such an occasion as he described nearly a year after his arrival:

Lee came up and asked me to go down to the camps and take Brockman's place for a week or so while he went to San Antonio. Well, I went down some six or seven miles from the ranch. On arriving I counted at the commissary tent nine niggers, sixteen Mexicans, seven hounds, twenty-one six-shooters, four desperadoes, three shotguns, and a barrel of molasses. Inside there were a good many sacks of corn, flour, meal, sugar, beans, coffee and potatoes, a big box of bacon, some boots, shoes, clothes, saddles, rifles, tobacco and some more hounds. The work was to issue the stores to the contractors as they sent for them, and was light and easy to do. . . . The few days I was there I was treated more as a guest than one doomed to labour. . . . Had an offer to gamble from the nigger cook, and was allowed as an especial favor to drive up the nice, pretty horses and give them some corn. And the kind of accommodating old tramps and cowboys that constitute the outfit would drop in and board, and sleep and smoke, and cuss and gamble, and lie and brag, and do everything in their power to make the time pass pleasantly and profitably —to themselves. I enjoyed the thing very much. [16]

Tenderfoot though he must have remained in the eyes of the hired ranch hands, Will came to be liked and accepted by them. His droll facility with words and his pleasing bass voice found among the unlettered cowboys an eager audience, so that in due course—as Betty Hall's brother reported—he was initiated into the cowboy fraternity: an event which he himself was later to chronicle proudly:

Three nights after that Curly rolled himself in his blanket and went to sleep. Then the other punchers rose up softly and began to make preparations. Ranse saw Long Collins tie a rope to the horn of a saddle. Others were getting out their six-shooters. . . .
Half a dozen six-shooters began to pop—awful yells rent the air— Long Collins galloped wildly across Curly's bed, dragging the saddle after him. That was merely their way of gently awaking their victim. Then they hazed him for an hour, carefully and ridiculously, after the code of cow camps. Whenever he uttered protest they held him stretched

over a roll of blankets and thrashed him woefully with a pair of leather leggins.

And all this meant that Curly had won his spurs, that he was receiving the punchers' accolade. Nevermore would they be polite to him. But he would be their "pardner" and stirrup-brother, foot to foot.[17]

Will tried, after that, to dress in a manner becoming his new status. "If long hair," he wrote back to Greensboro, "part of a sombrero, Mexican spurs, etc. . . . [and] my wild, untamed aspect had not been counteracted by my well-known benevolent and amiable expression of countenance, I would have been arrested long ago by the Rangers on general suspicions of murder and horse stealing." [18] His actual usefulness on the ranch—despite such an impressive appearance—seems to have taken two more prosaic forms. First, he was the obvious candidate for the weekly ride of fourteen miles to Fort Ewell to get the mail. His second function was, even if undramatic, somewhat more important. Betty Hall, reared as she had been on a Louisiana plantation, was more competent at supervising servants than at turning out meals with her own hands. Conditions on the ranch were, however, "too appalling for the average negro man or negro woman to bear, and Mexican servants were unreliable." [19] When the current Negro cook reached the end of her endurance—a bull snake had fallen from the rafters to the table where she was working—Betty was in despair. But Will had had to learn his way about a kitchen in Miss Lina's home and, as became evident many times later in his life, he enjoyed cooking. He was glad, therefore, to jump into the breach, and from that time forth he presided in the kitchen during the all too frequent hiatuses between cooks. "Please," he wrote to Mrs. Hall back in Greensboro, "send by express to this ranch 75 cooks and 200 washwomen, blind or wooden legged ones preferred. The climate has a tendency to make them walk off every two or three days, which must be overcome." [20]

Although the mail ride was in general a tedious errand, it yielded Will two experiences he was never to forget. Caught once in a violent thunderstorm, he had to spend the night with a band of desperadoes, or at least they seemed so to him under the circumstances. They "cursed and blasphemed at every stroke of lightning" through the long night, and the terrified Will afterward reported to Betty Hall that there had been actual "balls of fire fall-ing" around them.[21] The experience proved a genuinely traumatic one. More than twenty years later in New York, Porter was to emerge from a restaurant with a woman friend "to find," as the woman reported it, "the sky black, the thunder rolling and the lightning flashing. We looked at each other in consternation and mutually confessed a nervous terror of a storm. He hastily called a cab, and we rode home in absolute silence, each shivering in a corner whenever there was an especially vivid flash of lightning." [22]

The second break in the tedium of the mail ride to Fort Ewell was furnished by a sixteen-year-old girl named Clarence Crozier, like himself a recently arrived visitor. Her uncle and aunt, the Kerrs, owned the only store in a settlement composed of the storekeeper's family and a scattering of Mexicans, under which circumstances it is not hard to understand why, for lack of anything better to do, Clarence sometimes welcomed the chance to take a turn behind the counter. She happened to be in the store one day when a young man who "wore cowboy clothes with a swagger" [23] arrived to fetch the mail for Richard Hall's ranch. Having received the mail, he lingered, ostensibly to consider the *dulce galleta* (sweet wafers stocked for the Mexican sheepherders), but actually to devise a means of striking up a proper acquaintance with the new clerk, whom he was to remember as "an imported girl with fixings on." [24] Finally he risked the remark that he had once sold candy himself in a drugstore. "But my customers didn't always come back," he con-cluded boldly. "Now if a pretty girl had been behind the counter, maybe . . ." [25]

After that day Will developed a new zeal about keeping the ranch mail delivery on schedule. "I rode over to see her once every week for a while"; he was to write in a reminiscent story, "and then I figured out that if I doubled the number of trips I would see her twice as often." [26] But the store, with a wide counter between them, was hardly a proper setting for social calls. Soon Will changed his schedule so as to leave the ranch not in the morning but late in the afternoon. Although he usually arrived at the Kerr home before supper was over, he would never join the family at the table. (He must have sensed that Mrs. Kerr was not enthusiastic about the unknown "pale fellow who works for the Halls." If he wanted to make purchases in the store, she had told her niece, that was fine. "But I'd be a little more careful about bringing him in here. What do you two find so much to talk about, anyway?") [27] As soon as supper was over, Clarence and her cousin Mary Kerr and Will took over the parlor, where with Clarence at the organ they found considerable to sing and talk about until the time came for Will to say good night—often as late as ten o'clock—and start the long ride home. On one of these occasions he wrote in Clarence's scrapbook:

> Thy looks, thy words, each well-remembered smile of light,
> Like precious gems, or jeweled caskets rare,
> In memory's vault are hid from human sight.
> And oft she counts them o'er from year to year;
> As misers count their golden coins at night,
> Or pale sweet nuns their rosaries in prayer.
>
> Truly your friend,
W. S. Porter. [28]

In spite of Will's facility with second-hand verse the courtship was a short-lived one. Not only did Mrs. Kerr find Will "a queer sort of fellow, not a regular Texan," but she also objected to his being in arrears in his account at the store. She promised, if Clarence would go home to Brenham and forget young Porter, to give her as a going-away present the large white plume which had made Mrs. Kerr the arbiter of fashion in the neighborhood. Her strategy was successful, but the unscrupulous aunt "must have been bluffing," as Clarence ruefully wrote many years later; "she never gave it to me after all." [29]

Mrs. Kerr's disapproval of Will Porter as a suitor was the only discordant note in the general welcome extended to him in La Salle County, and there is no indication that he was serious enough about the girl to be more than casually disappointed when she cut short her visit. Several months after the event he wrote his own version of it, referring first to his continuing relationship with "a gentleman who for amusement and recreation, and not altogether without an eye to the profit, keeps a general merchandise store," and who, it seems, had for some time been "trying to sell me a little paper, which I would very much like to have, but am not anxious to purchase." The purchase, finally made, was a charge item of course, and Will was still in arrears.

You are right [he continued], I have almost forgotten what a regular old, gum-chewing, ice-cream-destroying, opera ticket vortex, ivory-clawing girl looks like. Last summer a very fair specimen of this kind ranged over about Fort Ewell, and I used to ride over twice a week on mail days and chew the end of my riding whip while she "Stood on the Bridge" and "Gathered up Shells on the Sea Shore" and wore the "Golden Slippers." But she has vamoosed, and my ideas on the subject are again growing dim.[30]

In addition to his regular trips to Fort Ewell, Will occasionally rode the forty miles to Cotulla, which, as he wrote Mrs. Hall in Greensboro, "has grown wonderfully since you left; thirty or forty new houses have gone up and thirty or forty barrels of whiskey gone down. The barkeeper is going to Europe on a tour next summer, and is thinking of buying Mexico for his little boy to play with."[31] A different side of Cotulla was represented by a lawyer named Frank Earnest, a cultivated man who carried on a correspondence with Mark Twain and owned autographed copies of Twain's books as part of a library whose remnants, after it was partially destroyed by fire, still included volumes by Byron, Dickens, Gibbon, Goldsmith, Hugo, Irving, Locke, Macaulay, Milton, Pepys, Scott, Shakespeare, and Smollett. Earnest made his library available to Will Porter. As always, however, Will chose not to confine himself to one stratum of society. Betty Hall apparently was mistaken when she said that he never drank in La Salle County, because another of his friends in Cotulla (a Mrs. Gilmer, herself a North Carolinian, who ran the local hotel and with whom Will felt a bond because her maiden name had been Porter too) later had a story about an evening when he entered the lobby of her hotel in a somewhat intoxicated condition. When reproached by Mrs. Gilmer, he admitted that one of the boys had given him a drink. When asked whether he had any whisky on him, he said not a drop, and solemnly assured the woman that he was not going to drink any more. Mrs. Gilmer urged him to go upstairs and go to bed in one of the rooms. He thanked her profusely, but instead of turning in immediately, sat in the lobby awhile and finally dozed in his chair

27

—until suddenly there was a telltale crash. At his feet were the broken fragments of the flask which had slipped from his pocket.

"Well," he said sheepishly, "I told you that I wasn't going to drink any more, and I'm not." [32]

Farther afield, Will gained an entree into the society of Friotown, in the adjoining county, where he was reported to be among the guests at a celebrated New Year's ball sponsored by the British settlers in this rich cattlemen's community. Of the splendor of this occasion the invitation gives a very inadequate idea:

HOP
— Given by the —
Ladies and Gentlemen of Friotown
— at the —
Court House, January 1, 1884
Refreshments will be served
To ———
Bring this programme with you. [33]

Fourteen-year-old Artie Slaughter, whose cherished invitation was to become the only written record of the affair, reported many years later having seen an impressively well groomed Will Porter dancing complacently with the belle of the ball under the glitter of oil lamps equipped with bright tin reflectors. The lamps must have paled in the dawn before the end of the long evening of waltzes, quadrilles, schottisches, polkas and lancers described by Mrs. Artie Slaughter Roberts, and after the dancing there was still a banquet of barbecued wild turkey and venison, with pastries and cakes of myriad-colored icings. Friotown, as the cultural center of the area, did itself proud that night.

One member of the cattle aristocracy whom Will may have met at the ball—at any rate he knew her well enough to use her as the model for at least two of his Western heroines—was Amanda Burks, the Queen of the Old Trail Drivers. By way of helping her husband rise to wealth and power, she had shot Indians in her day. ("Josefa while riding her pony at a gallop could put five out of six bullets through a tomato-can swinging at the end of a string.") [34] And she had driven nine-month stints on the old Kansas cattle trail. ("Again she made the cast, while the aroused cattle milled round the four sides of the corral in a plunging mass. This throw was fair; the white cow came to earth again; and before it could rise Santa had made the lasso fast around a post of the corral with a swift and simple knot, and had leaped upon the cow again with the rawhide hobbles.") [35] In Will's day the widowed Amanda lived in an imposing brick ranch house, from which she ruled over one of the greatest of the cattle empires.

Spread out over two years, of course, Will's social activities were few and far between. For one accustomed to the succession of people flowing in and out of a drugstore, ranch life must have consisted mainly of long stretches of monotony and loneliness, presenting day after day only the meager prospect of a pioneer hut, not far from which "were the horse corrals; and still farther the wool sheds and the brush-topped shearing pens, [beyond which] were the grass-thatched jacals of the Mexicans." [36] At night the darkness must have seemed darker and vaster than any Will had ever known, with nothing to break the far-reaching silence except "a flock of sheep [which] lay silent until a groundless panic would send a squad of them huddling together with a drumming rush." [37] On the rare nights when both Betty Hall's husband and her brother had to be away from the ranch, it must have been a comfort to them both to have Will's sleeping cot placed under her window. His services were required only once, it seems. Hearing something in the night, Betty called to him. It took a long time to rouse him, she reported, but finally he woke and went to investigate. There was another delay, followed alarmingly by pistol shots. Then Will was back with the anticlimactic report, "I've killed a coon." (It turned out by daylight to be a possum.) [38]

In many ways he must have missed the kind of life he had known in North Carolina. "Yes," he wrote to Dr. W. P. Beall, a young doctor friend in Greensboro, "I wish I could come back to live in N.C. I know it's a better place than Texas to live in, but I've left it and I'm not going to crawl back; if I come it must be in a coach and four so I guess I won't have the pleasure for sometime." The ranch country, he went on, constituted "a silent but eloquent refutation of Bob Ingersoll's theory; a man here gets prematurely insane, melancholy and unreliable and finally dies of lead poisoning, in his boots, while in a good old land like Greensboro a man can die, as they do every day, with all the benefits of clergy." [39]

Perhaps there is to be found in his letter a hint of ambivalence. At any rate, the fact that his feeling was not unmixed nostalgia is made clear enough in a letter he had written some months earlier: "Won't you please in your next letter mention some more about those ice cream & watermelon & 10th of May Celebrations & Soda water & Presbytery Concerts & picnics & dog fights and other summer amusements. The more I hear about such things the better I love this country & the more content I am to stay here." [40] He had no intention of returning, he wrote in another letter, "unless I can find . . . a wealthy cattle man asleep with his ill-gotten gains in his pockets and fall heir to his cash." [41] In Will's letters at this time there are entirely too many references to money—the means by which he hoped to gain the status which he had so conspicuously lacked in Greensboro—for his attitude to be taken as merely jocular.

In considering his attitude toward Greensboro, there is another matter to be remembered. In the eight extant letters written from La Salle County—and references within the eight indicate that the total number he wrote was probably not much greater—the reader is struck by the complete absence of any expression of loneliness or homesickness. Secondly, there is not a single reference to his family. Granted that he perhaps wrote to his father or his aunt, a son with any real solicitude for a father in Dr. Porter's situation would surely have wanted candid reports from a physician-friend whom he knew as intimately as he did Dr. Hall. There is no record that Will ever mentioned his father to any of his friends until once, commenting to Anne Partlan in New York on his unhappy early years, he remarked that his father had had no sense of responsibility whatever. Nor did Will's mother-in-law in Austin—who was later to report so fully and so favorably on the man whom she and her husband had continued to befriend even after her daughter's death—make any mention of any sorrow shown by the newly married Will at the time his father died in 1888.

For the time being he seemed content merely to be away from the drugstore and his aunt's grimly silent home. The accounts of him at this time make him seem unambitious and shiftless; yet throughout his years in Texas people were impressed by his abilities and went out of their way to be of assistance, as if they sensed something of what lay behind the exterior aimlessness. Thus while still on the ranch and without lifting a hand to seek such a thing, he got his first chance at a professional art job.

Will had, from childhood, drawn pictures and written sketches and verses. In one of his letters to Dr. Beall during his first year in Texas he had enclosed a rather broad burlesque of a genre which had already become its own best burlesque. "Lord Oakhurst's Curse," as he entitled it, tells of the aftermath of the death of a nobleman during whose last hours "His young wife, whom he loved with a devotion and strength that the presence of the king of terrors himself could not alter, moved about the apartment, weeping and sorrowful, sometimes arranging the sick man's pillow and inquiring of him in low, mournful tones if anything could be done to give him comfort, and again, with stifled sobs, eating some chocolate caramels which she carried in the pocket of her apron." By the time Lord Oakhurst has breathed his last, Lady Oakhurst uses an ax on his cabinet of private papers, only—on finding the document she wants—to collapse on the floor "with a wild, unearthly shriek that would have made a steam piano go out behind the barn and kick itself in despair." The property, it seems, has all been left to an institution which is to further research on possible methods of turning sawdust into peach brandy. The physician in attendance seizes this chance to pocket some valuable jewels, but as he emerges from the castle Lord Oakhurst's dogs attack him, "burying their fangs in his lower limbs and seriously damaging his apparel." Whereupon the irate physician "gave vent to a most horrible and blighting CURSE and ran with great swiftness to his carriage and drove off toward the city." [42]

On the strength of this story—as well as of a play ("a regular high art full orchestra, gilt-edged drama") [43] and a group of poems (which "will compare favorably with Baron Alfred's latest on spring") [44]—the literary-minded Dr. Beall had Will elected to honorary membership in the Vesper Reading Club of Lenoir. (Beall had only recently moved from Lenoir to Greensboro.) In reply to the secretary's letter announcing his election, Will wrote an overlengthy and overstrained exercise in humor, regaling the club with such choice bits of information as the fact that "the people of the State of Texas consist principally of men, women and children, with a sprinkling of cowboys." He also gave a still valid account of that Texas phenomenon known as the "norther":

You are riding along on a boiling day in September, dressed as airily as etiquette will allow, watching the fish trying to climb out of the pools of boiling water along the way . . . when a wind as cold as the icy hand of death swoops down on you from the north. . . . Where do you go? If you are far from home it depends entirely upon what kind of life you have led. . . . Some people go straight to heaven while others experience a change of temperature by the transition.[45]

Not only did Will's literary efforts bring him recognition back in North Carolina. His renown as an artist spread so far afield in Texas that he was sought out to illustrate a now famous but non-existent book which was to have been entitled *Carbonate Days*, by Joe Dixon. The author, a former mining prospector in Colorado, had been persuaded by John Maddox, an Austin businessman (later to become one of Will's closest friends), to put his experiences into a book which Maddox would pay to have illustrated and published. By the time the manuscript was completed, Maddox had heard about "a young fellow here who came from North Carolina . . . who can draw like blazes," who would be just the man to illustrate the book. Dixon made the trip from Austin to the Hall ranch, where he found "a young, silent fellow with deep, brooding blue eyes, cynical for his years." For three weeks the two worked together, during which time Will produced forty illustrations and Dixon became "much interested in the boy's personality . . . a taciturn fellow, with a peculiar little hiss when amused, instead of the boyish laugh one might have expected, and he could give the queerest caustic turn to speech, getting off epigrams like little sharp bullets." Hearing from Betty Hall that the boy wrote as well as drew, Dixon read some of the stories he had written and urged Will to submit his work to magazines. But Will, he found, "had no confidence in himself." [46]

The outcome of his first professional undertaking must have elicited several of Will's "caustic turns of speech." Dixon, it seems, re-read his story on returning to Austin, and coming to the conclusion that what he had produced was not art but trash, disposed of it accordingly. He dumped the ripped-up manuscript into the Colorado River. His would-be patron fished it out again and even took it to New York for an expert to try to reassemble the pieces. The attempt proved futile, though, and it is not improbable that Dixon's judgment was a wise one. As things were to turn out, Will's work was far from wasted. The indirect connection with John Maddox furnished him one of the two entrees with which he was to go to Austin.

The decision to leave the ranch was, characteristically, not Will's. He had found sanctuary and had gained complete acceptance in the community, and there is no indication that he had had any plans for leaving. The Hall brothers, however, were ready for a change, confronted as they were with the end of the cattle boom. In March, 1884, Richard closed a deal on some land in Williamson County and prepared to move his family and his sheep. He and his wife might understandably have felt that it was about time their young guest began to try his wings, but their attitude seems to have remained protective. They found another home for him when he decided to stop in Austin instead of going on with them to an even less civilized area. Will was thus able to move from the home of one Greensboro family into that of another, the Harrells, who were at the time among the prominent citizens of Austin.

In an attempt at disinterested analysis after his death, Betty Hall observed that the young man she had known both in La Salle County and afterward in Austin had had "no sense of responsibility or obligation or gratitude." To his aunt and his grandmother, she said, he "showed no gratitude" for his upbringing; likewise to herself and her husband he "never expressed any gratitude or repaid them for money advanced." Betty Hall, with her pioneer stamina, considered Will a young man who "lacked physical and moral courage." [47] As one of his truest friends, she did not mean to pass harsh judgment, and her words cannot be lightly dismissed. Perhaps, however, a more perceptive statement is that of Robert H. Davis, a friend in New York, who called Porter "a childlike individual, absolutely without guile, and at times utterly helpless." [48] Any of the surviving portraits of the artist as a young man— journeyman photographs though they are—plainly betray, behind the careful tailoring and the Western-mustached assurance, something oversensitive and vulnerable in the eyes. From the Richard Halls, as from his later benefactors in Austin, he accepted protective care as a child would, taking for granted something which is a child's birthright but which his own childhood had not brought him. In the kindly environment of Texas he not only followed the line of least resistance; he relaxed into a sort of irresponsibility which, chronologically, he should have outgrown.

CHAPTER THREE

· ᝓᜣᝑᜣᝒ ·

"Expect my next letter from the busy marts of commerce and trade,"
Porter wrote Mrs. J. K. Hall on March 13, 1884 (almost exactly two
years after leaving Greensboro), and in late March or early April
the Richard Halls, en route to Williamson County, presented him to
the Joe Harrells, into whose big, comfortable home at 1008 Lavaca
Street in Austin he was received as a member of the family. "Come
on in and make yourself at home with my four sons and let there be
five instead of four," [1] Harrell is reported to have said; and,
apocryphal though the speech may be, it expresses accurately
enough the welcome which Porter found in Austin.

Compared with Greensboro, the capital of Texas was a city—the
fourth largest in the state. (In the 1880 census, Galveston had a
population of some 22,000, San Antonio 20,000, Houston 16,000, and
Austin 11,000.) Although Austin supported forty-three saloons and
fewer than half that many churches, the city was nevertheless more
Southern in its genteel traditions than wild and woolly San Antonio.
In "Aristocracy and Hash," published several years later in his
humorous weekly paper, Porter described a stranger's vain search
for a reasonably priced boardinghouse in Austin:

I found [the unfortunate newcomer reports] nine widows of Supreme
Court Judges, twelve relicts of Governors and Generals, and twenty-two
ruins left by various happy Colonels, Professors, and Majors, who valued
their aristocratic worth from $90 to $900 per week, with weak-kneed
hash and dried apples on the side. . . . I want to find a boarding house
where the proprietress was an orphan found in a livery stable, whose
father was a dago from East Austin, and whose grandfather was never
placed on the map. . . . Is there such a place in Austin? [2]

Bordered on the south by the Colorado River and on the west by the cedar-covered hills of the Edwards Plateau, the city had spread out from the intersection of the two main streets (both unpaved). Congress Avenue—lined with two main hotels, five banks, the newspaper office, and many business establishments and saloons —ran north from the river and the Union Depot to the grounds of the present capitol and on for a mile out to City Park. (The old wooden capitol had burned in 1881; in 1885 the cornerstone was laid for the present granite structure, said upon completion five years later to be the world's seventh largest building.) Crossing Congress Avenue six blocks north of the river was Pecan Street (now called Sixth Street), with almost an equal number of business establishments. On one Saturday afternoon, according to the count of a local reporter, Pecan Street was lined with 350 buggies and wagons; and on the Fourth of July the year after Porter's arrival it was jammed with more than 4,000 people for the laying of the cornerstone of the $400,000 Driskell Hotel, soon to become known as the Southwest's finest.

By 1886 there were seven miles of track for the horse-drawn trolleys. In 1884 John L. Sullivan fought an exhibition bout in Millet's Opera House, which about this time spent $1,500 for new scenery for such productions as *Only a Farmer's Daughter, Peck's Bad Boy, The Mikado,* and *Adrienne Lecouvreur* (a one-night stand featuring the celebrated Modjeska). A second theater, the Novelty, was largely a vaudeville house. In 1883 the University of Texas, on a forty-acre tract north of the capitol, opened for its first session with a faculty of eight "eminent scholars." Edward's Circulating Library had nearly 1,000 subscribers at two dollars a year, and Gammel's Book Store maintained a stock of 10,000 volumes. A Miss Barber, in an "Art Depot" on Congress Avenue, offered instruction in drawing and painting. Austin was the annual meeting place of the Texas Live Stock Association, which stirred up almost as much local interest as the State Legislature did. Some 70,000 bales of cotton were ginned annually in Austin. In addition to the native American population (along with a scattering of Mexicans and Negroes) there was a fairly large colony of Germans (immigrants who had been given land grants by the Republic of Texas), who joined their fellow countrymen from all over the state in an annual *Saengerfest*. (Porter's rival for the hand of the girl he married three years later was the son of the wealthy Zimplemann family.)

"Judge, come on in and mix with us," Joe Harrell, Jr., is reported to have said on first meeting Porter, and later he explained: "His expression called for that name the first time I looked at him and nothing else would fit him." [3] The need of the solemn-faced young man for the security of family life is measured by his success in establishing himself as the fifth son he had been invited to become. "He was just like a brother to me," said David Harrell,[4] whose bed Porter shared in one of the big high-ceilinged rooms upstairs. He was never allowed to pay for his room and board, even after he went to work. He met the friends of the Harrell sons, who furnished him with an assured position in local society. In short, Porter found his situation so much to his liking that he held on to it for nearly three years. Now and then, during the latter part of his stay, he would rent a room downtown with Will Anderson or Ed McLean or some other friend for a trial period ("keeping bachelor hall," he called it), but he always came back home to the Harrells'.

Appropriately enough, Porter was midway in his twenty-first year when he reached Austin, and on arrival he went briskly through the motions of making a start in a career. Being a registered pharmacist, he wrote back to North Carolina for references. By the end of May he was in possession of two documents which left nothing to be desired. One, from the Clerk of the Supreme Court of North Carolina, testified that he was "undoubtedly a young Man of good Moral Character and reputed to be a No. One druggist and a very popular young man among his many friends": [5] a statement endorsed by the Register of Deeds and the Postmaster. The other letter read as follows:

PORTER AND DALTON
DEALERS IN DRUGS

Greensboro, N.C., May 26, 1884

To WHOM IT MAY CONCERN:

We have known the bearer, Mr. W. S. Porter, intimately, both as druggist and citizen. His character here was above reproach, and as a druggist we unvariably found him careful, painstaking and accurate.

37

We feel sure that he will acceptably fill any position he is willing to accept.

(Signed) B. A. CHEEK, M. D.
JNO. E. LOGAN, M.D.
W. P. BEALL, M. D.
JAS. K. HALL, M. D., EX. PRES.
Med. Asso. N.C.[6]

With such credentials as these, Porter had no trouble landing a job as drug clerk in the Morley Brothers' Drug Store on East Pecan Street. One would naturally expect that, after a two-year rest cure, he would make his second start in the business world with the self-assurance of previous experience and the enthusiasm of ambitious young manhood. If such was the case, his enthusiasm waned rapidly. Working in a drugstore in Austin proved to be the same combination of tedious work and long hours that it had been in Greensboro, and since it was no longer a matter of grim necessity for him he gave up the uncongenial job within two or three months.

After this, he volunteered his services occasionally as a relief man in the cigar store operated by Joe Harrell, Jr., but for nearly a year—reverting to the habits he had formed at the Halls' ranch—he idled around the Harrell home, reading, sketching, or strumming a guitar in the intervals between his unhurried and consistently unsuccessful efforts to think up some more congenial sort of work. As had happened before and as was to happen again, he not only impressed people as a superior young man deserving of special consideration; he aroused their protective instincts as well. In addition to furnishing his board and keep, the Harrells offered to send him to New York to study art, but either Porter doubted his ability or the prospect seemed too strenuous for his mood at the time. The months went by, but they brought him no closer to any recognizable purpose in life. He sketched so assiduously and impertinently that he had to be threatened with no serving at the table unless he desisted from caricaturing Mr. Harrell in the act of carving meat. "A great part of our nights and rainy days," David Harrell later remembered, "used to be taken up in trying to find a word in Webster's Unabridged Dictionary that he couldn't spell. But if anyone ever found a word that he couldn't spell or didn't know the full meaning of, I don't remember it. And when asked where he learned all this, he replied that he carried an unabridged dictionary under his arm for two years while herding sheep for Dick Hall in La Salle County." [7] Another portion of his ample leisure Porter devoted to writing skits and verses, which by now he was beginning to submit to magazines as Joe Dixon had advised him to do. Lollie Cave—the girl whose hand he had crushed in the Houston railway station and with whom he now resumed his acquaintance at her aunt's home in Austin— later spoke of the rejection slips he was accumulating at this time.[8]

It was the association with Lollie, whom he jokingly called Polly-O, that led to Porter's first recorded use of the pseudonym O. Henry. He could never entice the family cat (which he had named Henry the Proud) to come to him until one day he called out impatiently, "Oh, Henry!" For some reason the cat responded, and being thus recognized at last, Porter said, "Well, O. Henry, you have bestowed on me the honor of your name." In playful moments thereafter he began calling himself O. Henry, as is evidenced by an entry in Lollie's autograph album: "O. Henry—Polly-O. 1886. W. S. Porter." [9]

Yet, "if W. S. P. at this time had any ambitions as a writer," one of his friends later commented, "he never mentioned it to me. I do not recall that he was fond of reading. One day I quoted some lines to him from a poem by John Alexander Smith. He made inquiry about the author, borrowed the book and committed to memory a great many passages from it, but I do not recall ever having known him to read any other book." [10] Inaccurate as this impression no doubt was, it must have been the impression that most people had of him at the time. He had, the same friend felt, "got interested in society," and "was accomplished in all the arts of a society man; had a good bass voice and sang well; was a good dancer and skater; played an interesting game of cards; and was preeminently an entertainer." [11] To play the role of unexceptional young man about town, indistinguishable from the others of his new station, must have satisfied a deep need in Porter. At any rate, for several years he played the role so successfully that he fooled not only other people but almost himself as well.

By the latter part of 1885 he had become well enough known around town for his pleasant voice to win a place in the Hill City Quartette.[12] According to one of the other members, "Porter was the littlest man in the crowd, and, of course, basso profundo. He was about five feet six inches tall, weighed about one hundred and thirty pounds, had coal black hair, grey eyes, and a long, carefully twisted moustache." [13] A surviving photograph indicates that the sartorial standards of the group were high, set no doubt by the strikingly handsome H. H. Long, much of whose clothing was furnished him by local haberdashers with an eye for the advertising value of such a public figure. By this time the Quartette had become a well enough known musical group to begin making appearances in churches and at various public entertainments. It had begun, though, as a serenading organization, of which main function the gay young gentlemen never lost sight, especially after Porter became the dominant spirit in the group. (One of the members, C. E. Hillyer, later spoke of the leadership Porter exercised, although he was "so unassuming that we did not feel that he was leading us.") [14]

Naturally one of the girls to be chosen by Porter for a serenade was Lollie, who later wrote that his voice had the sort of "vibrant quality that 'crooners' have today." [15] On the occasion in question, as Lollie was to report it, she and her sister and two girl friends mischievously kept the house dark during the entire serenade. When the performance was over, they still gave no sign but watched from their second-floor window while Porter, filling one of his gloves with gravel, sang out, "There was a little girl, she had a little curl . . ." Without warning the missile sailed through the window to plump at their feet. Still in the dark, the girls emptied the glove and, after inserting a nickel in each finger, tossed it back. Thereupon they turned on the lights and invited the courtiers in, with Lollie's aunt playing the piano while they sang and danced. Porter disappeared at one point during the evening to reappear with his trousers rolled up and his socks rolled down, Lollie's best point-lace handkerchief around his neck, and a lace corset cover around his middle. From his shoulders trailed a Mother Hubbard wrapper, on his head was a nightcap belonging to Lollie's grandmother, and with Lollie's black-and-tan terrier in his arms he swung into the waltz which was in progress.

From Austin in afteryears emanated numerous stories of Porter's high-spirited gaiety as a young bachelor. According to a typical story, Porter and several fellow National Guardsmen had leave, during a military encampment at Lampasas, to attend a dance at a local hotel. Although their pass was to expire at midnight, so beguiling were their partners that it was something past midnight before one of them thought of the time. And before they could make up their minds how to handle the situation, the corporal of the guard arrived from camp and marched his squad into the hotel to arrest them. Thinking quickly at last, Porter had someone meet the soldiers at the ballroom door to warn them against frightening the ladies with firearms. Incredibly, the plan worked; the squad stacked arms before entering the ballroom. Simultaneously Porter maneuvered the delinquent group into the hall; they unstacked the rifles, and those who remained unarmed marched in the center as prisoners. Approaching the camp gate, Porter barked at the sentry: "Squad under arrest. Stand aside!" Again incredibly, the trick seems to have worked. Not only were the unidentified men allowed to enter and slip away to their respective tents, but when the corporal of the guard and his squad returned without arms or prisoners they were arrested as impostors.

Nearly all of such stories about Porter's bachelor pranks have somehow a suggestion of falsity about them, either as if the stories were doctored in the process of transmission or as if Porter himself had worked a little too hard at the role he had set himself to play. The latter guess seems the preferable one, since so many different stories from so many different sources are enough of a piece to tend to corroborate one another. Porter himself is on record, moreover, with some testimony of his own. Writing to David Harrell, who was out of town more than once in 1885, Porter (now twenty-three years old) recounted one of his latest exploits:

Our serenading party has developed new and alarming modes of torture for our helpless and sleeping victims. Last Thursday night we loaded up a small organ on a hack and with our other usual instruments made an assault upon the quiet air of midnight that made the atmosphere turn pale.

After going the rounds we were halted on the Avenue by Fritz Hartkopf and ordered into his *salon*. We went in, carrying the organ, etc. A large crown of bums immediately gathered, prominent among which

41

were to be seen Percy Hicks, Theodore Hillyer, Randolph Burmond, Charlie Hicks, and after partaking freely of lemonade we wended our way down, and were duly halted and treated in the same manner by other hospitable gentlemen.

We were called in at several places while wit and champagne, Rhine Wine, etc., flowed in a most joyous manner. It was one of the most recherche and per diem affairs ever known in the city. Nothing occurred to mar the pleasure of the hour except a trifling incident that might be construed as malapropos and post-meridian by the hypercritical. Mrs. Charles Sims on attempting to introduce Mr. Charles Hicks and your humble servant to young ladies, where we had been invited inside, forgot our names and had to be informed on the subject before proceeding.[16]

For all of his consistent efforts, Porter was not entirely successful in the attempt to keep his back turned simultaneously to both past and future. In a page of drawings (dated September 25, 1886) in Lollie's autograph album is a cow with a small black bird perched on the tip of one of her horns. The cow was presumably a Texas stage prop, on which had settled—as Porter explained the drawing to Lollie—"a little black crow, and somehow or other I feel it will follow me all the days of my life, as it has been hopping along with me so far. . . . First I lost my mother when I was a baby, and I have missed her all my life. . . . Here I am among strangers in a faraway land with not a soul who is kin to me. You know, it is a lonely feeling and sometimes it gets close to a fellow's heart." [17]

Apocryphal as some of Lollie's stories clearly are, it would be unchivalrous to disbelieve entirely her statement that Porter proposed to her about this time (presumably in 1886, the year in which he was writing and drawing in her album).[18] Lollie's account of the incident is marred by the impossible statement that, to make amends for turning Porter down, she decided on the right girl (Athol Estes) for him to court. The fact of the matter is that Porter had met Athol as early as the spring of 1885, and by the time in question had been busy courting her for over a year. His suit may not have seemed to be going too well, however, on account of the opposition of Athol's mother, and he may well have impulsively proposed to Lollie while in one of the moods that prompted the drawing of the crow. He very successfully covered up his disappointment (if any) when he heard about Lollie's engagement to another man.

MISS LOLLIE [he wrote her]

Good Bye!

Am very sorry we didn't get to tell you so before you left. Hope we'll see you again soon. Tell Miss Rosa Good Bye.

The "Upper Ten" miss you and reserve two chairs for you in the "charmed circle." I've found out what the great event is that is going to happen. Isn't it nice though? You'd never guess how I came to know— I expected it all the time.

Wishing you both a pleasant winter, and no earthquakes, I am

Very truly

W. S. PORTER [19]

We do not get many glimpses of Porter's loneliness in Austin. He kept himself busy not merely with serenading parties but with a varied social schedule, including amateur theatricals. On April 28, 1885, he wrote to David Harrell: "As you will see by this morning's paper, there is to be a minstrel show next Wednesday for benefit of Austin Grays. I attended the rehearsal last night, but am better this morning, and the doctor thinks I will pull through with careful attention." [20] And on July 24, 1886, the *Statesman* reviewed the previous evening's performance of *The Doctor of Alcantara* at Millet's Opera House, a comic opera in which Porter took the small part of Don Pomposo. Many years later, writing to Mabel Wagnalls, Porter added a few details:

Down in Texas at one time I belonged to a first-rate musical association (Amateur). We toured the state with Pinafore & the Bohemian Girl & the Black Mantles & the Mikado & the "Chimes" etc. Me? Oh, in the chorus, of course. Except once. Sang the part of Don Hypolito Lopez Pomposo Antonio Riccardo Doloroso in the Black Mantles. I put in the next 2 years living it down, & finally succeeded.[21]

In addition to his dramatic reputation Porter was already making for himself a reputation as a "sport." True, his very proper Quartette associate, C. E. Hillyer, said in later years that he "was always pure minded. He never told a vulgar joke even on camp or military trips [because] he had too much respect for women." This much is confirmed by the testimony of friends later in life. But it is clearly another matter to pretend, as Hillyer did, that Porter "never drank in saloons" and that "when the boys ordered drinks in a saloon,

Porter usually took a seltzer or a lemonade." [22] According to Dixie Daniels, a later associate on the weekly humorous paper he published in Austin, Porter "could drink more beer than any man his size I ever knew, without showing the effects in the least." [23] Hillyer apparently said more than he meant when he added, "I never saw him gamble, although I have heard that he gambled in a sort of private gambling place owned by Will Anderson." Later reports make all too plain the extent to which Porter drank and gambled in Austin, but however gay his evenings may have been at this time, he was a very proper-seeming young man. Unconcerned though he was with religion, he attended church regularly (usually to sing in the choir), and his speech was not only careful but almost entirely free from slang.

By now Porter's social life was such that he began to feel the need of a regular income. He still shied away from a druggist's work, but sometime in the fall of 1886 John Maddox (who had selected him to illustrate *Carbonate Days* and with whom he had become good friends) offered him a job as bookkeeper in the real-estate firm of Maddox Brothers and Anderson, one of the leading firms in the state. According to a Quartette associate, there had been one earlier and short-lived business venture:

For a time previous to his employment by Maddox Brothers and Anderson, Porter did some kind of work for the law firm of Ward, Hill, and Green. Mystery was attached to this work, and we boys spent lots of time conjecturing as to its character. We finally decided that it must be detective work. This conclusion was perfectly natural in view of the type of boy Porter was. He never told us about his past life; we never knew even where he came from. . . . [But] his past was of no consequence since he had the friendship and backing of the Harrells.[24]

The Maddox connection was to become as important in Porter's life as the Harrell connection, which it gradually superseded. Maddox employed Porter as a bookkeeper at the generous salary of $100 a month, and since he was completely inexperienced in this kind of work, turned him over to the third member of the firm, Charles E. Anderson, for instruction. Later on, Maddox was to offer to finance an art course in New York for Porter, and Anderson not only proved of great help at the time of Porter's marriage but took the young

PORTER AS A YOUNG BACHELOR IN AUSTIN

PORTER WITH ATHOL AND MARGARET

couple into his home for the first six months of their married life.
For little over a year Porter seems to have repaid the kindness of
his benefactors by working conscientiously at his job. "He learned
bookkeeping from me," Anderson later said, "and I have never
known anyone to pick it up with such ease or rapidity. He was
number one, and we were loath to part with him." [25] Another friend
commented on his serious attitude:

As a business man his face was calm, almost expressionless; his demeanor was steady, even calculated. . . . [He] was prompt, accurate,
talented, and very efficient; but the minute he was out of business—that
was all gone. He always approached a friend with a merry twinkle in his
eye and an expression which said: "Come on, boys, we are going to have
a lot of fun," and we usually did. The story of "The Green Door" in its
spirit and in its fact was just such a thing as might happen with him
any night. [26]

In the year 1886 a salary of $100 a month would have seemed all
a young man needed to start a home of his own, and by the time
Porter began making this salary he had for over a year been courting
a high-school girl named Athol Estes. Born in 1868 on a farm outside
the town of Clarksville, Tennessee, Athol seemed—as clearly as
Porter himself—marked for misfortune. The Clarksville of Reconstruction years ("Little Haiti" it was called because of the large
Negro population) was such a turbulent place that soon after Athol's
birth the Estes family fled from the threat of Negro uprisings to the
comparative safety of Nashville. Here, six months later, Athol's
father died of tuberculosis, having bequeathed to his daughter his
fatal weakness. When Athol was six years old her mother decided to
marry P. G. Roach, a well-to-do Nashville widower (originally from
Pittsburgh) with two daughters of his own, Nettie and Effie. Shortly
before the marriage was to take place, Roach had sudden financial
reverses; in fact, he lost everything he had. He offered to release
Mrs. Estes from the engagement; she insisted on sticking to her
bargain, and in due course Roach decided to make a new start in
the West. Having made the trip to Texas in the company of one of
Horace Greeley's young relatives, he selected Austin as the city in
which he would settle, and in 1879, after he had bought a farm out
from town and made a few investments with what money he had

been able to save up during the five years since his reverses, his family moved out to join him. Eventually Roach was to prosper, both on the farm and in the grocery business he established on East Pecan Street, but for the first few years things were tight, so much so that in 1881 Athol had to be taken out of private school and enrolled in public school, or "free school" as it was called. Many of her new playmates, though, turned out to be as well bred as herself, and her two remaining grammar-school years were happy and successful.

In high school Athol again became an outstanding student, and in her third year, when construction began on the new state capitol, she was chosen by her classmates to place in the cornerstone the souvenirs which they had contributed for the purpose (including a lock of her own hair). At this ceremony, held on March 2, 1885, some 20,000 people assembled to witness the placing of the huge granite rock (it weighed 18,000 pounds) which had been hauled from the quarries at Marble Falls on a specially built railroad. The occasion was marred by a shower of rain, which was particularly distressing to Athol because in spite of her mother's protest she had worn the beruffled dimity dress which had been bought for her to wear that night. The dance sponsored by the Austin Grays company of the state militia was an event to which she had looked forward even more eagerly than to the cornerstone celebration. By some quick work on the part of a colored laundress the dress was reconditioned, and it was at this dance—according to Frances Maltby, Athol's school desk mate in those days of double desks—that Athol met Porter.[27] The date would seem to be accurate, in view of the society-page notices during the winter of 1885–1886 of gatherings where both of them were listed among the guests.

The surviving pictures of Athol do not make clear what it was about her that attracted Porter. She had a conspicuously overdeveloped chin, with a jutting underlip and a sulky stare in the eyes. "But," Frances Maltby pointed out, "it is hardly fair to Athol to give her photograph to the public. Her beauty was chiefly that of coloring and expression"; and such was her vivacity that "Athol was a belle from babyhood to maturity by sheer right of charm." [28] With her light brown hair and blue eye, she had the "peach-bloom" complexion often associated with early tuberculosis, and she wore

46

dimity so consistently that in later years, when Porter was asked why he invariably dressed his heroines in either dimity or crepe de Chine, he said: "That is all I know about women's clothes. Athol always wore dimity. We couldn't afford anything better. It always looked good to me. And my second wife wore crepe de Chine." [29]

Whatever it was about her that caught Porter's interest—her animated charm, her not altogether fancied likeness to his sharp-witted mother, the similarity of her interests to his own—he was very shortly enrolled as a regular suitor and worried by the discovery of a rival (Lee Zimplemann) who had the inside track with Mrs. Roach. Having from time to time sung, without previous preference, in the choirs of the Baptist, Episcopal, and Presbyterian churches, Porter now gave his allegiance to the Presbyterian, where Athol was a choir member of long standing. And schoolgirl though Athol was, he was soon managing to see her so often even on school nights that during her senior year her friends looked forward to the almost daily reports on what the couple had done the previous afternoon or evening. In the only surviving note to the girl he married, Porter wrote (evidently fairly early in their courtship, perhaps during the spring of 1886):

MISS ESTES,

Tempted by the lovely weather, which with its genial and balmy influence seems already to herald the approach of Spring, I think no welcome to said approaching Spring could be more appropriate than to drive out among the green lanes and breathe the exquisite fragrance of the early violets and wild onions. So if you can and will, may I call for you at 2 o'clock this aft.? Or if circumstances prevent today, would Miss Estes favor me by suggesting the earliest afternoon I may have that pleasure? The absence of dust will make a drive more pleasant than usual.

Hoping Miss Estes will consent to go, or at least to name a day when she will,

I remain
Very truly
W. S. PORTER.[30]

Sometimes Porter helped Athol with her English homework, on one occasion fulfilling the assignment to describe some local entertainment by writing a sketch which began: "The tableaux were all on a large scale, intricate, elaborate, and very elegant. Colored lights were burned, and the young ladies in their groupings and graceful draperies were very beautiful." [31] If this is a fair specimen, we are at liberty to wonder how much Athol's grades were improved by Porter's help. She and her schoolmate Frances Maltby seem, however, to have been duly impressed by Porter's linguistic readiness, a characteristic for which Athol herself was noted. During her senior year, while a new high-school building was under construction, classes were held in the basement of the Baptist Church across from the Governor's Mansion, and often Governor Ireland, on his way home to lunch, would pass a group of the girls sitting near a rock pile behind the church. He repeatedly invited them to bring their lunch over to the shady yard of the Mansion, an invitation which Athol is said to have answered with various bits of repartee. "All shade and no rock pile is bad for the young," she quipped on one occasion, and again, "Oh, but then we would be out of sight, and don't want to be out of mind." [32]

In addition to his intellectual attractions, Porter seems to have had others even more telling. Sometimes he would visit the rock pile at noon, and in Frances Maltby's words, "as he continued up the hill with his dignity and his waxed moustache, there would be murmurs of: 'Isn't he adorable?'" [33] Then, of course, there was the inevitable serenading, combined with what all the girls seemed to have regarded as his inimitable drollery. The combination is illustrated in a double cartoon which he drew in one of Athol's textbooks. The first picture depicts the struggle of Mr. Roach, in sleeping garments and with a candle in one hand and a pistol in the other, to break away from Mrs. Roach, who is pleading with him to "Spare the artists," while overhead Athol and her two stepsisters, Nettie and Effie Roach, watch from a window. In the second picture Porter and his fellow serenaders (the Jolly Entertainers he called this group, presumably a somewhat livelier one than the Quartette) are making their getaway, two of them astride the horse and the other two in the surrey, all of them still performing on their instruments. The caption reads: "The only time the Jolly Entertainers Ever Declined an Invitation to Stop." [34] Actually, Mr. Roach was an easygoing man, formidable only to the extent of being "irritable when awakened," as Mrs. Roach once explained to Porter.[35] Mrs. Roach was the one who opposed Porter's suit. Not only was Porter poor and unknown (whereas Lee Zimplemann was the son of a wealthy German family), but he seemed to Athol's mother entirely too "sporty" to make a very promising husband for her daughter.

In spite of her mother's wishes Athol gradually gave Porter the edge over Zimplemann, who, though he is said to have been very handsome, no doubt lacked Porter's verve. According to Frances Maltby, the couple became engaged at a rehearsal for a social event reported by the *Statesman* on Sunday, June 5, 1887:

WAITER DRILL

Last night at Turner Hall the Southern Presbyterian Church gave the entertainment that the rain broke up on Friday night. The Waiter Drill of the young ladies was very good. They executed the manual of arms very nicely, and the marching was excellent. The officers were as follows:

Captain	W. S. Porter
First Lieutenant	Miss Laura Driscoll
Second Lieutenant	Miss Maggie Howard
First Sergeant	Miss Athol Estes
Second Sergeant	Miss Ellen Borroughs.[36]

Zimplemann had given Athol a lock bracelet (as well as an opal ring), which she was overheard at one of the waiter-drill rehearsals to tell Porter she was going to have removed. The engagement was unofficial, however, and there were no plans for marrying in the immediate future.

At the high-school graduation exercises on June 10 (an occasion on which "orations" were delivered by the boys and "essays" by the girls), Athol spoke on the topic "Three Fold Is the Pace of Time," and her performance is said to have been recorded by her fiancé in a cartoon captioned: "Walk, Trot and Canter," in which she was shown demonstrating in kind. Porter was involved in the commencement in another way too: he had lent his services as adviser in the selection of a parting gift which the class had chosen Athol to purchase and to present to the school principal. "Before the exercises closed," reported the *Statesman* next day, "Miss Estes, on behalf of the graduating class, called Professor Bryant to task for his many delinquencies during the past session and presented him with an elegant combination gold pencil and toothpick." [37]

A week later the *Statesman* society page contained a notice of one of the many parties given at this festive season, one of special interest in view of the home where it was held: "Last evening the residence of Mr. C. E. Anderson was a scene of merriment. The occasion was a german given to Miss Lizzie Thornton. The evening was spent by those present in the most enjoyable of dances, the german. Among those present were the following—Misses Walker, McCarthy, Brush, Perry, Boak, Estes . . . Messrs. Anderson, Goldman, Booth, Moore, Long, Porter." [38]

Less than a month later the same paper carried the announcement of Athol's surprise marriage to Porter. It had to be a surprise marriage because of Mrs. Roach's strongly stated stand in the matter of Athol's two suitors. (Her official objection to Porter was his mother's reported death from tuberculosis, the same heritage which Athol had from her father.) Porter was not deterred by Mrs. Roach's wishes. He had gained considerably in self-confidence in Austin, and he seemed to be as comfortably situated as could be desired by a not overly ambitious young man making his own way in the world. During the summer of 1886, when Richard Hall had been nominated in the democratic primary for Land Commissioner, Porter had written to his former friend asking for a job. In September, Hall had promised him a job in the drafting department if he could prepare himself in the three months remaining before the change of administrations. Porter worked so diligently and so successfully that Betty Hall later spoke of his remarkable feat in becoming, on such short notice, "the best in the force." [39] When Hall took over the Land Office in January, 1887, he made a place for Porter, who left Maddox Brothers and Anderson to become a draftsman at the same salary he had been making ($100 a month). Porter maintained his personal friendship with Anderson, however, to the extent of accepting an invitation shortly afterward to move into the Anderson home, where he seems to have been regarded (as he had been in the Harrell home) as a member of the family. [40] With a good job, a secure position in local society, and a foster family as prominent as the Andersons, Porter must have felt that marriage was no rash step. And yet it was not this or any other line of reasoning so much as the impulse of the moment which motivated him. Mrs. Roach was getting ready to send Athol to Nashville for the summer as a precautionary measure when Porter took charge of the situation.

Late in the afternoon of Friday, July 1, Mrs. Roach happened to need a spool of thread. As she gave Athol the money for the purchase, she noticed that the girl had somehow torn her skirt. "You certainly cannot go out of the yard in that torn skirt," she said.[41] But Athol, insisting that she would see no one she knew, hurried off to run the errand before the stores closed. For several reasons it may be safely assumed that what followed was entirely unpremeditated on her part. She was still wearing Lee Zimplemann's lock bracelet (he had so far refused to surrender the key, she had told Porter). Further, no girl would choose to be married in a torn skirt. Finally, no Southern girl in those days, exposed as children were to the superstitions of their black mammies, would have dreamed of marrying on a Friday. By pure chance Athol met Porter downtown, and between the end of the afternoon and mid-evening they not only made their fateful decision but, with the help of the cooperative Andersons, secured an after-hours marriage license from the county clerk, worked out their plan, and rented a carriage from a liveryman named Miller.[42]

The Reverend R. K. Smoot, pastor of the Southern Presbyterian Church, had been to a church meeting that evening, according to his son, and "having walked the mile and a half to our home, he came in about ten o'clock." [43] Actually, it must have been no later than nine o'clock, as will appear. At any rate, on this hot July night the Smoot family had turned out the lights and were sitting on the dark porch to cool off when a carriage drove up and stopped at the gate. Charles Anderson came up the walk, as the pastor's son remembered it, and announced: "There's romance in the air. I've got a couple down at the gate that want to get married." After a brief consultation, Anderson went back to fetch Mrs. Anderson and the bridal pair. "Oh, Will, my dress is torn," Athol said, suddenly remembering as they got out of the carriage. But Porter found a pin and expertly concealed the tear before they entered the house.

The pastor tried to reason with Athol. As Betty Hall commented later, the girl had been "almost raised by Dr. Smoot in Sunday School and the choir," and he was unwilling to perform the ceremony. But in the face of their determination he saw that opposition was useless. He examined the license. He asked Athol her age. "Well," he said finally, "I suppose you're old enough to know your own mind." [44] (Athol was nineteen, Porter twenty-five.) The ceremony that followed was reported by the *Statesman* next day:

HEARTS UNITED

It will be a matter of surprise and pleasure as well, for friends to know that last evening Mr. Will S. Porter and Miss Athol Estes were joined in the holy bonds of matrimony. The solemn and impressive ceremony was performed by the Rev. Dr. Smoot at his residence at 9:30 o'clock last evening in the presence of Mr. and Mrs. Anderson, the Rev. Mr. Murrey, and Mrs. Smoot. The young couple immediately repaired to the residence of Mr. and Mrs. Anderson, where they will make their home for the present. Both Mr. Porter and his charming young bride have numerous friends in the city who will join in extending to them most cordial congratulations and good wishes for their future happiness and prosperity.[45]

Up to the climactic point of the ceremony itself, the young couple had been carried on a mounting wave of excitement. As soon as the deed was done, even while they stood partaking of the teacakes and cool drinks which Mrs. Smoot had brought in, they must have been overtaken by a dread of the first consequence that had to be faced. It took no great effort of the imagination to picture the state into which Mrs. Roach had worked herself after at least five hours of waiting—waiting first in mere annoyance at the girl's delay but finally in genuine alarm for her safety. (The Roaches had a telephone, but not enough other people did for her to canvass all of Athol's friends.) As soon as possible the wedding party returned to the Anderson home—where the newlyweds were to live for six months—and Anderson went forth on his errand of conciliation.

Years later, in recounting the episode, Anderson remembered only that it was late, possibly as late as one o'clock in the morning when he reached the Roach home.[46] He tried to break the news gently, but, according to Frances Maltby, Mrs. Roach was indignant: "It took Mr. Anderson some time to make her see that it was her duty to receive the young couple and give them her blessing." [47] As Dr. Smoot's son reported the incident from Anderson's own account of it to the minister, Mrs. Roach "lost her self-control and simply raged. She vented her anger upon one after the other and finally lighted on my father. 'He had no business marrying them,' she said. 'As my pastor, he should have come here and asked my permission first.'

It was . . . months before Mrs. Roach would speak to my father. She refused to attend church during that time." [48]

It was not a particularly auspicious beginning for Porter's marriage.

CHAPTER FOUR

· ❦ ·

Eighteen years after his wedding, and eight years after Athol's death, Porter wrote a story about a sight-seeing bus in New York, among whose passengers were "James Williams, of Cloverdale, Missouri, and his Bride":

Capitalize it, friend typo—that last word—word of words in the epiphany of life and love. The scent of the flowers, the booty of the bee, the primal drip of spring waters, the overture of the lark, the twist of lemon peel on the cocktail of creation—such is the Bride. Holy is the wife; revered the mother; galliptious is the summer girl—but the bride is the certified check among the wedding presents that the gods send in when man is married to mortality. . . .

Dear kind fairy, please cut out those orders for money and 40 H. P. touring cars and fame and a new growth of hair and the presidency of the boat club. Instead of any of them turn backward—oh, turn backward and give us just a teeny-weeny bit of our wedding trip over again. Just an hour, dear fairy, so we can remember how the grass and poplar trees looked, and the bow of those bonnet strings tied beneath her chin—even if it was the hat pins that did the work. Can't do it? Very well; hurry up with that touring car and the oil stock, then.[1]

As Porter wrote these words, his first biographer tells us, his own elopement "came back to him touched with pathos but radiant and hallowed in retrospect." [2] And according to another writer, Porter and Athol "were admirably suited for each other. Will's pride in Athol and his love for her stimulated him to greater efforts, while Athol, despite the fact that she was never strong and was frequently ill, proved a devoted wife." [3] It is worthy of note, however, that it was the idea of a bride which excited genuine feelings in Porter's mind when he wrote "Sisters of the Golden Veil," whereas the words *holy* and *revered,* for wife and mother, suggest willed attitudes more than spontaneous feelings.

This is not to say that Porter's marriage proved a complete disillusionment, but only to suggest that it was considerably less idyllic than has usually been supposed. Many years later in New York, discussing marriage with his editor-friend Robert H. Davis, Porter said that if it were up to him to establish a code of courtship, he "would state plainly, via the preamble, that in all matters of the heart the word o-w-n-e-r-s-h-i-p be expunged." He went on to lament a state of affairs whereby "a gent supposedly living a free and unencumbered existence casts a languishing eye upon a fair woman, lets a few kind words slip into his conversation, allows her hand to repose in his for a split second and then finds himself on a par with the leading character in *Uncle Tom's Cabin.*"

Why [he demanded, warming to his subject] should a caress carry with it the assurance of vassalage? . . . Let it be understood that two souls with but a single thought should regard the culmination of that illusion as both the beginning and the end of the heart's desire, rather than to classify it as the inauguration of a permanent alliance with all its attendant and unhappy obligations. Would it not be a complete solution to look upon realization as a triumph so beautiful that it could not in this life recur, instead of announcing that under new management the business would begin to boom? [4]

These seem hardly the reflections of a man who "spoke of Athol so seldom . . . because the sacred things, like the love he bore his young wife, were too personal, too precious, to be talked and written about." [5] On the other hand, the first few years of the marriage were unquestionably happy. Athol's pride in her husband was "unbounded," Frances Maltby went on to say, "and his name was ever on her lips." [6] Later in New York, Porter told Anne Partlan (perhaps his closest confidant) that Athol was the only woman he had ever loved. [7]

Through the summer and fall months of 1887 the young couple stayed on in the Anderson home, sheltered from the problems of the workaday world. It has been said that Athol stimulated Porter to write more persistently than he had been doing, as evidenced by the fact that only three months after his marriage he received his first surviving letter of acceptance. But it is possible that Athol was not so much the cause of his success as the preserver of the kind of letter which Porter himself had never bothered to keep, for the acceptance letter (dated September 3, 1887, from the editor of the Detroit *Free Press*) is clearly a reminder from an editor who had been dealt with before:

MY DEAR SIR:
Please send your string for the month of August. And it would please me to receive further contributions at once. Send a budget every week.
Sincerely,
A. MOSLEY.[8]

Porter was now publishing narrative skits and jokes and verse consistently if not very profitably. Early in December the editor of the *Free Press* wrote again to promise a check in a few days and to inquire: "Can you not send more matter—a good big installment every week? . . . After you get a better idea of the things we do not want, the quantity to be returned will be very small." [9] The question of the kind of payment Porter was receiving is answered by a communication (undated but written about the same time) from a New York periodical named *Truth:* "We have selected 'The Final Triumph' and 'A Slight Inaccuracy,' for which you will receive a check for $6." [10] According to Frances Maltby, such was Athol's delight when this acceptance arrived that she "kissed him, congratulated him, and danced about him," and Porter remarked, "It will keep the chafing dish bubbling and buy steak and onions." [11]

It must not be assumed, however, that this was the beginning of the literary career of O. Henry. Ten years were to pass before the writer of humorous skits was to have his first real short story accepted by a national publication. Meanwhile, Porter and his bride were concerned less with literary matters than with the same round of dances and parties which had kept them occupied before their marriage. In addition to their choir singing in church, they became members of the Austin Musical Union, which, under the direction of Professor William Besserer, gave frequent concerts (of which the programs carried the notice: "Admission, 25 cents. Refreshments

Served").[12] Athol, who is reported to have had an unusually sweet soprano voice, read music with such facility that at rehearsals she often sang three or four different parts to fill in for absent members. Porter, with his untrained bass, was content to stay in the background, from where, "proud of her quickness and versatility, [he] would look on with possessive pride." He always added to the general good time with his "humorous comments," but Athol seems to have dominated the scene at such gatherings. "Between solos Athol would steal back to the rear line where we stood and exchange pithy repartee with her husband and admonish me [Frances Maltby] to keep him in hand." [13]

Already, though, there must have been—unknown to most of their friends—another side to the marriage. Betty Hall, who was to resume her friendship with Porter after her husband's election as Land Commissioner brought them to Austin, found that the young couple were not quite as harmoniously mated as people thought. Athol, she reported, was still a spoiled child, who "would lie on the floor and scream if he [Porter] was late." [14] Later there were to be other witnesses to more serious conflicts.

Soon after the first of the year, because of Athol's pregnancy, Porter rented a small house in the 500 block of East Fourth Street, the same street on which the Roaches lived. The Roaches and various friends donated odds and ends of furniture, and with "hilarious pride" they showed off the new bedroom suite which they were buying on the installment plan—a set of heavy, ornamented pieces with mirrors in both the dresser and the wardrobe. "So Will and myself can dress simultaneously and harmoniously," Athol explained pertly.[15] But the carefree gaiety of the young couple was interrupted by a double misfortune. When the baby, a boy, was born on May 6, it lived for only a few hours, and Athol was left so ill that at first Porter and her parents feared for her life too. During her daughter's slow convalescence Mrs. Roach took charge of the little household, and no doubt Mr. Roach helped substantially with the medical expenses. If so, it was the first of a long series of occasions when he was to assist Porter more than generously. Long before now Athol's parents had forgiven the runaway couple, and Mrs. Roach was to become and always to remain one of Porter's most loyal champions. "I consider those mother-in-law stories the falsest kind of laughs," he said with some feeling when such a joke was once told in her presence, and long after the death of her daughter and her son-in-law Mrs. Roach was to remember his kindness and essential goodness.[16]

Ever since they had moved from the Anderson home, Porter's salary of $100 a month had been proving a less and less luxurious income for a married man. In fact, he was already beginning to spend his salary before he earned it: by the end of the month for which he was to be paid he had invariably drawn most of it in advance. Increasingly he was to have financial problems, but for the time being he had a congenial and not too taxing job. On the whole his four years in the Land Office were the happiest of his life.

Whenever you visit Austin [he wrote in "Bexar Scrip No. 2692"] you should by all means go to see the General Land Office.

As you pass up the avenue you turn sharp round the corner of the court house, and on a steep hill before you you see a mediaeval castle.

You think of the Rhine; the "castled crag of Drachenfels"; the Lorelei; and the vine-clad slopes of Germany. And German it is in every line of its architecture and design. . . .

People living in other states can form no conception of the vastness and importance of the work performed and the significance of the millions of records and papers composing the archives of this office.[17]

In this building—now a museum but still very much as he described it—Porter became aware of an aspect of Texas life that was new to him. As he explained it in the same story:

The honest but ignorant settler, bent on saving the little plot of land he called home, elbowed the wary land shark who was searching the records for evidence to oust him; the lordly cattle baron, relying on his influence and money, stood at the Commissioner's desk side by side with the pre-emptor, whose little potato patch lay like a minute speck of island in the vast, billowy sea of his princely pastures, and played the old game of "freeze-out," which is as old as Cain and Abel.

On one occasion Porter took advantage of a chance to buy for $50 a piece of "stray land" which he had located in Wilbarger County and which he sold a few months later for $900. A shrewd and unscrupulous speculator could—as is explained in another story, "Georgia's Ruling"—have found many such "tracts of unappropriated public domain, generally invisible upon the official maps, but actually existing 'upon the ground.' The law entitled any one possessing certain State scrip to file by virtue of same upon any land not previously legally appropriated. Most of the scrip was now in the hands of the land-sharks. Thus, at the cost of a few hundred dollars, they often secured lands worth as many thousands." [18] Porter himself—rather than risk further speculation—characteristically preferred to toy with the idea of buried treasure. His brother later had a story about a lost gold mine the location of which was shown on an old map which Porter came across while in the Land Office. Shirley Worth (to whom Porter must have turned because of his construction-camp experience, not out of any fraternal magnanimity) said he declined the invitation to "come out, load up a burro or two, and make a try at finding this particular mine," [19] but Porter is said to have hired a wagon full of equipment and driven eighty miles to a neighboring county to conduct the search which he later described in his story "Buried Treasure":

I and the grandson of the treasure examined those cedar-covered hills with the care of a lady hunting for the wicked flea. We explored every side, top, circumference, mean elevation, angle, slope and concavity of every one for two miles up and down the river. We spent four days doing so. Then we hitched up the roan and the dun, and hauled the remains of the coffee and bacon the one hundred and forty-nine miles back to Concho City. [20]

Some years later, at a low ebb in his fortunes, Porter was to resurrect this fond hope of finding buried treasure. Meanwhile another, presumably not very lucrative, undertaking was the series of twenty-six illustrations which he did for a book by J. W. Wilbarger, *Indian Depredations in Texas. Reliable Accounts of Battles, Wars, Adventures, Forays, Murders, Massacres, Etc. Etc.*, published in Austin in 1889. Since Porter's drawings of appropriate depredations were turned into woodcuts by a local engraver, it is hardly fair to judge them, but unless the engraver was completely incompetent, Porter's drawings were clearly amateur work.

In the main, during his years in the Land Office, Porter confined his attention to his day's work as a draftsman and left his financial problems to take care of themselves. His spare time in the office

Porter seems to have spent in ornamenting the borders of his maps with drawings of appropriate birds, animals, cowboys, and steers (several specimens are still on display in the Land Office). He even drew sketches on the recently painted walls of the office which he shared with some fifteen other workers; one such sketch is said to have depicted, first, a man bent conscientiously over his desk (labeled "The Newcomer") and second, a man smoking and reading, with his feet propped up on his desk (labeled "Old Timer").[21] His co-workers liked him, but—with the exception of Herman Pressler—he made no intimate friends among them. His Land Office co-workers, like his associates at every stage of his life, were struck mainly by his reticence, which kept them from feeling that they really understood him.

Early in the year 1889 Athol found that she was pregnant again. By now they had moved into a cheerful little cottage at 505 East Eleventh Street, with altheas and pomegranates growing in the yard, and it was here that their second child was born on September 30, a daughter whom they named Margaret Worth. In an attempt at appropriate jollity Porter remarked to Athol, as soon as he had seen his daughter, "Do you think she'll ever develop an intelligent, human expression?"[22] But there was little occasion for jollity. Again Athol was ill, this time so desperately that it was a matter of weeks before her family felt certain that she would live, and even then, Frances Maltby remembered, "she mended so slowly that the fear of the disease of which her father had died filled her loved ones with anxiety. She, too, was tortured with the thought that this shadow was coming into her life."[23]

As soon as it seemed safe to move her, Mrs. Roach persuaded Porter that the place for the sick girl was her mother's home. Probably not much persuasion was required, although it must have been a bitter disappointment to give up the home they had made for themselves. He carried Athol to the carriage, and with the baby in her lap they drove to the Roach home on East Fourth Street. Their own furniture Porter put in storage.

They lived in the Roach home for several months, while Athol gradually regained her strength. When she seemed well enough, they rented a house almost next door and took their furniture out of storage. But almost by the time they were settled it was decided best that Athol should be spared the long, wearing summer in Austin. Going first with her mother to Nashville, she and her baby later went to visit Porter's aunt in Greensboro. (Miss Lina was living alone since the recent death of her mother.) In October Porter joined them. Unfortunately, no details about the visit have survived, and it is possible only to surmise what Porter's attitude must have been: whether, as has usually been suggested, he wholeheartedly enjoyed showing off his vivacious wife and infant daughter, or whether he merely took advantage of a free vacation for his family. He had not returned in the coach and four which he had written would be necessary before he would return. In fact, as he had learned during the summer, he was soon to be out of even the modest job he had. Richard Hall, who had opposed James Hogg for the gubernatorial nomination in the democratic primary, had lost not only the nomination but also his post as Land Commissioner. Since, therefore, Porter would be looking for another job in January, it could not have been a carefree vacation trip that he made to Greensboro to fetch his wife and child. No doubt his own feelings are suggested in a story he was to write a few years later for his humorous newspaper, the *Rolling Stone*:

I got off at the old depot, and then commenced the strange feeling of loss, depression and change that so much alteration wrought. I walked down the old familiar streets and gazed in deepest wonder at the scenes around me. The streets seemed narrower, the houses smaller and meaner; every prospect had shrunken and grown into ruin and decadence. I met men in the street by whose side I had grown up from my earliest boyhood. They all passed me with either a curious stare or a careless glance. . . . I reached home, and entered the old gate. Shrubbery had grown into trees; some trees had died and been cut down. The old house was the same, except it needed paint and repairs. . . . Of course, after I had made myself known, my welcome was warm enough, and after a few days my old friends about town came trooping about me and made my stay as pleasant as they could.[24]

Athol and Margaret are said to have visited in Greensboro again the following summer, and in 1891 Porter's brother was struck by the difference one year had made in her appearance. "Her disease," he said later, "was getting the upper hand." [25] There was some talk of having Miss Lina visit in Austin, but she never did so.

On January 21, 1891, after working his last day in the Land Office, Porter drew two-thirds of a month's pay ($66.66) and walked out into the streets of a city where everything seemed to be progressing except his career. At the head of Congress Avenue, in the center of a parklike tract of which one corner was occupied by the Land Office, stood the huge new tawny-granite capitol, completed and opened with gala festivities in September, 1888: it was the largest state capitol in the country and taller even than the Capitol in Washington. The horse-drawn trolleys running up the Avenue and around a circuit of several miles were gradually being replaced by electric cars. The population had grown to 15,000. But among all these busy-seeming people, Porter—now a man with no visible means of support for his wife and child—must have walked down the Avenue in a frame of mind to tempt him to stop in Four-Eyed Brown's or some other saloon instead of going home to Athol.

Before the end of the month he had accepted the only work he could find, a temporary job as inventory lister in the annual stock taking at Tobin's Drug Store. The fact that he was reduced to such poor-paying work is attested by the inventory book he used, on the last pages of which he doodled in characteristic fashion and even wrote a trial opening for a story.[26] But once again his welfare became the concern of one of his friends. In February—thanks to the efforts of Charles Anderson—he got a chance at another hundred-dollar-a-month job as teller in the First National Bank, located at the intersection of Congress Avenue and Pecan Street. Since Porter had Anderson's backing, and also because he seemed to have better eyesight than his bespectacled rival for the job, he was successful.[27] Clearly he was in no position to choose among jobs, but even if he had been he might well have chosen what any responsible adviser would have told him was a good business opportunity, one which could easily lead to better things in the bank. His new job, however, was to confront him not with advancement but with the crucial experience of his life.

Even if Porter had been a more skilled bookkeeper than he was, he would have found himself up against a nerve-racking job.

Founded as a bank catering largely to wealthy stockmen, the First National was still operated with the free and easy informality of the Old West. Not only were overdrafts allowed freely, but even the use of checks was often too much trouble for officers of the bank, who simply helped themselves from the cash drawer, with only a word to the teller if he was on the spot and sometimes not even a written memorandum in his absence. In his story "Friends in San Rosario," Porter was later to give an accurate enough account of the kind of banking practice prevalent in the First National. When a federal bank examiner invades one of the two banks in San Rosario, the president gets a hurried message from the president of the bank across the street. He then detains the examiner with a long-drawn-out explanation of an apparent shortage in his own funds. At the end of the story the reader discovers that there is no actual shortage; the reason for detaining the examiner has been the following note from across the street:

DEAR TOM:
I hear there's one of Uncle Sam's greyhounds going through you, and that means that we'll catch him inside of a couple of hours, maybe. Now, I want you to do something for me. We've got just $2,200 in the bank, and the law requires that we have $20,000. I let Ross and Fisher have $18,000 late yesterday afternoon to buy up that Gibson bunch of cattle. They'll realize $40,000 in less than thirty days on the transaction, but that won't make my cash on hand look any prettier to that bank examiner. Now I can't show him those notes, for they're just plain notes of hand without any security in sight, but you know very well that Pink Ross and Jim Fisher are two of the finest white men God ever made, and they'll do the square thing. You remember Jim Fisher—he was the one who shot that faro dealer in El Paso. I wired Sam Bradshaw's bank to send me $20,000, and it will get in on the narrow-gauge at 10:35. You can't let a bank examiner in to count $2,200 and close your doors. Tom, you hold that examiner. Hold him. Hold him if you have to rope him and sit on his head. Watch our front window after the narrow-gauge gets in, and when we've got the cash inside we'll pull down the shade for a signal. Don't turn him loose till then. I'm counting on you, Tom.

> Your Old Pard,
> BOB BUCKLEY,
> Prest. Stockmen's National [28]

Under such circumstances the balancing of the books would have been a feat, even if Porter had not been, according to an acquaintance at the time, "a man who neglected his duties at the bank because of a constantly itching pen." [29] Another acquaintance, who had dealings in the bank almost daily, noted: "He was a dreamer, would hide sketches when I came to the teller's window." [30] As he had done as a boy in the drugstore in Greensboro, and again as an unhurried draftsman in the Land Office, Porter was still enough of a prankster at heart, it seems, to use a good deal of his employer's time in recording the foibles of the people coming and going around him in the bank.

Whether he seriously neglected his work is another matter. Admittedly he made mistakes, of the kind illustrated by Mrs. Roach's account of the time he came home to lunch deeply troubled over his discovery that in a blank moment that morning he had counted out $500 to a farmer instead of the $50 called for by the man's check. (Although he conducted a frantic search for the man, it was in vain and he reportedly had to pay the difference himself.) [31] Anderson, however, said he was an excellent bookkeeper, and Mrs. R. J. Brackenridge (wife of the cashier, Dr. R. J. Brackenridge, who was a brother of the bank president, Major Tom Brackenridge) later stated that whenever she took her little daughter downtown to meet her husband after work, Porter "was always at the bank, even after hours, for he was very conscientious in his work." [32] Perhaps the reason Porter had to work overtime was that he wasted part of his time, but there is no room for doubt that he had a taxing job. Once, for example, he spent two days working on a $100 shortage, only to discover that one of the bank officers had withdrawn it for a trip to San Antonio without bothering to leave a slip for the amount. In his last year at the bank he hardly took time to eat his lunch when he came home at noon. "I have to get back," he would say. "I don't know what is going on while I'm gone." [33] And he would change his limp collar and hurry back to work. He often talked of quitting, but things were not the same as in the days when he could walk out of a job if he did not care for it.

Even under these difficult circumstances Porter's characteristic kindness was in evidence. A young employee just out of business college at the time has reminisced about his Spencerian penmanship and the many flourishes with which he ornamented his figures for the first few days in the bank.

The first day or two I turned in my report together with checks and cash to O. Henry as he was my superior officer. He said nothing but they balanced but about the third day called me over and in a confidential tone told me that he thought my writing and report were well gotten up and complimented me on learning to write such a fancy hand. Then he pointed to Dr. Brackenridge, cashier and chief Executive of the Bank, and told me that he was a very plain man and that he was sure he would like the statement and especially the figures made in just the plainest manner. O. Henry then made a few figures such as 2, 3, 5 and 8 and said that while I made nicer looking figures than he made that he knew Dr. Brackenridge would much prefer very plain figures without any flourishes. I knew this was a nice way he had of correcting me.[34]

Porter's work was not his only worry. There was his marital situation as well. No doubt it was partly his own fault. One of his friends at the time was to comment: "I regarded him as something too sporty for a good husband." [35] He seems to have still gone out on the town occasionally for an evening with his thirsty cronies. He is said to have been a poker player of esoteric skill. And whether he had earlier confined his drinking to beer, as several friends later claimed, now was as likely a time as any other for him to have branched out and learned—among other things—about the "strange, exalted sense of non-participation in worldly affairs" [36] which he later described as the effect of absinthe. After he left Austin there were many stories about his "dissipation." One acquaintance even reported having seen Porter, about the time in question, "in the presence of a bad woman at the train." [37] But very clearly the basic trouble at home was another matter entirely. Athol's later pictures show her as increasingly gaunt and hollow-eyed, and her nervous tension seems to have mounted steadily with the progress of her tuberculosis. "Will won't quarrel," she told her mother: [38] which amounted to an admission of the frequent occasions to do so which she gave him. Characteristically Porter seems merely to have withdrawn from the fray, doing everything possible to conciliate her. "Will was always a good father and a kind husband," according to Mrs. Roach.[39] According to Betty Hall, he "did for Margaret many things a mother should have done," for he was "supremely devoted" to his daughter.[40] In addition to bathing and dressing and feeding her a good deal of the time, he read Uncle Remus stories to her endlessly. In afteryears Margaret remembered his amusement at her antics. "Sitting on his knee I would feel him shaking, and look around to find him breathless with laughter. Sometimes the softest of chuckles would reveal him ruddy with suppressed mirth." And after putting her to bed there was the game of "drumming the rhythm of a melody against the wooden headboard of the bed, me guessing the tunes in turn" [41] until he could substitute some toy for his tightly gripped thumb and make his escape.

Athol seems to have been as busy socially as she had been in their carefree childless days. She took part regularly in the activities of the Musical Union, but by now—one friend was to remember— "Will Porter would bring his wife to the door [of the rehearsal room in the Driskell Hotel]; she would nod to him knowingly; and he would leave to come back when he thought the practicing was over. If he got back too early he would go over quietly and sit in one of the chairs reserved for visitors. He was just like that. He would take her to places, take good care of her, but he would not stay with her." [42] Mrs. Roach, too, commented on Porter's generosity in staying at home with Margaret while Athol went to her rehearsals.

Once, at least—in June, 1893—Porter joined Athol in a production of *Pinafore* on the occasion of the five-day International Regatta which officially opened the thirty-mile-long Lake McDonald (named for the mayor), a newly completed by-product of the $1,400,000 dam finished in 1891 to provide water power for the city. During the regatta—for which oarsmen came from as far away as Australia—five paddlewheel steamers, equipped with music for dancing, each carried as many as five hundred passengers up and down the lake. For the staging of *Pinafore,* Porter helped to design a ship which actually rested on the water, with a grandstand built facing it on the shore of the lake, and he took the part of an able seaman while Athol sang in the chorus. "Fully 1500 people witnessed the performance," said the *Statesman* of one of the performances. ". . . The originality of the scheme and the successful execution of the same is something that will cause all visitors to the city to speak in high praise of the ability of the Austin Musical Union

. . . and the Statesman would advise everyone, both stranger and home people, to go out and see this great performance . . . one of the greatest undertakings ever conceived." [43]

There were times when husband and wife recaptured some of the tenderness of the past—but always with a difference. Now their tenderness must always have been tinged with—in fact, must have been largely motivated by—a sense of the shortness of the time left to them. By the spring of 1893, if not before, they had moved into a cottage at 308 East Fourth Street (across the street from the Roaches), the home in which they lived longer than in any other. "Athol," wrote Frances Maltby, "always industrious, neat and orderly, was inclined to overdo her strength. Will Porter, recognizing this fact and fearing a return of the ill health that had so alarmed him, helped about the house in every way he could." This impulse could lead to moments of self-forgetful gaiety, as when Porter would insist on cooking a meal for their guests. "He prided himself on being able to broil a steak. Onions cut in cubes and served in vinegar was his own exclusive dish. He would urge you to partake, declaring it a dish fit for the gods. 'Both palatable and pungent,' he would say." [44]

But by now the marriage was not always, even in public, a seemly affair. For a time the Porters were among the group which boarded in the home of Richard Hall, located three miles from downtown across the river in South Austin. One of their fellow boarders later commented that Porter and Athol had frequent disagreements, especially over the handling of their three-year-old daughter— disagreements in which Athol "usually carried her point by a scene before the whole household, to his intense humiliation and shame. Afterwards I heard he was drinking." [45] Betty Hall, too, remembered Porter as "pitiable" at this time. Athol, she said, was a shrewish wife who seemed to delight in embarrassing him by starting quarrels in public.[46]

And yet Athol still had her appealing side. During the summer of 1893 the World's Fair in Chicago created a tremendous stir among Austinites. Never before had the country been exposed to showmanship on such a scale, to such high-pressure promotion tactics; and the glowing stories of people who had been and returned added even more fuel to the fire. Porter himself could not get away from his work, even if he had had the money for both of them to make the trip, but he wanted Athol to go. The Roaches encouraged the idea by offering to keep Margaret so that Athol could go with a group of friends, and Porter turned over to her the money to make her arrangements. As Mrs. Roach later told the story, she noticed one morning a pair of new muslin curtains blowing from the front window of the Porter home across the street. When she went across to investigate, the little front porch boasted two new wicker rocking chairs, and inside was a new floor matting with a Japanese pattern. "I just couldn't go on a jaunt and leave Will here to work all summer and not have any fun. Now he'll have just as much fun out of the money as I do." [47]

There were other pleasant interludes, furnished by the never failing kindness of Porter's friends. For one and perhaps two of the summers during his years at the bank the Richard Halls (Richard was now studying law in Austin) went back to their ranch for the hot months and turned over to the Porters their large brick home in South Austin. Situated in a cedar grove overlooking the capitol dome and the spires and roofs of the city, and within walking distance of a swimming resort known as Barton Springs, this beautiful home served as the equivalent of a distant vacation resort for Porter and his family. Especially nice, he thought, was the chance for Margaret to "know the joy of chasing chickens and getting redbugs on her legs," [48] and after leaving the bank at four o'clock Porter would hurry home to go swimming and to sit with his family after supper on the cool lawn.

It was at this stage of his career—after he had worked in the bank for three years and after his marriage had become a source of tension and even humiliation—that Porter seized upon the opportunity, which presented itself in March, 1894, to buy the press of the *Iconoclast*, a radical and vituperative monthly paper which had been edited by William Courtney Brann. The *Iconoclast* had not found favor in conservative Austin (the *Statesman* had called it a "skinning machine" and a "roasting mill"), but by turning it into a comic sheet Porter evidently hoped to supplement his bank salary and perhaps in time to free himself from the bank altogether. James P. Crane, the real-estate man and friend who went into the enterprise with him, afterward explained: "We created, as a vehicle to give vent to our foibles, *The Rolling Stone,* which I had the honor to name and design the heading. It was one of the means we employed to get the pleasure out of life and never appealed to us as a money-making venture. We did it for the fun of the thing." [49] Perhaps Crane was speaking for himself rather than for Porter, or perhaps he sensed that the *Rolling Stone* served partly as a means of escape from the impasse which Porter's life seemed to have reached.

The idea of publishing a paper of his own was one which Porter had toyed with before the Brann press came up for sale. As much as a year earlier—according to an acquaintance who had some money to spare—"he sounded me on the question of my financing such an enterprise, but I did not encourage him. . . . I am compelled to say, and with some degree of shame, that I was never able to discover any indication that fame was beckoning in his direction." [50] Now, suddenly, here was his chance. For the sum of $250 he was able to buy a printing press (getting two Land Office friends, Herman Pressler and Will Booth, to sign his note for the amount), and with Crane as his first associate he began weekly publication in April, 1894. After two issues published under the name the *Iconoclast,* Brann asked if he could have back the name for another newspaper he was going to publish in Waco, and Porter and/or Crane renamed the paper the *Rolling Stone,* of which the first surviving issue, on April 28, is numbered Vol. I, No. 3. Brann's new *Iconoclast,* incidentally, took a new lease on life in Waco; between the time his first issue appeared in 1895 and the time Brann was shot in a street brawl in 1898, his paper had reached a circulation of 90,000.[51] Porter's paper, on the other hand—published by "The Rolling Stone Company, 113 East 7th St., Driskell Hotel Block"—never during the single year of its life reached a circulation of over 1,500 [52] in spite of such appeals as the following:

The Rolling Stone is a weekly paper published in Austin, Texas, every Saturday, and will endeavor to fill a long-felt want, that does not appear, by the way, to be altogether insatiable at present. The idea is to fill its pages with matter that will make a heart-rending appeal to every lover of good literature, and every person who has a taste for reading print and a dollar and a half for a year's subscription; six months, $1; three months, 50c; single copies, 5c; in advance. Our Special Premium. For the next 30 days, and from that time on indefinitely, whoever will bring two dollars in cash to *The Rolling Stone* office, will be entered on the list of subscribers of that paper and will have returned to him on the spot Fifty Cents in Cash. Don't fail to take advantage of this opportunity at once. Each number will contain stories, humorous sketches, poems, jokes, properly labeled, side-splitting references to the mother-in-law, the goat Governor Hogg, and the States of the Weather and Texas.[53]

Except for the syndicated column of Bill Nye and such bits as were borrowed from *Truth, Life,* and other magazines, the entire content of the eight-page paper was produced after banking hours and at night by Porter himself,[54] who also helped with the mechanical side of the work. Crane soon left town for bigger and better things in Chicago (his contribution seems to have been somewhat nebulous from the beginning), and Porter's next associate was a printer named Dixie Daniels, who had drifted into town that spring. Hearing that Porter was looking for a printer, Daniels "talked things over with him, the proposition looked good, and we formed a partnership then and there. . . . Our idea was to run this weekly with a lot of current events treated in humorous fashion, and also to run short sketches, drawings and verse." [55] Porter's feat was a remarkable one, considering that he was also holding down a full-time job. Soon, though, instead of furnishing a release from the tension at home, his work on the paper only made things worse than ever.

This was the year (1894) when the city installed a new system of electric street lights: twenty-nine towers 150 feet tall, each equipped with enough lamps to produce 2,000 candle power, so that in the artificial moonlight a man was supposedly able to read the time from his watch anywhere in the city. No doubt as a consequence the streets furnished a livelier panorama for footloose wanderers. In the Bismarck Café—with its mahogany bar, its alarmingly proportioned cuspidors, and its portraits of the Kaiser and the Iron Chancellor—Porter became such a regular patron that he staked out a headquarters for himself by carving a wedge out of the table where he liked to sit. In addition to beer, Crane reported, he had a great fondness for Hungarian goulash, preserved ginger, sweetbreads, and cream puffs, not to mention a taste that slightly puzzled some of his friends: "He had a wonderfully discerning longing for rare perfumes and always purchased the finest to be obtained." [56] Speaking of his habits at this time, Daniels later wrote: "One of his favorite amusements was lounging about a cafe, eating caviar sandwiches and throwing the dice for beers." On many evenings, after they had finished their work on the paper,

he would call to me to come along and "go bumming." That was his favorite expression for the night-time prowling in which we indulged. We would wander through the streets and alleys, meeting with some of the worst specimens of down-and-outers it has ever been my privilege to see at close range. I've seen the most ragged specimen of a bum hold up Porter, who would always do anything he could for the man. His one great failing was his inability to say "No" to a man.[57]

There seem to have been other failings, too, which Daniels refrained from mentioning. He did confide that Porter was so fond of beer that he "could drink ½ gal. without taking the vessel from his mouth," but in writing to an early researcher he concluded his account: "The rest of my personal relations with Porter had better be confided to you personally." [58] In addition to his heavier and heavier drinking, it would appear that for some time Porter had been supplementing his income by means of his skill at poker. Betty Hall remembered his "enormous extravagance" at the time he and Athol boarded with the Halls, and how horrified she was to discover that the large sums of money he spent had been won in gambling.[59] The Raatzes, Porter's neighbors on East Fourth Street, afterward told of his "regular gambling sprees" in the office of the *Rolling Stone*. They also told, confidentially, of certain occasions when Athol would arrive at midnight and try to smash in the door because she believed ("and here they lift their eyebrows," interjected the early researcher, who did not embarrass his informants by publishing such findings) that her husband had a woman in the office. The confidential testimony of other acquaintances makes it quite clear that the woman was not a figment of Athol's jealous imagination. But no details have survived except for an unverified story (recorded by the same researcher) about this or some other woman who made a scene at the railroad station when Porter was leaving to go to prison in 1898; reportedly she tried to go with him and had to be forcibly put off the train.[60]

This not very attractive picture had a reverse side. At home Porter had fixed up for himself a study in an old barn in his back

71

yard. Here he did much of his writing and apparently a good deal of reading as well, for at the time the barn burned in 1912 Porter's library of some 1,000 volumes was still there.[61] Moreover he lavished attention on his five-year-old daughter and her playmates in the neighborhood, playing games with them and telling them stories. At the proper season each child nailed to his gate a box in which his playmates deposited the comic drawings they called valentines, many of which Porter drew for Margaret. One of his more ambitious efforts, meant to be given to Arthur Raatz, shows a woman working with scissors on a huge pair of pants, while a man (with cotton pasted to the paper for his hair and whiskers) looks on glumly. Arthur (but they called him Tom because it wasn't his name) "worked so hard that he grew so fast that he became so much larger than his father that one day Mrs. Raats got a pair of Tom's old trousers and cut them down to fit Mr. Raats. . . . Let all parents take warning and not make their children work when they should be playing." [62]

The dichotomy in Porter's life at this time makes clear how formidable was the impasse he had reached, an impasse to which he reacted in much the same way he had reacted as a boy in Greensboro. He backed away from it, reverting to his "sporty" bachelorhood in ways which gradually got out of hand.

At this stage of his life—it was his thirty-second year—Porter should have been a man seasoned by trials and responsibilities, and his strengths and weaknesses should have been reasonably clear to him. Actually this was not the fact. The crucial testing was yet to come. Until now Porter had drifted according to circumstance, possessed of no fixed destination and no clearly defined ethic of procedure. Repeatedly he had accepted the overgenerous aid of friends, and his acceptance had been childlike: without compunction beforehand and without a sense of indebtedness afterward. He had no real conception of the value or handling of money, of which he was in particular need now that he was trying to make a success of the chronically unprosperous *Rolling Stone*. Working in a bank whose officials frequently borrowed cash for their own use, would such a man begin to avail himself occasionally of the money he needed, and even doctor his books to cover up his actions until he should be in a position to make repayment? Or would such actions be out of the question for the well meaning, law-abiding man who could and did obtain from his friends the highest sort of character testimonials?

Whatever the cause, the fact is that in October or November of 1894 the problem of balancing the books reached an acute stage. Meeting him on one of her trips back to Austin, his former sweetheart Lollie Cave (now Mrs. Wilson) sat with Porter on a bench in the capitol grounds and listened to his troubles. In addition to the occasional missing sums which turned up when the borrower remembered to replace them, he told her, money was regularly disappearing from the bank. In fact, Mrs. Wilson reported, Porter told her that he had discovered who was taking the money: "a friend who has been just like a father to me. . . . I told him I was short and asked him what I should do with the items—if I was to charge them to loss or what. To my utter amazement he told me to carry them along. . . . I went to him again, and this time he told me to carry it in a dead account or switch it around until they could charge it off. So there it stands, and if the bank examiner finds it my name will be Dennis." [63] This is the only detailed statement by a contemporary who claimed to have known, before the outcome, about the shortages which led to Porter's loss of his job. It is not a statement which several other contemporaries would have accepted as a true account of what had happened. To support it, there is the fact—to which Porter's predecessor, J. M. Thornton, later testified—that there had been discrepancies in the books before Porter took them over.[64] And Betty Hall later said that Porter told her it was Dr. Brackenridge's "trifling with the books that caused the trouble, but [he] did not consider Dr. Brackenridge meant to do wrong." [65]

The evidence will be considered as the chronology of the story makes it available. Meanwhile, on December 20, Porter wrote to Crane in Chicago: "I quit the bank a day or two ago. I found out that the change was going to be made, so I concluded to stop and go to work on the paper." [66] What had happened was that a federal bank examiner had found discrepancies in Porter's books, and suspicion had pointed to Porter himself. District Attorney Robert U. Culberson later broke a thirty-nine-year silence on the matter to tell an interviewer: "I was playing bridge at an Austin club one night in 1894 when Frank Hamilton, who with George W. Bracken-ridge, owned the First National Bank in Austin, came to me. He told me there was a shortage in the accounts of Will Porter, a teller. But he said, 'Bob, I'm to blame.' By this he was referring to the lack of system in the bank for handling cash. Actually there was no system." [67]

According to the bank examiner in the case, F. B. Gray:

> The American Surety Co. was on his [Porter's] bond and of course could have been held for the full amount of the shortage, but when Mr. Frank Hamilton the Vice-President of the bank, and a representative of over three fourths of the stock of the bank called on Mr. Carr Lucy the representative of the Surety Co., for payment of the shortage, it is my theory that Lucy declined to pay the amount or any part of it until Hamilton should prove conclusively that Porter got the money. This to my mind would not have been a hard thing to do but since Dr. Brackenridge, the Cashier, attended the window while Porter was at dinner it looked a little formidable to Hamilton and he saw at once that he had a law suit on his hands with the possibility of losing the case. He then applied to Porter and a Mr. Roach who is a relative of Porter's wife and gave them to under-stand that he must have his money. Circumstances go to show that, to avoid the law suit, the three, Hamilton, Lucy and Roach, held a confer-ence and agreed upon the following settlement:
>
> Roach agreed to pay $1500.00 provided Lucy would pay $1500.00 and the Bank lose the remainder and provided further that both Hamilton and Lucy should use the utmost endeavors to get Porter released from the complaints I had filed against him. Hamilton told the U. S. Att'y. that it was his opinion that Porter intended no wrong, what he did was only *a series of mistakes* and that he should not be prosecuted.[68]

Porter, of course, resigned from his job, and for the time being the pressure eased. Culberson, convinced by Hamilton of Porter's in-nocence, agreed to let the matter drop. The bank examiner had demanded, however, that the case be prosecuted, and everybody concerned must soon have known that a grand jury hearing could not be avoided at the next term of court in July.

According to one source, when Mr. Roach went home to lunch on the day of the bank examiner's finding, he took word to Athol that Porter was going to be held responsible for shortages at the bank. Later in the afternoon Mrs. Roach went across the street to find her daughter "crumpled up on the bed . . . crying as if her heart would break." But then the clock struck four. "Instantly Athol was on her feet. She seemed suddenly electrified with courage and determination. 'It's four o'clock,' she said. 'Will will be home any minute. I mustn't act like this. He shan't find me crying.' And he didn't. He found her dressed in a crisp blue dimity that he loved, sweet and fresh and dainty, her head held a bit higher than usual." [69] No doubt the spirit of the story is true, for Athol rallied to her husband's defense. But from another source comes the more likely story that the bank examiner's findings were not publicized the same day, and that Porter in his deep distress kept the news from Athol for some time, leaving home and returning at his usual hours.[70]

By the time he left the bank Porter was already doubtful about making a success of the *Rolling Stone*. Writing to Crane in Chicago from "the City of Tomales" [*sic*], to which he had come "last night to work up the *Rolling Stone* a little over here," he put the matter bluntly:

. . . I tell you what I want to do. I want to get up in that country some-where on some kind of newspaper. Can't you work up something for us to go at there? If you can I will come up there any time at one day's notice. I can worry along here and about live but it is not the place for one to get ahead in. You know that, don't you? See if you can't get me a job up there, or if you think our paper would take, and we could get some support, what about starting it up there? [71]

Apparently no encouragement was forthcoming from Crane, for by the beginning of the new year Porter was beginning an all-out campaign to make a go of the *Rolling Stone*. In January, 1895, he took as co-editor an Englishman named Henry Ryder-Taylor and undertook to publish the paper simultaneously in Austin and in San Antonio, with a San Antonio page edited by Ryder-Taylor. Introducing his new associate as a former editor both of the *Texas Figaro* and of the San Antonio *Daily News,* as well as a former city editor of the San Antonio *Daily Light,* Porter informed his readers that the addition to his staff was intended to attract "a large influx of subscribers, that our advertisers and those intending to advertise will appreciate." [72]

According to Dixie Daniels (but not, it seems, according to the facts of the matter), the *Rolling Stone* was rolling along very nicely until Porter made two mistakes. He alienated the German element in Austin with his undue levity in cartoons and skits directed at their alleged capacity for beer, and he became involved—through Ryder-Taylor's influence—in the Callaghan mayoralty campaign in San Antonio, thus losing most of his San Antonio subscribers. Daniels seems to have been particularly annoyed by the new addition to the staff. "How Ryder-Taylor," he later observed with some asperity, "had any influence on him [Porter] I never was able to make out, for he used constantly to make fun of him. 'Here comes that man Taylor,' he would say, 'got a diamond on him as big as a two-bit piece and shinin' like granulated sugar.'" [73] Even if this is not Daniels's own scorn attributed to Porter, evidently Porter was less concerned with his personal feelings than with the addition of a man he considered a valuable staff member. In England, Ryder-Taylor had been—according to his own account at least—an amanuensis of Charles Dickens, and in San Antonio the first issue of his short-lived weekly paper had carried on the first page his picture with the caption:

HENRY RYDER-TAYLOR
Editor of the *Texas Figaro*
Former dramatic editor of the London *Telegraph*
Amanuensis of Charles Dickens. [74]

In answer to a question on the subject, one of Dickens's sons is said to have replied: "I am well acquainted with the affairs of my father. But I know of no one named Ryder-Taylor who had anything to do with his work. In fact, I have never heard the name before." [75] But Dickens's son was far away, and although Ryder-Taylor had reportedly been kicked by a gambler whom he had tried to expose he seems to have made a place for himself with his diamond stickpin, silk hat, frock coat, checked trousers, and spats.

Having opened a branch office at 903 South Presa Street in San Antonio, Porter was in the city conferring with his co-editor often enough to become a familiar figure among the newspaper men there. After Austin, with its familiarly Southern ways, San Antonio was a

RTER IN THE TELLER'S CAGE IN THE FIRST NATIONAL BANK
IN AUSTIN

MARGARET PORTER

new experience. As he was to write in his story "The Enchanted Kiss":

Here were still the Spaniard's forbidding abodes of concrete and adobe, standing cold and indomitable against the century. From the murky fissure, the eye saw, flung against the sky, the tangled filigree of his Moorish balconies. Through stone archways breaths of dead, vault-chilled air coughed upon him; his feet struck jingling iron rings in staples stone-buried for half a cycle. Along these paltry avenues had swaggered the arrogant Don, had caracoled and serenaded and blustered while the tomahawk and the pioneer's rifle were already uplifted to expel him from a continent.[76]

San Antonio was a well known refuge for tuberculars, some of whom Porter was to describe vividly in his story "A Fog in Santone," and in parts of the city there were still to be found "coquettish *senoritas*, the music of the weird Spanish minstrels, and the strange, piquant Mexican dishes . . . the glitter of eyes, jewels, and daggers, the ring of laughter and coin." [77]

In the main, though, Porter's mind was doubtless on less picturesque matters. In a bar which he frequented not far from his South Presa Street office, he became acquainted with Frank H. Bushnick, managing editor of the San Antonio *Express*, whom he asked for a job as a reporter. "He admitted," Bushnick recalled, "that he had had little experience in reporting, so I could not see my way clear to employ him." He did, for a time, substitute for the Austin correspondent of the *Express*, "sending items about his friends, which showed imagination but did not have much news in them." [78] And in addition to these efforts to augment his income in San Antonio, Porter made at least two visits to the nearby German settlement of Fredericksburg. "They are all German people who live in Fredericksburg," he later wrote in his story "A Chaparral Prince." "Of evenings they sit at little tables along the sidewalk and drink beer and play pinochle and scat . . ." and one rich citizen "smoked a meerschaum pipe three feet long and had wiener schnitzel and hassenpfeffer for dinner every day in the week." [79]

The *Rolling Stone*, however, was an Austin enterprise. Porter campaigned sporadically against loose-swinging signs above the downtown sidewalks, for a clearing of the weed-choked capitol grounds, against lotteries, for increased wages to pipe-laying city workmen, against the express-wagon owners' neglect of their horses, and for shorter sermons (which might result in "less courting in the choir and more souls awakened—or kept awake." [80] Even if there had been any definite policy behind it, however, editorial matter was of minor importance in the paper. As Porter put it:

> The politics of *The Rolling Stone* is Independent, with an inclination toward Presbyterianism, and the theory that the world is supported on the back of a mud turtle. Our platform might be stated in the following words: We believe in treating everybody square all around, backing the winning horse, and closing all open accounts with a note when hard pressed. We will hew to the line, provided the chips fall our way. [81]

What appealed mainly to the reader of 1894–1895, as well as to the present-day reader, is the farcical-satirical account of life in and around Austin, a city which—according to Porter's story—was founded by Stephen F. Austin, Daniel Boone, Davy Crockett, Ed Morris, Ponce de Leon, and Ben Thompson, a group which "got a gun and killed off the Indians between the lunatic asylum and the river and laid out Austin. It has been laid out ever since." [82] Porter explored Austin in the same spirit which was later to guide him in New York:

> Like the Califf al Raschid, but without his power of relieving distress or punishing wickedness, I often stroll about Austin studying nature and reading many pages in the great book of Man.
>
> Like the Califf, too, I am somewhat incognito, as the public as a general rule take me for no more than an idle, somewhat lazy young man, and once or twice I have been frightened by having work offered me. [83]

The general run of Porter's humor in the *Rolling Stone* is on an elementary level—the level of a run-of-the-mill college magazine. At his worst Porter was capable of a good deal of the kind of thing illustrated in "The Power of Poetry," an account of Eulalle Mc-Girlygirt's melancholy reflections: "Rupert will not come today. I shall not feel his strong arms around me, taste the nectar of his lips in a pulsing, passionate kiss, not quaff the aroma of his Cedar Run-copper-distilled-two-drinks-for-a-quarter breath. . . . I must not doubt him. I will not rack my soul with the thought that he could be untrue to me." Retiring to her boudoir, Eulalle seated herself on a damask-covered fauteuil and rang for her femme de chambre to fetch her a volume of Tennyson's poems—for the solacing of her tender feelings, we suppose. Instead, Eulalle "placed the book under the corner of the fauteuil, and saying to herself, 'Well, I guess I have fixed that pesky short-legged sofa now,' was soon wrapped in the sweet slumber of innocence." [84]

At the other extreme is "Bexar Scrip No. 2692," [85] a story almost as finished in manner as much of the later work of O. Henry. This story stands apart in the *Rolling Stone*. The highest level Porter was able to maintain with any consistency is illustrated by the burlesque crime stories featuring Ticqocq, the great French detective,[86] or by such a story as "The Confession of ——," in which a girl named Lynette has returned home to America after six years at an aristocratic young ladies' school near London. Lynette, her mother tells her, has "changed very much from the little girl who left me six years ago, but I am much pleased with you. You have acquired that aristocratic calm and poise that only comes from association with the best people." The problem of the story has to do with the authenticity of a suitor who calls himself Lord Cranston and who has "almost convinced me of the genuineness of his title and his wealth. But still, some undefinable doubt, some intuitive skepticism, held me back." Lynette tries strategy. Lord Cranston's castle is at Seaview, he has said; surely then he must know her dear friend Lady Augusta Trever? But no, Lord Cranston only replies with perfect candor: "There is no family or place of the name in the country. You must have been misinformed as to her residence, Miss Lynette." Would not, she asks herself, an impostor have fallen into her trap? "That night I came very near promising my hand to Lord Cranston on the south balcony among the oleander bushes." Before she makes up her mind, however, Lynette and her suitor and her mother happen to be out riding one day, and at the railroad station, where they stop to see the newcomers, they behold "a short, stocky young man wearing a rough pepper-and-salt suit and a tweed cap, and a handsome young lady in a traveling dress and a steamer cap." The mother's face immediately begins turning red and pale by turns. "Lynette!" she cries, springing from the carriage, while the stocky young man takes a good look at Lord Cranston and says sharply: "Higgins, you scoundrel! where are my trunks and papers? I will give you fifteen minutes to produce them, or I will hand you over to the police." In a low voice Lord Cranston says to his companion: "Farewell, Miss Lynette; I wish it had all been true." But as he turns to go, she stops him. "Wait a moment, Mr. Higgins. I think I am going your way." As they walk down the platform together she hears the newly arrived young lady saying: "And Mama, dear, let me introduce Lord Cranston, who has been so kind and attentive. His valet had stolen all of his things and run away with them." [87]

This, of course, is the same plot O. Henry was to use in such a typical story as "Transients in Arcadia." The difference between the two lies less in the perception involved than in the somewhat more convincing execution of the later story. Of the same basic situation O. Henry was to work out different angles in such stories as "While the Auto Waits," "Lost on Dress Parade," "The Caliph and the Cad," and "A Night in New Arabia." The situation of the impostor thus figures not only in the stories Porter wrote after his prison experience. It is as if throughout his life he somehow regarded himself as an impostor, as one who had no real right to the position he occupied.

In any event, his strenuous efforts to increase the circulation of the *Rolling Stone* proved unavailing. He had to borrow money repeatedly to keep the paper going—not only from his generous father-in-law (who put, all told, $1,000 into the paper before it folded), but also from at least one friend, Ed Smith, who later said: "I loaned him money to publish *The Rolling Stone.* . . . Porter always made his approach for these loans with a humorously turned remark. The money he repaid me was usually the proceeds of a story sale. . . . I did not expect to be fully repaid by him." [88] The "stories" referred to were probably the same kind of skits and bits which Porter had been selling as early as 1887. Now that he was out of a job and in debt too, he seems to have turned them out in quantity, for his neighbors remembered passing his house at night and seeing him writing after most people were in bed. [89]

So great was the need for money that Porter seems at this time to have resurrected his old interest in buried treasure. Unless Daniels's brother dated the episode carelessly in his account, it was in 1895 that Porter and the two Daniels brothers began trailing the legendary funds ($20 gold pieces to the number of 20,000) of a murdered paymaster of the Mexican Army. The trail led to a spot on Shoal Creek a couple of miles from downtown, where the searchers found mystic signs cut into the bark of a tree and where, under cover of darkness, they began digging. Strengthened by several libations from the bottle brought along for moral support, they had made remarkable progress (the hole they were digging had reportedly reached a depth of seven feet) when they were interrupted by a violent scream, which kept repeating itself from successive points in a circle around the scene of their activities. Completely unnerved, they packed their digging equipment on the rented horse and made their getaway, only to learn next day that the disturber of the peace had been not the ghost of the paymaster or of one of his murderers, but an escaped inmate from the nearby state asylum.[90]

This incongruous episode is a fitting prelude to the farcical circumstance which seems to have been the immediate cause of the demise of the *Rolling Stone*. In the issue of March 30, 1895, after two issues had failed to appear, Porter wrote:

The person who sweeps the office, translates letters from foreign countries, deciphers communications from graduates of business colleges, and does most of the writing for this paper, has been confined for the past two weeks to the underside of a large red quilt with a joint case of la grippe and measles. . . . People who have tried to run a funny paper and entertain a congregation of large piebald measles at the same time will understand something of the tact, finesse, and hot sassafras tea required to do so. We expect to get out the paper regularly from this time on, but are forced to be very careful, as improper treatment and deleterious aftereffects of measles, combined with the high price of paper and press work, have been known to cause a relapse.[91]

Whichever of the two causes was involved, Porter is said to have actually had the threatened relapse and to have returned to bed for a more cautious convalescence. The *Rolling Stone* gave up the ghost without more ado.*

* As the earliest body of work which Porter produced, practically none of which is available to the reading public, the *Rolling Stone* deserves fuller treatment than seems appropriate in the narrative of Porter's life. See Appendix.

CHAPTER FIVE

· ⟨≈⟩ ·

Between the end of April, when the *Rolling Stone* suspended publication, and the middle of October, when he went to work for the Houston *Post*, Porter was dependent on his father-in-law to an extent which must have been humiliating even to one accustomed to accepting help. For nearly six months he was without any kind of earned income except the five- and ten-dollar payments for the humorous bits he continued to grind out for the Cleveland *Plain Dealer* and other newspapers. Athol seems to have rallied to his defense as sharply as before she had badgered him; her parents and all of his friends clearly regarded him as the unfortunate victim of circumstances beyond his control; nevertheless he must obviously have felt stigmatized—even if the matter had been allowed to drop after the shortage was made up at the bank. But the whole question still had to be considered by a grand jury at the July term of court. As his ordeal approached, Porter is said to have retired more and more into himself, so much so that he even avoided his friends.

The details of what happened when the grand jury considered the case in July are disappointingly few. According to District Attorney Culberson's later statement, "Hamilton [vice-president of the bank] requested permission to appear before the grand jury and explain conditions in the bank and intercede for Porter. I granted Hamilton's request, and the grand jury returned a no-bill. . . . The examiner was bitter against me for permitting Porter to be no-billed. He wrote to the treasury department." [1] The only other first-hand information comes from bank examiner Gray's letter to the Comptroller of the Currency.[2] Having "reported to

Hon. R. U. Culberson, U. S. Attorney for the Western District of Texas and spent ten days assisting him in preparing several cases to the U. S. Grand Jury at the July term of the U. S. Court at Austin, Texas," Gray informed the Comptroller, on July 13, 1895, that out of the four cases involved, in only two were indictments brought, although "it is my opinion that indictments should have been obtained against each of the persons accused. I shall attempt to give you a full report of the cases and if, in giving my impressions I appear to be personal and you elect to use the information given, I trust you will not do so in such a way as will make it unpleasant for me if it can be avoided, but at the same time my convictions are positive and I do not shrink from the responsibility in any way." Gray proceeded to charge Culberson with either incompetence or indolence, and to back up his charge as follows:

As an illustration of what I mean will say that when I first preferred charges against Richardson and Porter I furnished to the U. S. Atty and his assistant a full list of all the witnesses needed and they both assured me that they would subpoena all witnesses and have them on hand the day the Court convened. About two weeks before that time [mid-June, this would have been] I happened to pass through San Antonio on my way to Laredo and having a little time to spare between trains I called on the Attorney to remind him again about our witnesses for I had been warned that he was neglectful and he again assured me that they should all be served in due time and that I need not give myself any uneasiness on that score. Court convened Monday morning, July 1st, and you can imagine my surprise on going to the Court room about 9 o'clock to find that not a single witness had been served with subpoena in any one of the cases in which I was interested and of course none were on hand. He had simply neglected to attend to the matter and had no good excuse to offer. I made him up another list of such witnesses as could be had for that sitting of the grand jury and officers were sent after them in all directions. Some of the witnesses were out of the state, however and could not be reached in time but we got all we could reach.

When the Porter case was finally heard, Gray explained, he proved to the seeming satisfaction of the jury that Porter had on exactly fifty occasions embezzled bank funds totaling a sum of $5,654.20. As an example of how the embezzling was done, Gray cited an item of $608.36 which the Fort Worth National Bank had sent to Porter's bank for collection and for which Porter had failed to give due credit. When Fort Worth protested, Porter said he had erroneously credited the amount to a Dallas bank "and that he would correct this by charging Dallas and crediting Fort Worth which he did but as a matter of fact Dallas had never been credited and he simply transferred the shortage from one account to another." Gray also cited an item of $554.48, a draft on the San Antonio National Bank, which he said Porter sold but failed to credit. For witness he "had the purchaser of the draft on hand to prove that he bought and paid for it, also had the cancelled draft to show that it had been paid by the San Antonio Nat'l Bank. The monthly statement rendered by the San Antonio Nat'l Bank had been checked by Porter and reported correct though this check appeared charged in the account. Cash account in none of these instances showed over, hence it was to my mind conclusive evidence that he embezzled the money."

To balance Gray's evidence, however, Hamilton testified to his belief in Porter's innocence of anything except an unfortunate series of errors. Similar testimony was offered by J. M. Thornton, Porter's predecessor as teller in the bank and a nephew of Dr. R. J. Brackenridge; according to Gray, "Thornton interested himself a great deal with those who were working in the interest of Porter, had frequent long private interviews with them and I am confident that he used his influence with the jury in his, Porter's, behalf and to him mainly is chargeable the failure to indict the thief." Such an outcome was so disappointing to Gray that he recommended to the Comptroller that he be instructed to appear before the next grand jury in February, 1896, "and make another effort to indict Porter."

As a result of Gray's letter, Attorney General Judson Harmon notified Culberson on July 25 "that the Comptroller of the Currency complains of serious irregularities, or perhaps I should say lack of either vigor or intelligence, or both, in the conduct of your office, with respect to various persons charged with the violation of the national banking laws." [3] In a lengthy reply to his superior, dated July 29, Culberson denied that he had failed to subpoena witnesses except on one occasion (not the Porter case) when he did not send for a witness from Kansas City because the witness had already written letters which would prove all that could have been expected from his oral testimony, "and as I saved the Government something I cannot see in what respect I have done wrong." [4] Culberson proceeded to defend himself so vigorously that on August 2 the Attorney General wrote to inform him that "your statement completely vindicates you and leaves nothing to be desired on the part of this Department." [5]

So ended a dispute which there is now no way of judging, and so also—it seemed at the time—ended the Porter case. Porter had been no-billed by the grand jury as the result of testimony by at least two high-ranking fellow citizens, one of them the vice-president of the bank in which he had been employed. No doubt of his innocence seems to have been entertained by anyone except the federal examiner, the man whom O. Henry must have had in mind when he described J. F. C. Nettlewick, National Bank Examiner, "short in stature, but strongly built, with very light, closely trimmed hair, smooth, determined face, and aggressive, gold-rimmed nose glasses. . . . His air denoted a quiet but conscious reserve force, if not actual authority." [6]

As if to put the seal on the closed book of the past, in the same month that the grand jury exonerated him there came to him exactly the kind of opportunity about which he had sounded out James P. Crane after losing his bank job back in December. Now, through the influence of Crane's brother, the columnist Dr. Frank Crane, Porter was offered the editorship of a humorous paper in Washington, D.C. He jumped at the chance. Excited as two children, he and Athol sold their furniture and made final preparations for the move. Only then, at the last possible moment, did the threat which had for so long hung over Athol fall with disconcerting abruptness. She was taken gravely ill, too ill for Porter to consider leaving her. All their plans had to be canceled.

Earlier in the summer Athol had been in the habit of visiting almost daily a poor family down the street whose sixteen-year-old daughter had been dying of tuberculosis. The sick girl had pathetically admired Athol's two diamond rings (one stone from a pair of Mrs. Roach's earrings, the other from a stud Porter had given her), and on the day she died she had asked to wear them just once. Mrs. Roach, after her own daughter's death, once said, "I have often wondered if Athol's frequent visits to that sick girl, and allowing her to wear her rings, had anything to do with Athol developing the disease." [7] But Athol's own case of tuberculosis had been a long-standing one, and the contact with another victim could have had no connection with the beginning, at this time of particular stress in her life, of the final stages of the disease.

It must have looked to Porter as though Fate had reached down to block his escape. Surely *escape* is the right word too. Exonerated though he had been, his situation in Austin could not have been an enviable one. Even if it had been only a matter of failure and inadequacy as breadwinner and husband, it would have been bad enough. But, as became evident later, there still remained doubts as to his innocence of the charge which had been brought against him.

In August, as if to gain a brief respite from his situation, he is reported to have made a trip to the ranch country where he had lived during his first two years in Texas. Evidence that he made such a trip was found in the Friotown courthouse, scene of the gala New Year's Ball of 1884. On a blackboard upstairs (the building had for a time been used as a temporary schoolhouse) a former acquaintance found scrawled one day a nostalgic reference to bygone days:

> Gone but not forgotten.
> W. S. PORTER.[8]

Things took a sudden turn for the better in the fall.[9] Athol began slowly to mend, and another opportunity came his way. Ed McLean, one of his earliest Austin friends and now secretary of the Railroad Commission, had sent a copy of the *Rolling Stone* to Colonel R. M. Johnston, editor of the Houston *Post*, with "the suggestion that Porter would be worth considering for a place as a writer on the *Post*," as Johnston later explained. "After reading *The Rolling Stone* I made an appointment through Mr. McLean with Mr. Porter . . . and made a contract with him to join the *Post* editorial staff." [10] Since no vacancy existed at the time, a place had to be created for Porter—that of general utility writer at a salary of fifteen dollars a week.[11]

Such a salary was not enough to support his family, but Porter gratefully accepted the offer. It gave him something to do after the long months of idleness and depression, and he must have understood that if he made good his salary would be increased. In fact it was raised on November 28 to $20, and again on May 14, 1896, to $25, which was the highest salary paid to *Post* reporters.[12] For the present, he could support himself on the fifteen-dollar salary, since Athol was not strong enough yet to move but would for the time being stay on with Margaret at the Roach home. In mid-October (his first column appeared on October 18) Porter moved to Houston; his financial condition is indicated by the railroad pass given him by McLean.[13]

From the start his work seems to have been appreciated on the *Post*. Judge E. P. Hill, president and majority owner of the paper, later commented: "He was one of the most gentlemanly men I ever knew. He had a low, gentle voice, graceful, easy manners, and he knew how to be really courteous." [14] Colonel Johnston afterward wrote: "Mr. Porter was a lovely character and one of the brightest men that I have ever come in contact with. He was modest, almost to the fault of self-effacement. His leaving the Houston *Post* was an irretrievable loss to the paper." [15] Johnston, in fact, after raising Porter's salary to the top figure he could pay, advised Porter that he owed it to himself to go to New York, where he could earn the kind of money his ability warranted. Another colleague was former Governor W. P. Hobby of Texas, who remembered Porter as "a very shy, reticent man. He never made friends offhand, but required some little time to size them up. He was slow and soft-spoken. I always enjoyed his stories." Nor, said Hobby elsewhere, was it only the stories Porter wrote, "but those he would tell me made a deep impression on my mind." [16]

Porter's duties on the *Post* were, as Johnston put it, "somewhat of a varied nature." In addition to doing special assignments and running the society column (which he detested and with which Athol helped him after she came to Houston later in the fall or winter), he wrote a daily column which at first was called "Tales of the Town" but which soon was renamed "Some Postscripts and Pencillings" and at last was called simply "Some Postscripts." He also did some cartooning for the paper; as Johnston later explained, "we were in the midst of a very warm political campaign in Texas and during the campaign he drew some of the most magnificent cartoons that I have ever seen in print anywhere. They attracted attention, not only in Texas, but were copied freely throughout the United States." [17] It was as "the Post Man," though, that Porter made a place for himself on the staff of the paper, as well as a name for himself in Houston.

Most of his column writing was a continuation of the kind of thing he had published in the *Rolling Stone:* a dig at Austin's Colorado River dam as the best in the world because a man caught nine four-pound catfish below it; jokes about the bloomered bicycle girl; a definition of San Antonio's Alamo as a business house which had been allowed to fall into neglect; racetrack episodes and night scenes in Houston; topical cracks about the rivalry between Houston and Galveston as seaports. To meet his daily deadliness Porter even reprinted skits from the *Rolling Stone:* for example, the one about the stranger seeking a moderate-priced boardinghouse in a city of aristocratic widows. Of the "Postscript" items the only ones of lasting interest are a few which furnished the germs of later O. Henry stories. The story "A Poor Rule," for example, is obviously based on the skit about a Houston girl who wanted to find out which of her flattering suitors was the really sincere one.[18] A better-known story, "The Enchanted Profile," stems from the "Postscript" paragraph about the marriage plans of Annie Williams of Philadelphia, the model for the head of Liberty on the silver dollar.[19] Finally, there is the skit about the advice seeker who told the Post Man his troubles. Hezekiah Skinner idolized his wife, who, however, was in love with William Wigstaff; in fact she had eloped with Wigstaff. "For two months," said the wretched man, "the home of Hezekiah Skinner has been desolate, and this woman and Wigstaff have been flying from his wrath." The speaker explained that although he no longer cared for the faithless woman, yet he was still tortured by what had happened—at which point a woman's voice was heard in the outer office. "Great heavens, her voice!" cried the man, rising to his feet apprehensively. "I must get out of here." The Post Man urged him to confront his wife bravely and denounce her for wrecking his home. But the Post Man had misunderstood the situation. "You do not understand," pleaded his guest as he climbed out the window. "I am William Wigstaff." [20] O. Henry was to use the same plot in his story "The Hypothesis of Failure."

In a less typical sort of "Postscript" item Porter aptly characterized his own humor as well as Bill Nye's on the occasion of Nye's death in February, 1896:

His humor was peculiarly American in that it depended upon sharp and unexpected contrasts, and the bringing of opposites into unlooked-for comparison for its effect. . . . Bill Nye's jokes never had a sting. They played like summer lightning around the horizon of life, illuminating and spreading bright, if transitory, pictures upon the sky, but they were as harmless as the smile of a child. The brain of the man conceived the swift darts that he threw, but his great manly heart broke off their points.[21]

About Porter's private life during his eight months in Houston, very little is known. His closest friend on the *Post*, W. R. Sinclair, later wrote reminiscently: "He and his wife and little daughter, about nine years old [actually Margaret was six at the time] boarded on Caroline Street. . . . Almost every afternoon we would take long walks together. . . . He made no effort at being funny—jokes just oozed out of him. He never laughed at his own humor. He seldom laughed, but always there was a smile playing on his face." [22] In Houston, Porter renewed his friendship with Lollie Cave Wilson, whose account of their activities together suggests, even more clearly than Sinclair's, that Porter—now that he had congenial work to do and now that his Austin misfortune was apparently a thing of the past—was beginning to regain some of the gaiety of the years before he went to work in the bank. At this point trouble struck again. "When he went away [from Austin] in October, 1895," Lollie Cave Wilson was later to write, "he most naturally thought the affair at the bank had been attended to. In fact, he gave it no further thought but went happily on his way, with peace of mind, to accept a position on the 'Houston Post.'" [23] Whether or not Lollie understood Porter's state of mind, it is apparently true that he thought the bank affair had been settled. But as a result of Gray's correspondence with the Comptroller of the Currency, Culberson received early in 1896 orders from Washington to resubmit the case when court convened in February. "I was instructed," Culberson remembered, "to speak to the jurors. This I did, and Porter was indicted." [24] According to one report, Gray had by now been replaced by another bank examiner named Logan, whose efforts were largely responsible for securing an indictment by the new grand jury.[25] On February 10, 1896, four indictments were filed in Austin, charging that:

One, W. S. Porter, being then and there the teller and agent of a certain National Banking Association, then and there known and designated as the First National Bank of Austin, and located and doing business in the City of Austin, County of Travis, and State of Texas . . . did then and there unlawfully, knowingly and feloniously embezzle certain of the moneys and funds of the said banking institution.[26]

Indictment No. 1145 charged the embezzlement of the sum of $4,702.94 on November 1, 1894; Numbers 1146 and 1147, the identical sums of $554.48 on October 10, 1894; and No. 1148, the sum of $299.60 on November 12, 1895 (a clerical error for 1894). Witnesses before the grand jury this time had been F. B. Gray and H. P. Pfaefflin (the assistant cashier of the bank, who had checked Porter's books).

Concerning Porter's arrest in Houston on February 14, only one detail has survived. In the words of W. R. Sinclair: "One day Captain Jack White, Houston's chief of police and an old friend of mine, met me on the street and informed me, 'I have your crony, Will Porter, down at the station. I'm locking him up, so you come down and see him in the office.' . . . . That night he was taken to Austin under arrest."[27]

Porter's Houston friends rallied to his defense as hearteningly as his Austin friends had done on the earlier occasion. *Post* editor Johnston telegraphed Ed McLean: "Porter arrested; meet him at train and make bond for him." According to McLean, Porter arrived in Austin "silent and noncommunicative." All he would say was, "I made a mistake of $500 in paying out money." Fortunately, arrangements had already been made for the posting of his bond. Once again his father-in-law, along with his closest Austin friend, came to his rescue: his bond of $2,000 was signed by P. G. Roach and Herman Pressler. As Sinclair heard the story in Houston, when Porter's train reached Austin at midnight Judge Maxey was at the station to fix his bond on the spot. According to a more likely account, Porter arrived in Austin on the night of February 14 but did not make bond until February 16, after which he returned to Houston.[28]

90

His arrest had prostrated Athol. During the fall and winter her health had improved almost miraculously, but now, in addition to being hopelessly caught in the toils of the law, Porter had a seriously ill wife on his hands. The only thing for them to do on a salary of $20 a week was to have Mrs. Roach come to Houston to take care of Athol while he tried to carry on his work. Even so, his column, which involved leg work on the streets in addition to writing time, appeared only four times in February and sporadically for his remaining time on the staff. Since on May 14 his salary was raised to $25 weekly, however, it is obvious (and it turns out to be the fact) that he was doing other kinds of work which required him to be away from home less than would have the daily preparation of his column.

For a full month Porter took no action in the matter of his indictment. On March 16 he filed an affidavit in Austin asking for a continuance of his case. Only two days before, he stated, had he been able to secure legal counsel. (This, of course, was a matter of money again, and rather than become further indebted to his father-in-law or some other Austin friend, he had gone to the owner of the *Post*, Judge E. P. Hill, for a loan of the $200 which the Austin legal firm of Ward and James had demanded before they would take his case.) [29] Porter also stated in his affidavit "that the charge embraced in the indictment is so general in its terms that it will require a critical examination of the books of the said bank during the entire time that the defendant was employed therein to enable him to ascertain exactly what transactions form the basis of said indictment."

The defendant further states that he resides in the City of Houston, where he has lived for about four months; that for the past thirty days his wife has been ill, a greater part of the time, being confined to her bed; that being a comparative stranger in said city, the defendant's presence at his wife's bedside was absolutely required, she having no friends or acquaintances in said city to give her necessary attention, and that she is now in that condition. That for the reasons stated, it has been beyond the power of the defendant to visit the City of Austin and spend sufficient time to make any personal examination of the books in said bank.[30]

The request for continuance was granted (the trial was now set for the July term of court), but Porter seems to have made no further efforts to prepare a defense. According to Herman Pressler, he did not consult with his attorneys nor ever get around to an examination of the bank books with them; and a cousin of Athol's later reported that, desperately worried though Athol was about the impending trial, Porter would never discuss it with her.[31] The only statement he is reported to have made at this time was quoted (obviously with some elaboration) by Lollie Cave Wilson:

"The guilty man, if charged, would take the stand and call me a liar. He is not, as I thought, a man of honor, or he would have kept his word to me and straightened the matter out when I left Austin and the bank. Therefore when he is caught in a trap he will take the crook's viewpoint and clear his own skirts. His word will be taken against mine, because my word is the only thing that accuses him—the books, those silent accusers, are pointing fingers of guilt at me. You know that those men at the bank are too close together to give an outsider a chance. . . . I was not cut out for that kind of work. But I took the job and held a position of trust. I failed that trust when I permitted such an outrageous thing to happen. Since I did not report the shortages as they occurred, I can legally be held as an accessory to the fact." [32]

This sounds less like the remembrance of an actual conversation than an attempt to put into Porter's own words the attitude which Mrs. Wilson had sensed on his part. Even so, and even if "the guilty man" existed only in the wishful thinking of Porter and his friends, nevertheless Lollie surely expressed accurately enough Porter's attitude toward the trial during his last months in Houston. Despite such an attitude, though, he seems to have been so uncommunicative on the subject and to have kept up such a successful front that most of his friends assumed he felt no real concern. He continued, moreover, to produce copy for the *Post:* a series of longer special features in addition to his now irregular "Postscripts" column.

A group of some fifty of these sketches and articles—unsigned for the most part—have been identified beyond any reasonable doubt as Porter's work.[33] Four of them, indeed, are signed "W. S. P." or "W. S. Porter"; in fourteen others the writer refers to himself as "the Post Man"; and in a good many of them are to be found themes or plots which recur in the later work of O. Henry.[34] It is this latter group which is of special interest to anyone trying to trace the development of Porter's personality and work.

In at least three of the *Post* items Porter toyed—as he had already done, of course, in the *Rolling Stone*—with what was later to become one of his favorite themes. "Sketched About Town" is the story of a tramp who fancied himself a scholar of wealth and position until, suddenly overcome by some inner change, he lapsed back into his true status "and with shaking hands drew from his pocket something wrapped in paper. He unrolled it, took something from between his thumb and thrust it into his mouth. The sickly, faint, sweet odor of gum opium reached the reporter." [35] This, of course, is a situation identical with that of Dopy Mike (Prince Michael) in "The Caliph, Cupid and the Clock," and similar to that of still another Mike (the Wandering Jew) in "The Door of Unrest."

In another *Post* sketch, "An Unknown Romance," a society man and a society girl, who have decided to play the respective roles of Alpine hunter and peasant girl while in Europe, happen to meet while thus disguised; they fall in love, but "Miss Augusta Vance, with a dowry of five millions, could not commit the folly of thinking of a common hunter of the Alps mountains," and as for Pelham Van Winkler, "society and family have claimed him, and today, at high noon, he was to marry Miss Vance, the daughter of the millionaire iron founder." [36] Without recognizing each other from their Alpine meeting, they end by making a marriage of mutual convenience. The same theme is handled in such later stories as "Lost on Dress Parade" and "A Night in New Arabia"; it is reversed in stories like "The Caliph and the Cad" and "Transients in Arcadia"; and both angles figure in one of O. Henry's best-known stories, "While the Auto Waits."

Still another *Post* story of mistaken or confused identity is "An Odd Character," [37] which is suggestive again of "The Door of Unrest" but even more particularly suggestive of "The Enchanted Kiss," a story with a San Antonio setting, the writing of which must have brought back to O. Henry something of what he felt in the spring of 1896 while waiting to be tried for embezzlement:

Nearly all of us [he wrote in the later story] have, at some point in our

93

lives—either to excuse our own stupidity or placate our consciences— promulgated some theory of fatalism. . . . Tansey had done likewise. . . . Each excursion that he had made had led to the one paramount finale. . . . Clearly, Fate was holding up to him the mirror that night, calling him to observe what awaited him at the end of whichever road he might take.[38]

By the time he reached New York, that is to say, and published such stories as "The Enchanted Kiss" and "Roads of Destiny," Porter seems to have understood himself well enough to express in terms of fatalism his inadequacy in dealing with the actualities of life. As a matter of fact, he did not have to wait until 1903 to gain this insight into himself. The same fatalistic attitude is expressed in the *Post* sketch "A Night Errant":

Life is neither tragedy nor comedy. It is a mingling of both. High above us omnipotent hands pull the strings that choke our laughter with sobs and cause strange sounds of mirth to break in upon our deepest grief. We are marionettes that dance and cry, scarce at our own wills; and at the end, the flaring lights are out, we are laid to rest in our wooden boxes, and down comes the dark night to cover the scene of our brief triumph.[39]

In the *Post* sketches, then, are to be found two of O. Henry's favorite motifs: the situation of the impostor or wearer of a disguise, and the idea of fate as the one unavoidable reality of life. Also to be found are other plot ideas that figure in the later stories—for example, the memento divided between two lovers: in the sketch "In Mezzotint" [40] it is a concert ticket for two, the pieces of which are reunited when the heroine commits suicide as an act of penance for forsaking her poor lover to marry a well-to-do doctor, and in "No Story," written in New York, it is the hero's half of a divided dime which identifies him. As in the later story "Dougherty's Eye-Opener," so in the *Post* sketch "How She Got in the Swim" [41] Porter dealt with a husband's belated discovery of the social charm of a wife whom he had kept immured at home. As in "Proof of the Pudding," so in the sketch "Unavailable" [42] we have the editor who rejects a story as wildly improbable because it is free of melodrama and sentimentality. And in the *Post* sketch "Nothing New Under the Sun" [43] a poor writer in his attic room views through a hole in the roof the blue-tinged star which was later to figure in "The Skylight Room."

It is possible to find in "Simmon's Saturday Night" [44] a recognizable predecessor of Jeff Peters in *The Gentle Grafter* stories. And even the underpaid shopgirl, of whom O. Henry was to become the champion in New York, is to be found in the *Post* sketches. Writing about the last evening of 1895 in "New Year's Eve and How It Came to Houston," Porter singles out among the people on the street "a lovely shopgirl, as neat and trim as a fashion plate."

Her big hat plumes wave, and her little foot heels beat a merry tictac upon the pavement. . . . Her bright eyes flash sidelong glances at the jeweler's windows as she passes. . . . She is thinking of the handsome, finely dressed man who comes so often to her counter in the big store, ostensibly to buy her wares. How grand he is, and what eloquent eyes and a lovely moustache he has. She does not know his name, but well she knows that he cares little for the goods she sells. . . . She wonders where he is now. She trips around a corner and meets him face to face. She gives a little scream, and then her face hardens and a cold glitter comes into her eye.

On his arm is a huge market basket . . . [and] by the hand he leads a cold-nosed but indisputable little boy.

She elevates her charming head to a supercilious angle, snaps out to herself the word "married!" and is gone.[45]

A final parallel is of particular interest since it is found in his last sketch published in the *Post* (on June 22, just a week before the opening of the July term of court in Austin). In "An Aquatint" (as in "Whistling Dick's Christmas Stocking," written in prison, and in "Compliments of the Season," written in New York) Porter writes about a tramp whose face is "sodden with drink, loss of hope, and the mark of the beast. The image of anything strong, manly or high had vanished from it forever." The Houston tramp saves a child from drowning, and when the terror-stricken parents reach the spot he "delivered up the child, and then he stood, shivering with ague, parched with thirst, wretched, vile, despicable and repulsive, with the dirty streams of water trickling from his rags." The father's hand goes to his pocket "with commendable quickness," but the mother is more perceptive.

She caught the arm of the duller man before he could bring the money to sight, and she offered the tramp—her hand.

"We thank you, sir," she said in a sweet and even voice, "more than words can tell you for what you have done. Please accept our lasting and sincere gratitude."

And while the excellent but duller man stood with one hand half drawn from his pocket wondering, the tramp had doffed his burlesque of a hat, bowed like a prince over the woman's hand, spoken a word or two in correct response and went his way with a surer step and the ghost of a forgotten smile upon his face. . . .

Later she mused when she and Dot were alone, and said to herself, "I wonder what he once was." [46]

This is sentimentality of a kind which O. Henry never overcame. Now, as later, it helped to furnish a refuge for a man confronted by a situation which he must already have known how he was going to face—or rather, not to face.

Unfortunately, it is not possible to assemble a detailed and coherent account of Porter's actions when the time came for him to stand trial in Austin. According to one report, Porter persuaded Athol to return to Austin ahead of him, and she and Margaret made a stopover to visit friends on the way.[47] Athol was still far from well. Another version of what happened is that she had already, as soon as she was able to travel, been taken back to Austin by her mother.[48] At any rate, *Post* editor Johnston raised for Porter, when he was ready to go back, the sum of $260 to help pay the expenses of his trial, which all of his friends confidently expected to end in his acquittal. His friend W. R. Sinclair took a walk with him on the afternoon of the day he was to leave, "and he told me that he had made all his arrangements for the event. He had secured money to pay his expenses, and left me saying, 'Adios, I'll be back in a day or two.' . . . I had inside information that acquittal awaited him if he went to trial." [49] The truth seems to be that Porter had made no plans for his defense, and presumably he had no intention of returning to Austin. All that is known for certain is that on July 10— some days after he had left Houston, long enough for him to be missed and sought in vain—the night editor of the *Post* wrote: "The reporters who went to see the Austin train off saw Mr. Porter there, and he has never been seen since. Our presumption naturally is that he took the east bound Southern Pacific, which leaves [Houston] about the same time. . . . We know he speaks Spanish fluently and think that a man who is a fugitive from justice might naturally try to bury himself in Cuba." [50]

The surmise of Frances Maltby, Athol's school friend, is that Porter, between trains, was looking around the town of Hempstead, fifty miles from Houston. This was Mrs. Maltby's home town and the scene of more than one notorious shooting, so that Porter had once said to her, "I'd like to have a look around at that place." During his exploration of the town, Mrs. Maltby surmises, his train pulled out and left him; faced with the accomplished fact, Porter impulsively followed it through. "On such small things," observes the writer, "are decisions made." [51] On the other hand, Hyder Rollins—one of the most careful writers on the subject—has expressed the opinion that Porter's flight "can hardly have been a last-minute decision but was evidently premeditated," and that it was the windfall of Johnston's $260 which "no doubt led to plans for flight. There appears to be no foundation for the story of Porter's sudden decision to change trains at Hempstead and skip his bond." [52]

This opinion is substantiated by two bits of evidence which have been overlooked by Porter's apologists. Herman Pressler, Porter's most intimate friend at this time, said later that Athol knew Porter was going to flee, and that when she left Houston she went to visit friends in Brazoria County and only returned to Austin after her parents had learned of Porter's disappearance.[53] In fact, according to Louis Kreisle (the Porters' next-door neighbor and close friend in Austin), Athol not only knew of her husband's plan to flee but, when they parted, even gave him her watch to help along with his expenses.[54]

All of this lends credulity to Lollie Cave Wilson's story of a talk she had with Porter a few days after Athol and Margaret had left Houston (according to Lollie, they had left about June 20):

When I met him he was perfectly calm and seemed anything but frightened. However, his expression was very serious and the old smile was gone.

His first words were, "Polly-O, the little black crow has alighted again, and again we fly away. . . . You won't agree with me—neither does Athol—but I am going away, maybe forever. . . . I will send for Athol and Margaret as soon as I am able." [55]

97

It was on July 6, 1896, according to Lollie, that Porter left Houston, ostensibly for Austin. Instead he went to New Orleans, from where he was able finally to take a boat to Honduras. Since he was convinced that he would be convicted if he went to trial, his intention apparently was to evade the issue until his case should be barred by the statute of limitation.

CHAPTER SIX

· ⟨∿⟩ ·

"I am like Lord Jim," Porter has been quoted as confiding to a friend in New York, "because we both made one fateful mistake at the supreme crisis of our lives, a mistake from which we could not recover." [1] If we are to consider Porter (regardless of his innocence or guilt of the embezzlement charge) as essentially a man of good intentions, then his flight from trial was a mistake, whether he was innocent or guilty. And yet "mistake" is not really the word. An action can hardly be called a mistake if it is the most characteristic action of one's life—the logical outcome of all that has gone before. When Porter was confronted with a showdown, when the actuality of his own character was to be placed in the scales before his own eyes as well as those of the world, surely the thing he did was the one inevitable thing for him to have done.

Evidently—whether his flight was premeditated or not—he had no properly worked out plan. New Orleans, being the nearest big city, was the most logical first stop, but once there Porter came to an irresolute standstill, even though he must have known that, if recognized, he could be arrested as easily there as in Houston. He did—according to Lollie Cave Wilson—drop the name Porter and assume the name Shirley Worth.[2] Instead of making plans to move on, though, he tried to conserve his funds by taking temporary newspaper jobs, first on the New Orleans *Delta*, then on the *Picayune*. Joe Monget, a local newspaper man, later reminisced:

I knew him, only casually, as a reporter on one of the big dailies (I think the *Picayune*). . . . The newspaper boys rented an old rookery down in the old French Quarter of New Orleans, where they slept and ate one meal per day,—dinner. They called this place "The Ranch." They had employed one of the best Creole cooks to be obtained in the city, and I considered it a rare treat to be able to drop in to one of those dinners, both for the company and the food. Whenever I did, which was frequently, O. Henry was there, but like some others, attracted little attention. . . . [He] seldom, if ever, told a story. Several of the boys were of a roystering disposition, [and] would go out on the town to have a royal good time. Only twice do I recollect O. Henry joining us, [on which occasions he was] the same good, jovial fellow, always appreciating a good story or joke, able to chamber his liquor.[3]

In what amounts to a very suggestive statement about himself, O. Henry later described a character who "saw himself an outcast from society, forever to be a shady stalker along the ragged edge of respectability. . . . He was self-condemned to this opinion, as he was self-exiled, through it, to this quaint Southern city a thousand miles from his former home. Here he had dwelt for longer than a year, knowing but few, keeping in a subjective world of shadows which was invaded at times by the perplexing bulks of jarring realities." This character's plight is the result of legal entanglement all too similar to what Porter's might have been:

It is no new tale, that of the gambler's declension. During one night's sitting he lost, and then he had imperilled a certain amount of his employer's money, which, by accident, he carried with him. He continued to lose, to the last wager, and then began to gain, leaving the game a winner to a somewhat formidable sum. The same night his employer's safe was robbed. A search was had; the winnings of Lorison were found in his room, their total forming an accusative nearness to the sum purloined. He was taken, tried, and, through incomplete evidence released, smutched with the sinister devoirs of a disagreeing jury.[4]

During his few weeks in New Orleans, despite his confinement to a world of shadows, Porter managed to get around a good deal, as is evident from such later stories as "Hostages to Momus," "Blind Man's Holiday," "Cherchez la Femme," "Whistling Dick's Christmas Stocking," and "The Renaissance at Charleroi." He made "the acquaintance of drinks invented by the Creoles during the period of Louey Cans, in which they are still served at the side doors."[5] He strolled around the old Place d'Armes to observe "the ancient Cabildo, where Spanish justice fell like hail . . . and the Cathedral, another provincial ghost . . . [and the] little, iron-railed park of flowers and immaculate gravelled walks, where citizens take the air of evenings." [6] He caught the characteristic notes of the Creole dialect spoken in the little cafés of the Quarter. ("H'what you say?" said Madame, cheerily. . . . "One tam I think those w'at you call calendair, wix ze l'il day of mont' below. But, no. Those wall is broke in those plaze, M'sieu Robbin.") [7] And he met and observed such local types as Grandemont Charles, "a little Creole gentleman, aged thirty-four, with a bald spot on the top of his head and the manners of a prince," who was a clerk "in a cotton broker's office in one of those cold, rancid mountains of oozy brick, down near the levee." [8]

No doubt Porter, like one of his later characters, lived in "a dim *chambre garnie* in Bienville Street . . . [and looked] down from my attic window from time to time at the old, yellow, absinthe house across the street" [9] while he pondered over his plight and wrote notes to Athol by way of Lollie Cave Wilson. The notes were usually unsigned drawings, Lollie reported, such as the one she particularly remembered of a woman holding a baby and looking across a river at a man who stood with arms outstretched and tears running down his face. Porter had a room, he wrote, near the famous restaurant of Mme. Louis Beguet. Since Lollie had known Louis years before, Porter went to see him, and it was through this connection that he met a French importer-exporter, "who sent him to South America and gave him the opportunity of making a living there in the import and export business." (Lollie's story is not to be dismissed because she seemingly made an error in her geography. As later details indicate, she meant South America to include Central America.) When Porter left New Orleans, he sent Athol "a large sketch of two hands clasped as if shaking good-bye, with a sailing vessel in the background. We knew then that he was on his way again." [10]

Fortunately, the country selected for him by Lollie's importer-exporter—if there was really such a person—turned out to be the only Central American country which had no extradition laws. In any event it was Honduras to which Porter went, as was attested by several close friends in Austin. Lollie, still having trouble with her geography, reported receiving three letters from him from "South America": one from Puerto Cortes, one from Trujillo, and one from Honduras! Moreover, Al Jennings (the notorious train robber who was to write a graphic if somewhat undependable account of his association with Porter at this time and also later in prison and in New York) arrived in Trujillo in 1896 with his brother Frank and the $30,000 loot of which the two had relieved a bank in Texas. Apparently they had made a hasty departure not only from Texas but from the American mainland. "My full-dress suit," Jennings recorded, "had lost one of its tails by this time; the white shirt was embossed with little hunks of dirt and splashes of whiskey. Only the rim of my stovepipe hat was left, an uncombed red mat stuck out through the ventilator." [11] Catching sight of the American flag above one of the "four life-sized houses" in the town, Jennings headed for it, and it was under that insignia that the two famous fugitives met.

On the porch of the squat bungalow that housed the American consulate, sat an ample, dignified figure in immaculate white ducks. He had a large, nobly-set head, with hair the color of new rope and a full, straight-glancing gray eye that noted without a sparkle of laughter every detail of my ludicrous makeup.

He was already serene and comfortably situated with liquor, but he had about him an attitude of calm distinction. A rather pompous dignitary, he seemed to me, sitting there as though he owned the place. This, I thought, is indeed a man worthy to be the American consul.

Porter took Jennings to the nearest cantina, where, in the process of getting acquainted, he finally, defensively inquired, "You probably wonder who I am and why I'm here?" Jennings reassured him at once: "Oh, God, no. In my country nobody asks a man's name or his past. You're all right." Aided further by one of the local beverages, Porter relaxed again. Honduras, he said, was an admirable location for a man who didn't want much to do. What line was he in, Jennings inquired.

"I entertain the newcomers."

"You must be a hell of a busy man," Jennings guessed.

"You're the first since my arrival."

They discussed possible investments for Jennings's bank loot: a cocoanut plantation, a campaign for the presidency of the country, an indigo concession. At this point in his account of the event, Jenning's memory seems to have begun playing him tricks. It was, he tells us, the Fourth of July (Porter had not left Houston on July 4, of course), and by way of celebrating the holiday the three of them (Frank Jennings had by now come up from the boat to join them) acted out the musical-comedy events which make up the plot of O. Henry's story "The Fourth in Salvador."

As a result of this prank, according to Jennings, the three of them were invited to leave the country, and after a voyage around the tip of South America and a stopover in Mexico City (where Jennings claims he saved Porter's life by shooting an insulted "Castilian" with whose fiancée Porter had unwisely flirted), the party ended up on a friend's ranch back in Texas. Here, in planning a new bank robbery to replenish their treasury, Jennings invited Porter to come in on the venture. "We didn't need him, but I had already grown very fond of the moody, reticent, cultured fellow. I didn't want him to be dependent on us and I wanted his company on the range." Porter demurred, it seems, and Jennings suggested he could just wait outside and hold the horses. After a moment's hesitation, Porter said, "I don't believe I could even hold the horses." [12] At this point, according to the story, the Jennings brothers parted company with Porter. Beginning with the Fourth of July episode in Trujillo, however, Jennings's narrative is fictional to the point of being wholly undependable.

Judging by the reports of his Austin friends, Porter seems to have stayed in Honduras until he decided to return to Austin. According to his friend and neighbor Ed Smith, he wrote to Athol about once a month while in New Orleans and Honduras. Knowing that the postal authorities would watch her mail, he sent his letters to a woman friend in Houston, who changed the envelopes before sending them to Mrs. Smith in Austin, who on receiving them would take them hidden in a book to Athol. If anyone else was present she would hand the letter over casually, saying, "Here's a book I'd like for you to read." [13] Athol, it seems, did not want her mother and stepfather to know about the letters; she was afraid that Mr. Roach, who was naturally concerned about the $2,000 bail which Porter had jumped, might communicate with the authorities.

Athol's friend Frances Maltby estimates that Porter had been gone some two months before Athol had any word from him. He begged her to join him, saying that he had been looking around for a school for Margaret, but Athol was too ill to contemplate such a trip. "The courage and loyalty with which she faced [his forfeiture of his bond]. . . and defended him against the clamor of censure that arose, filled the people of Austin with a new love and admiration for the wife." [14] Although she was running a daily temperature, she started a business course to prepare herself to make a living for Margaret. In the distress she felt over her situation, she tried to make money by doing fancy needlework, which she sold to a store-keeper she knew. Nothing in her life, it might be said of Athol, became her like the leaving of it. During her last year of life, faced not only with her husband's arrest and flight but also with the rapid progress of her own disease, she seems to have grown from a spoiled child into a woman of selfless courage. No word of bitterness or panic was attributed to her by anyone who knew her at this time.

Contrary to Mrs. Maltby's estimate of two months, the Porters' neighbor L. H. Kreisle later said it was only three weeks before Athol heard from Porter, who at first sent his letters through the Richard Halls but later, because the Halls lived so far out, through the Kreisles themselves.[15] Kreisle mailed some of Athol's letters to Porter, addressed with fictitious names, and on one occasion—presumably in response to a request—Kreisle telegraphed Porter $30: a loan which Porter later repaid. Porter never went to South America, Kreisle said, but wrote regularly from Honduras. (Anne Partlan, too, said that Porter talked to her about Honduras but never about any other Latin-American country.) [16]

As is indicated by the conflicting details in these accounts of his correspondence with Athol, Porter apparently sent his letters through different friends at different times. Unfortunately, Athol's caution led her to destroy the letters as soon as she had read them, but Mrs. Kreisle, to whom she read some of them "with the tears rolling down her cheeks," reported that Porter hoped to have his family join him in Honduras. At least at first he had to resort to manual labor to make a living, "digging ditches and doing just anything he could get to do. . . . I remember in some of his letters he told her about what a little bit he would have to eat some days, sometimes only one banana." [17]

Other than such scattered bits of information furnished by friends of the family, the only details about Porter's Honduran interlude are to be found in his later stories, particularly the series entitled *Cabbages and Kings*. Here Honduras becomes Anchuria, and Trujillo becomes Coralio, a town which "lay at the sea's edge on a strip of alluvial coast. It was set like a little pearl in an emerald band." From the main street, which parallelled the beach, the town dwindled into narrower side streets.

These side streets were covered by a growth of thick, rank grass, which was kept to a navigable shortness by the machetes of the police. Stone sidewalks, little more than a ledge in width, ran along the base of the mean and monotonous adobe houses. At the outskirts of the village these streets dwindled to nothing; and here were set the palm-thatched huts of the Caribs and the poorer natives, and the shabby cabins of negroes from Jamaica and the West India islands. A few structures raised their heads above the red-tiled roofs of the one-story houses—the bell tower of the Calaboza, the Hotel de los Estranjeros, the residence of the Vesuvius Fruit Company's agent, the store and residence of Bernard Brannigan, a ruined cathedral in which Columbus had once set foot, and, most imposing of all, the Casa Morena—the summer "White House" of the President of Anchuria. On the principal street running along the beach—the Broadway of Coralio—were the larger stores, the government bodega and post-office, the cuartel, the rum shops and the market place.[18]

Of an American exile in "this far land of the lotus," Porter wrote: "He was happy and content in this land of perpetual afternoon. Those old days of life in the States seemed like an irritating dream. . . . The climate as balmy as that of distant Avalon; the fetterless, idyllic round of enchanted days; the life among this indolent, romantic people—a life full of music, flowers, and low laughter; the influence of the imminent sea and mountains, and the many shapes of love and magic and beauty that bloomed in the white tropic nights —with all he was more than content." [19] One is reminded of the carefree spirit of the letters Porter wrote to North Carolina from the Halls' ranch in Texas. And that the story expresses—in part at least —Porter's own state of mind in the tropics is clearly indicated by Anne Partlan's later comment that he "spoke of Honduras as Mecca," where he had found "freedom . . . infinite peace. 'Let's go to Honduras,'" he would say to her in New York.[20] Mrs. Roach, too, said that "Will seemed to feel free and at ease there, with the exception that he did not have Athol and Margaret with him. He was planning to make a home there, and used to write Athol how hard he was working toward that end. Everything was being planned, but poor Athol was too sick to ever go there." [21]

Clearly Porter knew his wife's condition well enough to be aware, at one level of awareness, that his idea of moving his family to Honduras was unrealistic. But this fact he refused to reckon with. He took life as it came from day to day, and when he left Honduras to return home after some four or five months the decision was not entirely of his own making. What happened was that at Christmas time he received from Athol a box containing his overcoat along with some new clothes and delicacies she had bought with the twenty-five dollars netted by a point-lace handkerchief which she had made and some friends had raffled off for her. "It was not till a long time afterward," according to Mrs. Roach, "that he knew her temperature was 105 when she packed that box." [22] He did, however, receive letters about the same time—according to Lollie Cave Wilson, from both herself and Mrs. Roach—advising him that in view of Athol's condition he should come home, "for it was very plain to me [Lollie] that Athol was rapidly failing." [23] Betty Hall understood that Athol herself had been begging him to return and clear his name, but that Porter agreed only after his two bondsmen promised to go on a new bond for him and to help arrange for his defense.[24]

Whatever the exact details, Porter finally had to acknowledge the futility of the plans he had tried to make for the future. Faced with a dying wife and a dependent child, he made the only possible decision. No doubt it took some little time to accumulate passage money. Even so, by the time he reached New Orleans he was flat broke. On January 21, 1897, he telegraphed his father-in-law: "Wire me twenty-five dollars without identification quick. Can't get my check cashed. W. A. Bright." [25] On this humiliating note ended Porter's attempt to evade the charges which had been brought against him in Austin. The following day he received the money from Roach, and presumably on January 23 he arrived home to submit to the inevitable.

According to a still-widespread version of what happened after his return, the authorities, "out of sympathy for his sick wife . . .

pretended to be unaware of his presence in the city." [26] Actually, Porter appeared in court on February 1, having hastily arranged with his attorneys to file a demurrer to his indictment before the regular term of court was to begin on February 7.

Now comes the defendant, W. S. Porter, in his own proper person into Court and having heard the indictment read, says that the said indictment and the matters therein contained, in manner and form . . . are not sufficient in law. . . . Whereas for want of sufficient indictment in this behalf, the said W. S. Porter prays judgment, and that by the Court he may be dismissed and discharged from the said premises in the said indictment specified.[27]

In a Motion to Quash Indictment, also filed on February 1, the indictment is said to be "vague, indefinite, uncertain and insufficient" on seven points (which add up to no more than a legal stall for time). In consequence, on February 12 Judge Aleck Boarman granted Porter's request to be allowed to make a new bond. Although his earlier bond of $2,000 had been declared forfeited, his bondsmen had not been assessed, and the same two men now signed a new bond for a doubled amount.[28] After these legal steps had been taken, the case was allowed to continue in abeyance until the term of court following Athol's death.

For a time after Porter returned, Athol's new will to live brought about a remarkable improvement in her condition. His flight had seemed an admission of guilt, but when he returned of his own free will, "she fairly radiated with joy at the thought. People surely would acknowledge his innocence!" [29] During Porter's absence her stepfather had cleared out the hayloft in the backyard and insisted—because of the supposed curative power of the odor of hay—that she spend as much time there as possible. He had also sent her out riding in the family buggy as often as he could persuade her, and of this latter form of treatment Porter now took charge, going with her for long drives in the fresh air.

Athol's improvement was a very temporary one. Her new-found strength soon failed, but her spirit never failed. "I never saw such will power," Mrs. Kreisle afterward observed. "The only day she remained in bed was the day she died. . . . Toward the last she was too weak to get in and out of the buggy, so Mr. Porter would carry her in his arms and sit her in the buggy." [30] For the six months Athol survived after his return, Porter seems to have devoted himself exclusively to helping nurse her. Mrs. Roach said that "all his time and thought were given to her comfort. They were happy, yet they must have known that the end was not far away. . . . They would drive around in the cool of the day, and on Sundays they would drive up to the open window of the Presbyterian Church . . . and remain till church or Sunday school was over." [31]

Porter's true frame of mind, however, was one which he was unable to conceal entirely. According to Mrs. Roach, he "often intimated that he would kill himself rather than become a convict. All of it broke my girl's heart and she died quickly." [32] Surely this was the low ebb of Porter's life—to have to stand by and wait, himself facing imprisonment and disgrace, while his wife wasted away before his eyes. He must have given much remorseful thought to what ten years as his wife had done to her; and yet, now that her life was ending, what he must have felt most strongly of all was the helplessness which he later summed up in one terse sentence: "The lonesomest thing in all the world is a soul when it is making ready to go on its mysterious, far journey." [33]

In May, Aunt Lina died—an event which can have meant little or nothing to him under the circumstances. Two months later, at six-thirty on Sunday evening, July 25, Athol died, at the age of twenty-nine. She had, for the first time during her illness, spent the entire day in bed. Margaret, lacking only two months of being eight, was old enough to understand and completely go to pieces over her mother's death. "When no one else could soothe the child," Mrs. Maltby wrote, Porter "took her in his arms and away from the house. It was a hot, sultry night. With old Charley [the horse] and the buggy he drove Margaret out in the country." [34] Finally the child fell asleep, but back at home, as he started to lift her out of the buggy, she woke and began sobbing again. They spent another hour riding around aimlessly. It was almost midnight before Porter was able to carry her as far as the porch without waking her. He laid her in the hammock and spent the rest of the night swinging the exhausted child to keep her asleep. On the following night Margaret was again sleepless and hysterical until Porter repeated the process.

Funeral services were held at ten o'clock on Tuesday morning at the Roach home. Afterward Porter refused to go in the carriage with the Roaches, but drove alone with Margaret, with whom he sat at a distance until the graveside service was over and everyone else had left the cemetery. Only then did he and Margaret go to Athol's grave, where they spent a long time rearranging the flowers. "At the time of his wife's death," Mrs. Maltby wrote, "the abject misery of Will Porter was pitiable in the extreme. It was made more pathetic by an aloofness, a desire to be by himself, that he maintained."[35] In the words of the *Statesman:*

Mrs. Porter's death was a sad blow to all her relatives and friends. For some months now it has been evident that she was a victim of that dread disease, consumption, and while her end was assured, its fast approach when she was in the prime of life caused one and all to feel the pity that is ever attendant on the cutting off of life in the hour of youth. Mrs. Porter leaves a husband and one child to mourn her loss. She was a woman known and beloved by many. She made many friends while yet a young girl in this city, and her married life was but a continuation of that girlhood so far as the moulding of friendship's chain is concerned. All will regret her untimely end and will join the Statesman in extending sympathy to the bereaved relatives and friends.[36]

The remaining months of 1897 are an almost complete blank. Athol's death seems to have brought no change in Porter's relationship with the Roaches, who apparently never wavered in their belief in his innocence. As Mrs. Roach remarked after his death, "Will was a noble man with a true heart." [37] In the late summer or early fall he began writing again, in a room fixed up for him above Roach's grocery store. At about this time both he and Roach seem to have been hard pressed for money. On September 1 he signed a note to Ph. Hatzfield & Co., Importers, for the sum of $47.50, to be repaid within six months with interest at 10 per cent. (The money was not repaid, and Hatzfield later endorsed the note to J. W. Maxwell, presumably a lawyer, whose inscription across the bottom reads: "In Illinois [*sic*] Penitentiary. She is dead." The latter phrase was a slang designation for a dead account.) [38] The assumption that Roach too, at least temporarily, was in financial straits is based on an item in the *Statesman* of September 18, 1897. In the list of delinquent taxes for the year 1896, P. G. Roach is shown as owing the city the sum of $148.96. It is not hard to understand how he might have overextended himself financially, what with all of Porter's earlier difficulties and Athol's long illness. Many years later he stated that, all told, he "loaned" his son-in-law some $10,000 between the time Porter married Athol and the time he moved to New York.[39]

In December, Porter sold his first short story to a national publication. From the S. S. McClure Company he received a letter, dated December 2, making no mention of price but stating:

> Your story, "The Miracle of Lava Canyon," is excellent. It has the combination of humane [sic] interest with dramatic incident, which in our opinion is the best kind of a story. If you have more like this, we should be glad to read them. We have placed it in our syndicate of newspapers. The other stories we return herewith. They are not quite available.[40]

The story was not published until September 18, 1898, some five months after Porter had entered the Ohio Penitentiary, so that he later remarked, "My first story was paid for but I never saw it in print." [41] Appropriately enough it not only concerns an outlaw and a sheriff, but has to do with the characteristic situation of a disguised character. The hero, Sheriff Conrad, is a physical coward who has succeeded in concealing his weakness and even in gaining a reputation for courage and daring. In the presence of the heroine, Boadicea Reed ("she had never, no, never, felt the slightest sensation of fear or abashment at any person or thing since she could remember. Miss Boadicea despised and contemned all the little feminine weaknesses and terrors of her sex with all the prejudice of one who did not understand them"), Sheriff Conrad nerves himself up to hand-to-hand combat with Arizona Dan, the worst man in the country: a situation in which suddenly "valor and courage had come upon him. He felt that he would never know fear again. Something had passed into his blood that made him a man instead of the spurious thing he had been. He felt the two dark eyes above fixed on him, but he kept his own upon Arizona Dan's." He disposes of Dan, of course, and as he walks Boadicea back to her home, "a scream of fright came from the namesake of the battle queen of the Britons.

"'A horrid lizard!' she cried.

"The sheriff's strong arm reassured her. The miracle was complete. The soul of each had passed into the other." [42]

This first acceptance of a story must have brought Porter a certain exhilaration even in the months following the death of his wife and preceding the trial scheduled for February. Despondent he was to the point of contemplating suicide, and he avoided all of his friends. "He didn't want to talk with anybody," Charles Anderson remembered.[43] But even though he had not the heart to help his attorneys work on his defense, it later became clear that he had not yet given up that last shred of hope which remains even after all reason for hope is gone.

CHAPTER SEVEN

· ∽✙✙∾ ·

The February term of court opened on Monday the seventh, with Judge Thomas S. Maxey presiding. It was not until Tuesday of the following week, however (the day the battleship *Maine* was blown up in Havana Harbor), that Porter was taken into custody and technically, but not actually, committed to the Travis County jail. On the same day the *Statesman* carried an announcement that on the preceding day the trial of Zola and Perrieux had resumed in Paris.

Betty Hall had written to District Attorney Culberson asking him to be merciful in Porter's trial, but he had had his orders from Washington and could only press the case with due diligence. On January 23 he had written the Attorney General in Washington to request the authorization as a witness of F. B. Gray, whom he considered "absolutely essential and necessary on behalf of the Government for the proper trial of the case against Porter." [1] This authorization had been given, and Gray was on hand as one of the chief Government witnesses. In selecting the jury, Porter's attorneys, Ward and James, had struck from the list three names (J. R. Wutrich, George Boerner, and Emil Schultz) on the common assumption that Germans tended always to be on the side of authority. Boerner's was also one of the three names struck—for unknown reasons—by the attorneys for the Government (R. U. Culberson and Duval West). The jury, as finally constituted, included only one Austin man, the others being from outlying parts of the Western District of Texas. Since it was a federal case, one Negro happened to be on the jury: L. H. Washington, a minister from Giddings. The foreman was W. B. Barr. [2]

112

The four original indictments, filed on February 10, 1896, had been numbered 1145–1148, charging embezzlement as follows:

No. 1145: $4702.94 on November 1, 1894
No. 1146: $554.48 on October 10, 1894
No. 1147: $554.48 on October 10, 1894
No. 1148: $299.60 on November 12, 1895.

Two reindictments were now added, since Porter had failed to appear in July, 1896:

No. 1174: $554.48 on October 10, 1894
No. 1175: $299.60 on November 12, 1894 (correcting the date in 1148).

The prosecution began by moving that 1145, 1147, 1148, 1174, and 1175 (together involving a sum of $5,557.02) be consolidated (omitting 1146 as merely a duplicate of 1147). Later, in an apparent effort to strengthen its case, the prosecution moved that 1145 and 1147 be dismissed. Porter was therefore tried on three indictments involving two charges (since 1175 was only a correction of 1148), and the total sum involved was $854.08. The two new indictments, in order to bar an appeal to the statute of limitation, carried the statement "that between the days, the sixth (6th) of July, A.D. 1896, and the fifth (5th) of February, A.D. 1897, the aforesaid W. S. Porter was a fugitive and fleeing from justice to avoid a prosecution in this court for the offense herein set out." [3]

Unfortunately, the stenographic record of testimony—if there was one [4]—has been lost, so that there is no way to reconstruct the trial in satisfactory detail. Porter, it is known, had given his attorneys no real help in working up his defense, and not only did he ask his family and friends to stay away from the courtroom, but throughout the three days of the trial he seemed tired and indifferent as he "sat with his chair tilted backward and his hands clasped behind his head, looking on in a somewhat bored manner." [5] One of the jurors came closer to what was probably Porter's actual state of mind behind the mask of unconcern: "I felt sorry for Mr. Porter. He was a very nice-looking young man, quiet, calm, cool. He didn't speak at all in his own defense and acted as if he were cowed." [6] By now, whatever hope he may have allowed himself earlier, he had obviously accepted his conviction as inevitable. As he wrote Mrs. Roach after the trial: "After I saw the jury I had very little hopes of their understanding enough of the technical matters presented to be fair." [7]

In the absence of complete details, the usual version of the trial has substituted hearsay and wishful thinking. C. Alphonso Smith, in his authorized biography of 1916, began the process by stating that Porter's conviction was partly based on the error in the dating of indictment 1148, an error which "has remained to this moment unnoticed." [8] A careful reading of the printed *Transcript of Record,* available in connection with the appeal of the case to the Circuit Court in New Orleans, would have corrected such an impression, but in their zeal to exonerate Porter at any cost later writers have repeated Smith's error and added others of their own. It has been said that Porter's attorneys were incompetent, and that Porter was crucified by a malicious bank examiner who was determined to make an example of someone—in short, that the trial resulted in an obvious miscarriage of justice. "The whole case," according to Lollie Cave Wilson, "was so balled up that today, under similar circumstances, it would be thrown out of court. . . . It seems to me that the same rule of carelessness which characterized the running of the banks in Texas could be applied as well to the courts of Texas in those days." [9]

This impression needs to be corrected once for all. As one of Porter's own friends later commented: "Judge Maxey was the soul of honor . . . and [to suggest a miscarriage of justice is a] gross insult to the living and dead Grand Jurors . . . and to the Petit Jurors . . . who said he was guilty." [10] And Juror Mark Patterson said: "What impressed me most . . . was the clocklike precision with which the court was conducted. At exactly 9:30 A.M. the judge opened court, and we jurors had to be there on the dot. . . . The trial lasted three full days. . . . We examined all the evidence very carefully . . . thrashed the matter out completely. The jury was composed of what I should call fair-minded men." [11] The truth of the matter has been succinctly put by Hyder Rollins in pointing out that, whatever may be said of Porter's moral guilt or innocence, "there can be no possible doubt that his trial was conducted with all fairness, or that his attorneys used every available legal device to help him." [12]

The substance of the testimony of the chief Government witness,

F. B. Gray, may be gathered from his original charges in the letter he wrote to the Comptroller of the Currency on July 13, 1895. He had found in Porter's books, he stated, "exactly fifty instances where he had unquestionably embezzled the Bank's money." Of these, the transaction forming the basis of indictment 1174 was one in which Porter "sold a draft on the San Antonio Nat'l. Bank for $554.48 and failed to credit it. . . . The monthly statement rendered by the San Antonio Nat'l. Bank had been checked by Porter and reported correct though this check appeared charged in the account. Cash account in none of these instances showed over, hence it was to my mind conclusive evidence that he embezzled the money."

As elaborated at the trial, the ascertainable facts were that E. L. Gwartney, local agent for the Singer Sewing Machine Company, bought on October 8, 1894, a draft for $554.48 on the San Antonio National Bank. Gwartney testified that he had paid for it in cash and that he had bought it from Porter. In the words of the prosecuting attorneys' abstract of questions to be put to, or facts to be elicited from, the witnesses (a document preserved among the court records):

A. He bought draft.
B. He paid for it in cash.
C. From whom did he purchase?
   Porter generally absent at noon for dinner. Gwartney also went to dinner at noon—and will testify he never purchased at that hour. That he always bought from Porter "to the best of his belief and recollection."

The bookkeeper of the San Antonio bank next testified that the draft had been paid by his bank on October 10, and he was followed by John H. Whites, bookkeeper of the First National Bank in Austin, who testified first that Porter was absent from his window only at noon, and second that in recording the day's transactions he had not found, among the stubs of detached drafts, any entry for the draft in question. The cashier, Dr. R. J. Brackenridge, was next questioned as to the hour (noon) at which he customarily relieved Porter as teller, and as to the person to whom he customarily turned over the moneys received by him while acting as teller. Finally came the testimony of H. P. Pfaefflin, assistant cashier and

115

one of the directors of the bank, who was questioned, in part, as follows:

A. When employed?
B. Did he check any of Porter's work? . . .
E. Explain how postings were made.
F. Examine cash book. . . .
H. Did you examine Teller's cash—By whom kept. If you were acting as Teller and party purchased from you a draft for $554.48 and you received cash payment for same, but omitted to make entry on your books—In balancing cash, what would be the result? . . .
Q. Give full details of settlement of Porter's shortage.
R. State the conversation you had with him thereto.

From the testimony presented, the inescapable-seeming conclusion was that Porter had pocketed the cash and tried to cover up the theft by failing to record the transaction.

The second charge on which Porter was tried (1148, or, as corrected, 1175) involved a deposit of $299.60 sent to Austin by the First National Bank of Waco on November 10, 1894, in acknowledgement of which a credit slip was sent to Waco on November 12; the transaction was not, however, entered on the books, and again the cash could not be traced. First among the witnesses this time was J. K. Rose, in 1894 cashier of the Waco Bank, who testified that the credit slip and the letter acknowledging it were both in the same handwriting. John H. Whites followed on the stand to testify that all letters acknowledging such transactions were written by Porter. When W. L. Gilfallen, assistant cashier of the Austin National Bank, took the stand, the prosecution expected two bits of information from him:

A. Prove by him that on Nov 12/94—the First Nat. Bank—Deposited in Austin Nat. Bank $1581.27 all in checks and drafts—on Austin Nat. Bk.—
B. Included therein was draft $299.60.

After further testimony by the bookkeeper of the Austin National Bank, H. P. Pfaefflin concluded the case for the prosecution by testifying along lines indicated by such questioning as the following:

A. He made expert examination to discover irregularities. . . .
G. What should have Teller's cash shown in consequence of his failure to credit said item of 299.60—Did it show this amount over?
H. Examine Teller's cash on Nov 1/94—State whether short or over and how much.
I. Examine on Nov 11/94. State same. . . .
K. Examine on Nov 13/94.
L. That finishes Examination—he can state that no other item for 299.60 was received from any other source.

Since Porter refused to testify in his own defense, his attorneys could only attempt to sway the jury in a manner not very satisfactorily indicated by the notes they jotted down on a copy of the defendant's jury list:

Thornton and Bannermann [as witnesses?]
. . . If you give Porter 10,000 in the morning and only let him pay checks or receive deposits—
. . . Gone when error occurred [since the $299.60 discrepancy was not discovered until January 16, 1898, when J. K. Rose wrote to inquire?] [13]
. . . No evidence that no one knew where he was—[while a fugitive?]
. . . Suppose Dr. Brackenridge were to take out a note—
No suspense account
Circumstantial evidence
Reasonable doubt
Appealed to the Court to protect him.

In later years one of Porter's attorneys (Ward) was quoted as remarking: "How could I defend him? How could anybody have defended him when he wouldn't defend himself? He wouldn't talk." [14] The defense did not, however, leave any stone unturned in arguing the case. In a series of legal maneuvers they filed, first, a motion to direct acquittal on the ground that "said indictments show on their face that they were found more than three years after the alleged commission of the offense charged and said offenses are therefore barred by limitation under the laws of the United States, and the Government has offered no testimony to show that this defendant has ever at any time been a fugitive from justice or that he has fled beyond the jurisdiction of the United States to avoid prosecution." [15]
When this motion was overruled—since a search had been made

for Porter through the state after he fled in 1896—the defense filed a motion to dismiss indictment on two counts: "1. Because . . . the indictment in cause No. 1148, consolidated in this case, is based upon the same acts and charges the same offense as the one charged in indictment No. 1175. . . . 2. Because . . . no proof has been offered or even attempted by the Government to show the fraudulent conversion of legal tender money." This motion, in its turn, was overruled, and now the defense requested three special charges. Two of them appealed to the jury to find the defendant not guilty on the ground of substantially the same technicalities which had already been overruled; the third charged the jury "That to be a fugitive in the sense the indictment herein charges it is not necessary that the party charged should have left the State or the United States . . . but simply that having within a State committed that which is by law a crime when he is sought to be subjected to its processes he has left its jurisdiction and is found in the territory of another State." [16]

After refusing the three special charges, Judge Maxey delivered his Charge of the Court, a long, carefully explanatory, and scrupulously fair-minded statement. He began by reminding the jury that in the three remaining indictments only two charges were involved. "The two indictments, to-wit: Numbered 1148 and 1175, respectively, charge the defendant . . . with having embezzled, of the funds of said bank, the sum of two hundred and ninety-nine dollars and sixty cents ($299.60). The charge embraced in these two indictments and the evidence introduced relative thereto refer to the same transaction . . . and they constitute but one charge against the defendant." After pointing out that a person adjudged guilty of embezzlement was liable for a sentence of from five to ten years, Judge Maxey meticulously defined the technical meaning of the term *embezzlement:*

The crime of embezzlement is a species of larceny. . . . It involves two general ingredients or elements: First, a breach of trust or duty in respect of the moneys, properties and effects in the party's possession, belonging to another; and secondly, the wrongful appropriation thereof to his own use. In other words, there must be an actual and lawful possession or custody of the property of another, by virtue of some trust, duty, agency or employment, committed to the party charged; and while so lawfully

in the possession and custody of such property, the person must unlawfully and wrongfully convert the same to his own use, in order to commit
the crime of embezzlement.

In conclusion, Judge Maxey presented—in what would seem a
model of disinterested fairness—a summary of the duties and problems of the jury:

. . . It is your peculiar province to pass upon the controverted facts
arising upon the trial of the cause, and the Court will not invade the
province of the jury. . . .

If from the evidence you find that the defendant embezzled the moneys
of the bank . . . you are instructed that the subsequent repayment or
refunding by him or by any one for him or in his behalf of the moneys
embezzled . . . would not condone the offense nor relieve the defendant
from the consequences of his criminal acts. . . .

You are the exclusive judges of the credibility of the witnesses, and of
the weight to be given their testimony. . . .

You are further instructed that the presumption of law is in favor of
the innocence of the defendant until his guilt has been established by the
evidence to the satisfaction of all the jury beyond a reasonable doubt.
If, therefore, upon a full consideration of all the facts and circumstances
in evidence, you entertain a reasonable doubt of his guilt, you should give
him the benefit of it and acquit him.

Evidence has been introduced touching the general reputation of the
defendant for honesty, uprightness and integrity prior to the commission
of the offense charged in the indictment. Upon this point, you are instructed that good reputation and good character are generally facts
proper, like all other facts proved in the case, to be weighed and considered by the jury; it is an ingredient which may render that doubtful
which would otherwise be clear. If, however, the guilt of the accused is
plainly proved to the satisfaction of the jury, notwithstanding his good
character has been given its weight by them, it would be their duty to
convict him, irrespective of such proof of character; but when the evidence
is doubtful and conflicting, then the importance of the character of the
accused is increased." [17]

The deliberations of the jury were remembered differently by
different jurors after different time lapses. In 1914 L. B. Mallet said
that there was no dissent among the twelve men, who reached
their verdict of guilty within twenty minutes.[18] In 1935 Mark
Patterson said that they deliberated for a good part of the third

day of the trial.[19] According to the report in 1915 of one of Porter's friends, Foreman W. B. Barr had been heard to say that if he had known at the trial what he knew later, he would never have voted to convict; that he came over to the side of those voting guilty only because he was anxious to get back to his home.[20] Barr's reported statement is balanced by a written statement of Patterson's in 1935: "The money was gone. The defendant . . . offered nothing to show his innocence. When the ballot was taken, it was unanimous for a verdict of guilty. . . . If I had to go over it again, I should do the very same thing." [21] The statement made by L. B. Mallet includes one further bit of relevant information. On the morning after the trial, it seems, Foreman Barr circulated a petition for mercy, to be presented to Judge Maxey. Mallet refused to sign, and thought that none of the other jurors signed. The petition, which was never presented, did not charge injustice but only made the point that Porter, as an educated, well connected man, was deserving of mercy.

After the jury brought in its verdict of guilty, on the afternoon of February 17, the court ordered "that the defendant be temporarily committed to the County Jail of Travis County, Texas, at Austin, to await the further order and sentence of this Court, which is temporarily suspended." [22] On the following day the Austin *Evening News* carried a brief story:

Will S. Porter, well known in this city, and at one time teller of the First National Bank, was found guilty yesterday in the federal court now in session of embezzlement on three counts. The lowest penalty is two years in each count. Judge Maxey has not yet passed sentence upon him.

The news of Mr. Porter's conviction was a great surprise to his many friends here, as it was believed that the matter had been settled, all shortages being made good. It is not believed that an appeal to the U. S. Supreme Court will be taken. It was during Mr. Porter's time as teller that he was charged with misappropriating funds.[23]

Of Porter's moral guilt or innocence, it is clearly impossible, on the basis of existing evidence, to furnish absolute proof. It is possible, though, by facing the issue dispassionately, to come closer to a reasonable certainty than the O. Henry apologists of the past have come. First of all, their evidence needs to be presented.

It has been customarily suggested that Porter merely fell heir to a badly kept set of books, which he was never able to put entirely in order. The man who preceded him in the teller's job, J. M. Thornton, has been quoted as testifying that there were discrepancies in the books before Porter took charge of them.[24] "Old timers in Austin" are said to have often pointed out that there had been unexplained shortages in the books for several years.[25] Yet federal bank examiners had gone over the books regularly; surely charges, if warranted, would have been brought earlier than they were. Porter's own books had presumably been examined on more than one occasion during his four years in the bank; it seems gratuitous to assume that only in 1894 did an examiner demand an accounting and try to make an example of someone.

Porter's own story, insofar as he ever spoke of the matter, was that while he was technically responsible for the shortages he did not himself take the money. This is what Lollie Cave Wilson claimed he told her, and there are other versions of the same story. To Betty Hall he said that Dr. Brackenridge's "trifling with the books" was what caused the trouble, but he absolved Brackenridge of dishonest intentions.[26] Again, the understanding of Dr. John M. Thomas, prison physician, was: "His father-in-law was president of the bank, and he was the cashier. His father-in-law took the money, and O. Henry covered up the stealing by fixing the books. . . . It has been some little time since the conversation with O. Henry, so I may be mistaken in detail, but I am positive he mentioned the president of the bank, and as I always understood his father-in-law was the president, I naturally connected him with the bank story, although no name was mentioned by O. Henry." [27] Most indisputable of all is Porter's statement to Mrs. Roach in a letter written immediately after the trial: "Right here I want to state solemnly to you that in spite of the jury's verdict I am absolutely innocent of wrong-doing in that bank matter, except so far as foolishly keeping a position that I could not successfully fill." [28]

How is one to reject this categorical statement of innocence? Porter was quite obviously no thief at heart, and no one could suppose he had anything but the best intentions in the world. To buttress this point, various writers have stated that the opinions of Porter's own friends and fellow townsmen were overwhelmingly in

121

his favor. One writer assures us that of fifty-six old-time Austinites interviewed in 1937, only four said they believed Porter guilty; five others thought he might have been mixed up in the affair in some way; the other forty-seven maintained that the Will Porter they had known could not have been guilty of any dishonest act. The same writer tells us that D. H. Hart, clerk of the court in which Porter was tried, also believed him innocent of having personally used any of the money, and that the man who had been Porter's competitor for the bank job said afterward: "I thought Porter lucky and myself unlucky at the time, but later on I was thankful that I had not been given the job. If I had been hired instead of Will Porter, I might have been the one sent to prison." Of the group interviewed by the writer in question, the general feeling is said to have been summed up by a woman who had worked with Porter in the Land Office. She said, in answer to the question of his possible guilt, "Negligently, perhaps; criminally, never." [29]

Lawrence Smoot, son of the minister who married Porter, later remarked that if Porter had ever got hold of a couple of hundred dollars he would have spent it in entertaining his friends, who would thus have been aware of his windfall.[30] David Harrell, whose bed Porter shared when he first came to Austin, said, "I have heard Carr Lucy, agent for the American Surety Company, which went on O. Henry's bond, say a dozen times that Porter was not guilty but was a victim of circumstances." [31] The whole affair, Harrell maintained, was an amazing story of inefficiency paid for by the imprisonment and disgrace of an innocent man. And Ed McLean, who got the Houston *Post* job for him, reportedly said that if it had not been for Gray, who would not let the matter drop, Culberson would never have pressed charges.[32]

"I once asked him," Al Jennings wrote in 1912, "after we had been together years, what he 'fell' for. 'I was cashier, I bet that cotton would go up, but cotton went down.' The money was given to him by another fellow associated in the same institution. The fellow had a charming wife and two children; Porter was foot-loose. When the finger of accusation was pointed at the other man, Bill Porter, cold of face, stepped forward, saying easily, 'You are mistaken, it was I.' The other fellow said: 'O, Bill, don't do that.' (You know Porter.) The expression of his face never changed, and he said coldly, 'I don't believe we are on friendly terms.'"[33] This noble if somewhat theatrical story is marred by the reflection that, with a tubercular wife and a young daughter, Porter was hardly "foot-loose" at the time. Jennings, however, was convinced of his innocence.

C. Alphonso Smith, who first investigated and published the facts of the trial and imprisonment, expressed his belief in Porter's complete innocence. The verdict of the jury he explained as the result of one fact and one alone: "O. Henry lost his case at Hempstead, not at Austin . . . and the humiliation of it and the folly of it were so acutely felt by O. Henry that he remained silent."[34] The only other widely read biography followed Smith's lead in concluding that "the conceded facts are enough to justify posterity in rendering the verdict 'not guilty.'"[35]

All this adds up to a very impressive array of testimony in Porter's favor. Unfortunately, it does not include certain facts which the O. Henry apologists have either ignored or not known. To begin with, one of Porter's own lawyers (Ward) later said: "I had a high regard for him. Of course, someone else may have taken the money [but] I'm afraid he was guilty."[36] One of his friends and neighbors (Ed Smith) made in 1935 a more damaging statement: "I wrote insurance for Northwestern Mutual Life Insurance Company of Wilwaukee. . . . Porter took out a policy with me. He made himself a little younger than he really was to keep from paying higher premiums. The fact became known at Porter's death. . . . An adjustment was made." Commenting on his own opinion as to the embezzlement charge, Smith said: "Do I think he was capable, if he was really guilty, of writing the letters to Mrs. Roach that he did, declaring his innocence? Yes. Will Porter was a good actor."[37] Another friend, Brooks Haynie, remarked: "The handwriting tells the tale. He falsified the books and had no defense to make."[38]

Only one writer (Luther W. Courtney, whose brief article in a learned journal did not reach a wide audience) has ever expressed the belief that Porter was guilty. In a survey made in 1943 of people who had known Porter in Austin and in Houston, Courtney made a surprising discovery. Instead of an almost unanimous belief in his innocence, he found that nearly half of these people "admitted that Porter was technically guilty of the charge on which he was tried and convicted." One of them, a good friend of Porter's, said he believed Porter took the money to help finance the *Rolling Stone*, meaning to repay the bank as soon as the paper made enough profit. Such opinions, Courtney assures us, "could be extended at length were it not a violation of confidence to write what was told with the understanding that no publicity would be given." If belief in Porter's innocence had really been as unanimous as has customarily been stated, Courtney continues, why was so little effort made either at the trial or later at the appeal to present evidence of his integrity? Why, after his conviction, was there no concerted drive to gain for him a pardon? Blessed as the man was with loyal friends and generous benefactors, evidently his guilt was widely accepted, although many friends would not publicly admit the fact "because they felt that basically there was no purposeful design of wrongdoing." In the light of such findings, Courtney concludes: "This attitude toward a man who was without doubt technically guilty is a tribute of high order. When one considers all the facts which indicate O. Henry's guilt, one is best able to understand the conduct of a man who was innately good at heart." [39]

This conclusion was based on information gathered in 1943. Of considerably greater weight is a hitherto unpublicized group of statements collected by Hyder Rollins in 1914. District Attorney Culberson (who "felt kindly toward Porter, and it was a source of regret to me that the case was bound to go against him") wrote that in the event Rollins thought the verdict was an unjust one, "nothing could be further from the truth. The evidence against him was overwhelming, and no man who heard all the testimony could escape the conclusion that Porter was guilty. He was tried before one of the fairest of judges, he was ably represented, and there was no prejudice against him. . . ." Betty Hall, who had written to Culberson asking him to be merciful, confided to Rollins that she and her husband felt certain that Porter took the money, though they felt equally certain that he meant to return it when he was able. The Raatzes also had no doubt of their friend's guilt, though they did not wish to be quoted. D. H. Hart, clerk of the court—despite what later apologists may have heard of his opinions

—said at this time that anyone who saw the trial knew that Porter was guilty. Good friend and benefactor John Maddox admitted that Porter was clearly guilty. And, most damaging of all, Herman Pressler himself said: "At first, and even during the trial, I thought him innocent. But he would *never* go over the bank books with his lawyers, though they implored him, to clear up the matter." Even Dixie Daniels said there was no doubt about Porter's taking the money; and Daniels, along with Pressler and Ward and others, suggested a connection between his embezzlement and his "dissipation" during his years in the bank.[40]

Very clearly the traditional claim that there was a miscarriage of justice in Porter's trial is a myth. His flight to Honduras and his refusal to testify in his own defense are eloquent self-accusations. And the testimony at the trial, as well as the bank examiner's analysis of sample transactions, makes it all too plain that the irregularities in bookkeeping were not caused by carelessness but were deliberate jugglings to conceal the embezzlement of funds. As a last resort, of course, one may try to take refuge in Porter's story that he doctored the books to shield someone else. No contemporary, however, who had access to the facts in the case ever suggested such an "out" for Porter, and it seems incredible that his many influential friends would have stood by without lifting a hand while he was pronounced guilty and sentenced to a penitentiary term for someone else's theft. True, Betty Hall has been quoted as urging that Porter had no capacity for "self defense and even self assertion," so that he would not have taken the stand in his own defense even "if he had been accused of eating his grandmother." [41] But to go to jail for an accusation which rightfully belonged to another—would not such an experience call forth some reaction beyond an overmastering urge to conceal his record from the world? In none of the O. Henry stories—some of them written in the penitentiary—is there a line of bitterness or protest. Even in the two stories which depict the very kind of incident in which he himself came to grief, no personal involvement is even remotely suggested except in the slightly wry portrayal of the bank examiner. In "A Call Loan," the examiner is "a dyspeptic man, wearing double-magnifying glasses," who "inserted an official-looking card between the bars of the cashier's window of the First National

Bank. Five minutes later the bank force was dancing at the beck and call of a national bank examiner." [42] As for J. F. C. Nettlewick in "Friends in San Rosario": "There was something so icy and swift, so impersonal and uncompromising about this man that his very presence seemed an accusation. He looked to be a man who would never make nor overlook an error." Contrasting him with Major Kingman, president of the First National Bank of San Rosario, O. Henry wrote: "Two men of very different types shook hands. One was a finished product of the world of straight lines, conventional methods, and formal affairs. The other was something freer, wider, and nearer to nature. Tom Kingman had not been cut to any pattern." [43]

The inescapable truth seems to be that Porter took the money himself. "I am sure," a surviving fellow clerk has recently stated, "that the other clerks in the bank felt as I did that when he started taking the money he had no intention of keeping it. His little paper was not a financial success and I think that most of his friends thought he took funds hoping that a small investment in cotton futures would give him a good profit and that he could then repay the money taken. He was certainly not the criminal type." [44] This statement throws new light, incidentally, on the accounts of Porter's gambling and on his own later remark quoted (as if it were a mere joke) by Al Jennings: "I bet that cotton would go up, but cotton went down." [45]

What attitude, then, is one to adopt toward Porter's crime? As on the Halls' ranch, as during his bachelorhood in the Harrell and Anderson homes, Porter the bank teller had followed the pattern set up for him by his boyhood environment in Greensboro. His reaction to financial temptation, as to marital stress, had been less that of the responsible adult than that of the overprotected child (a role he was understandably but belatedly trying to play). With neither problem had he come to grips realistically. In the matter of the embezzlement he had not let his right hand know what his left hand did. His handling of money throughout his life is a clear indication of how he was unable to change or grow, and this immaturity is reflected in his writing. It was a cruel destiny for one with the natural endowments which Porter had.

126

On the first day of his two-month stay in the Travis County jail while he awaited sentence and then transportation to Ohio, the *Statesman* carried a news story about a group of unidentified men who had been digging for buried treasure in the Shoal Creek bottom where Porter and the Daniels brothers had tried their luck three years earlier. The rumor that the new diggers had found the treasure sent people rushing to the site, the *Statesman* reported, where they found the men gone but an empty iron casket three feet long and various pieces of digging equipment littering an area twenty feet square which had been dug full of holes three to four feet deep.[46] If Porter read the paper that first day in jail, he must have been struck with the irony of circumstances, of which he never tired of multiplying examples in his later stories. On the following morning he would have been interested, and no doubt disappointed, to read that Colonel R. M. Johnston of the Houston *Post* had declined to become a candidate for the democratic nomination for lieutenant governor.[47]

War was in the making, although it was not actually declared until April 21, and as the center of National Guard activities for the state, Austin became a busy place. Porter must have welcomed the excitement and wished that he could be more completely forgotten than in fact he was. Mrs. Roach sent him a writing table and chair, and from the Roaches and other close friends came pillows, books, newspapers, and clean clothes. In addition to visits from his friends, his lawyers came (after the sentence was pronounced) to discuss plans for an appeal. About Porter himself during these two months, nothing is known except that he seems to have settled down quietly to his writing again, and that he changed the spelling of his name from Sidney to Sydney and dropped the William: On April 25, 1898, the S. S. McClure Company (which had accepted "The Miracle of Lava Canyon" several months earlier) addressed him as Mr. Sydney Porter in writing to decline a new manuscript he had submitted.[48]

On March 25 "the defendant, W. S. Porter, was brought into open Court in charge of the Marshal for the purpose of having the sentence of the law pronounced." He was asked "whether he had anything to say why said sentence should not be pronounced against him, and he answered nothing in bar thereof." First of all, Judge Maxey overruled the motion for a new trial (filed by Porter's attorneys on February 19), after which came the moment Porter must have been awaiting with even more trepidation than he had awaited the opening of the trial:

. . . for said offenses by him committed [that he] be imprisoned in the Ohio State Penitentiary, at Columbus, State of Ohio, for the period of five (5) years from this date. . . . It is further ordered that the said defendant be temporarily committed to the Travis County jail to await a time when the Marshal can conveniently obey the directions of this sentence.[49]

It was the lightest sentence allowed by law, and under the law at that time Porter could not have been hoping for a suspended sentence. Even so, the finality of it was clearly a blow. Back in his cell, he wrote the following letter:

DEAR MRS. ROACH:

I feel very deeply the forbearance and long suffering kindness shown by your note, and thank you much for sending the things. Right here I want to state solemnly to you that in spite of the jury's verdict I am absolutely innocent of wrong doing in that bank matter, except so far as foolishly keeping a position that I could not successfully fill. Any intelligent person who heard the evidence presented knows that I should have been acquitted. After I saw the jury I had very little hopes of their understanding enough of the technical matters presented to be fair. I naturally am crushed by the result, but it is not on my own account. I care not so much for the opinion of the general public, but I would have a few of my friends still believe that there is some good in me.[50]

Another month passed before the sentence was put into execution. During this time Porter's attorneys filed two bills of exceptions: the first making the point that "there was no proof whatever that the funds embezzled were lawful legal tender money of the United States"; the second stating that only the following evidence had been offered in the fugitive-from-justice charge: "That on the 6th day of July 1896, W. S. Porter . . . failed to appear . . . and his appearance bond in said two cases was thereupon forfeited and an alias capias in each of said two original cases . . . were [sic] thereupon issued and the same placed in the hands of the United

States Marshal . . . and that the same were never executed." According to Porter's attorneys, "The Government proved by R. C. Ware that said two alias capiases were placed in his hands and that he made search and inquiry in the State of Texas for the defendant, W. S. Porter, and could not find him." Yet, continued the defense, Porter voluntarily appeared at the next term of court after the forfeiture of his bond, and the government offered no evidence at the trial that Porter had "ever been absent from the State of Texas, or had ever gone beyond the jurisdiction of this Court." [51]

These two bills of exceptions were allowed by Judge Maxey on March 31, and each carries the endorsement: "This bill has been examined and agreed to and it is hereby agreed that the same may be filed after term time and in vacation. [Signed] Culberson, United States District Attorney." On April 19 Porter's attorneys also filed a petition for a writ of error (granted on April 20), asking that the case be appealed to the Circuit Court of Appeals; and on April 21 a bond of $250 (with Ashby S. James, one of Porter's attorneys, and P. G. Roach as sureties) was filed to cover the costs of the appeal.

The sentence in the original record bears the endorsement: "Came to hand April 18, 1898 and executed by transporting the said W. S. Porter to the Ohio State Penitentiary and delivering the said W. S. Porter to the Warden of the Ohio State Penitentiary at Columbus O. on April 25, 1898, together with a true copy of this writ. [Signed] George Louis Siebrecht, U. S. Marshal, Western Dist. Texas." [52] On April 21 war was declared against Spain, and on Friday, April 22, Porter left Austin. At the railroad station, according to Mrs. Roach, "it looked like a state dignitary going, so many were the friends that came to see him off and so open were their expressions." [53] His eight-year-old daughter was not among those present. As he wrote her from Columbus, "I am so sorry I couldn't come to tell you good-bye when I left Austin. You know I would have done so if I could have." [54]

Ed Smith later recalled riding "by chance on the train with him as far as Taylor, Texas, when he was being carried handcuffed to the penitentiary. He preserved his demeanor but looked bored. I think for a local reason he may have welcomed his conviction." [55]

This last remark presumably has reference to Porter's involvement with a woman (a "bad" woman, one friend indicated), who, according to rumor, made a scene at the station. The only other first-hand account of Porter's trip to prison is a fictional elaboration in a story he published the year after he emerged from prison:

At Denver there was an influx of passengers into the coaches on the east-bound B. & M. express. In one coach there sat a very pretty young woman dressed in elegant taste and surrounded by all the luxurious comforts of an experienced traveler. Among the newcomers were two young men, one of handsome presence with a bold, frank countenance and manner; the other a ruffled, glum-faced person, heavily built and roughly dressed. The two were handcuffed together.

It appears that the pretty young woman has known the handsome young man in diplomatic circles in Washington; when the handcuffs come to her attention her expression changes to one of "bewildered horror." But at that moment the glum-faced man speaks up: "You'll excuse me for speaking, miss, but, I see you're acquainted with the marshal here. If you'll ask him to speak a word for me when we get to the pen he'll do it, and it'll make things easier for me there. He's taking me to Leavenworth prison. It's seven years for counterfeiting." The pretty young woman relaxes. She and the handsome young man talk about why he left the old crowd in Washington to go West and become a marshal. Finally the two men go down the aisle to the smoking car, and one of the passengers in a nearby seat remarks on what a good sport the marshal is.

"Pretty young to hold an office like that, isn't he?" asked the other.

"Young!" exclaimed the first speaker, "why—Oh! didn't you catch on? Say—did you ever know an officer to handcuff a prisoner to his *right* hand?" [56]

CHAPTER EIGHT

. ⟋⅏⟍ .

On Monday, April 25, 1898, Porter entered the Ohio Penitentiary as Prisoner Number 30664. It was recorded that his height was five feet seven inches, that his shoe size was six, that his hat size was 7⅛, that he had medium dark complexion and medium chestnut hair sprinkled with gray. His vocation he gave as newspaper writer. His nearest relative to be notified in case of death he listed as P. G. Roach. Whether it was a clerical error or whether Porter was already preparing for the time when he would try to conceal his prison record, his age was recorded as thirty-three instead of the thirty-five he really was. (His birthday was September 11, 1862.) "The records also show," a later warden wrote in answer to a query, "that he was . . . of good education and intemperate habits." [1]

The first impact of the place on Al Jennings (who not long afterward became a fellow prisoner after his conviction for a notorious train robbery) was "the heavy breath of the prison—the breath laden with evil smells." [2] To the fastidious Porter, with his predilection for a dash of perfume on his handkerchief, what must have been the effect of this smell—the enveloping, permeating, tainting aura of the place? Jennings remembered all too vividly his own first meal, with "the odor of slumgullion, of putrid meat, of millions of flies. . . . There was the clatter of tin, the shuffle of uneasy feet, the waving of upraised hands signaling the guards for bread. No sound of the human voice, but that God-forsaken, weighty, brutal dumbness imposed upon convicts in the penitentiary."

Many of the tiered cells where the prisoners slept were window-

131

less, so that the only ventilation came from the closed-in corridors. "The cells were entirely without sanitary equipment. On Saturday night the men were locked up and kept in this stifling confinement until Monday morning. Two men sleeping, breathing, tramping about in a walled space four by eight for 36 hours turned that closet into a hell. It was no longer air that filled the place, but a reeking stench." [3]

How much, if any, experience Porter had of the typical prisoner's routine is unknown. On learning that he had been a registered pharmacist, the authorities at once assigned him to a special niche, which he described to his father-in-law in a letter written three weeks after his arrival:

I accidentally fell into a place on the day I arrived that is a light one in comparison with the others. I am the night druggist in the hospital, and as far as the work is concerned it is light enough, and all the men stationed in the hospital live a hundred per cent. better than the rest of the 2,500 men here. There are four doctors and about twenty-five other men in the hospital force. The hospital is a separate building and is one of the finest equipped institutions in the country. It is large and finely finished and has every appliance of medicine and surgery.

We men who are on the hospital detail fare very well comparatively. We have good food well cooked and in unlimited abundance, and large clean sleeping apartments. We go about where we please over the place, and are not bound down by strict rules as the others are. I go on duty at five o'clock P.M. and off at five A.M. The work is about the same as in any drug store, filling prescriptions, etc. and is pretty lively up to about ten o'clock. At seven P.M. I take a medicine case and go the rounds with the night physician to see the ones over in the main building who have become sick during the day.

The doctor goes to bed about ten o'clock and from then on during the night I prescribe for the patients myself and go out and attend calls that come in. If I find anyone seriously ill I have them brought to the hospital and attended to by the doctor.

In spite of his privileged position, Porter's state of mind was such that there seemed "not one thing in life at present or in prospect that makes it of value. I have decided to wait until the New Orleans court decides the appeal, provided it is heard within a reasonable time. . . ." Even this hope was barely enough to make his situation endurable. His closing words were: "I can stand any kind of hardships or privations on the outside, but I am utterly unable to continue the life I lead here. I know all the arguments that could be advanced as to why I should endure it, but I have reached the limit of endurance. It will be better for every one else and a thousand times better for me to end the trouble instead of dragging it out longer." [4]

In confirmation of such a state of mind, Dr. John M. Thomas, chief physician at the prison, who became Porter's friend and benefactor, later wrote: "In my experience of handling over ten thousand prisoners in the eight years I was physician at the prison, I have never known a man who was so deeply humiliated by his prison experience." [5] Yet less than two months after expressing to Roach the most absolute despair, Porter was writing to Mrs. Roach (on July 8): "I often get as blue as any one can get and I feel as thoroughly miserable as it is possible to feel, but I consider that my future efforts belong to others and I have no right to give way to my own troubles and feelings." [6] By "others" he primarily meant Margaret, his eight-year-old daughter, who had been told nothing about his trial and imprisonment. To her he wrote, on the same day he wrote to Mrs. Roach:

You don't know how glad I was to get your nice little letter today. . . .

Well, I think it is a shame some men folks have to go away from home to work and stay away so long—don't you? But I tell you what's a fact. When I come home next time I'm going to stay there. You bet your boots I'm tired of staying away so long. . . .

So you just be as happy as you can, and it won't be long till we'll be reading Uncle Remus again of nights. [7]

Even after the Circuit Court of Appeals affirmed in December the verdict of the district court, Porter failed to carry out his suicide threat, although in his position as unsupervised night druggist he had every opportunity to do so. The contradiction between the two attitudes is characteristic of Porter's whole prison experience. The same fundamental contradiction is revealingly illustrated on a later occasion. In the words of Dr. Thomas:

One time we had a little misunderstanding about some alcohol which was disappearing too rapidly for the ordinary uses to which it was put.

I requested that he wait for me one morning so that I could find out how much alcohol he was using in his night rounds, and after asking him a few questions he became excited when he thought I might be suspicioning him. "I am not a thief," he said, "and I never stole a thing in my life." . . . I soon discovered that he was not the offender in the matter of the alcohol. But the question disturbed him and he asked me once or twice afterward if I really thought he ever stole anything.[8]

Even an unjustly sentenced man, if he had realistically faced the fact that he was a convicted embezzler, could hardly have been surprised that an official in the prison might think him capable of thievery. Characteristically, Porter averted his eyes from a situation with which he did not know how to deal. "It was very seldom," according to Dr. Thomas, "that he mentioned his imprisonment or in any way discussed the subject." He simply withdrew into himself, and one of the Columbus newspaper men regularly assigned to cover prison news was afterward to point out that, ironically, they all took special note of Porter "because of the elaborate precautions he took to prevent them from doing so. Not a moment during the years he was imprisoned did he relax an extreme solicitude to keep visitors, officials and associates from acquainting themselves with his identity. . . . He strove to have his personality appear as a negative, neutral one, which would merge, indistinguishable, with all the others. But he developed his technique to a point where it was apparent." [9]

He avoided even his fellow prisoners, and advised such conduct for Jennings on their first meeting—a Sunday when he was making the rounds of the cells with his kit of medical supplies. He had avoided even this encounter until nearly a month after Jennings's arrival at the prison. "Colonel, we meet again," he said, standing before Jennings's door. (Jennings was to remember the awkwardness of the moment. "I could not bear to look him in the face. I did not want to see Bill Porter in convict stripes.") Before the guard came within range, Porter said: "Be careful of the friends you choose. On the outside it may be safe to pick up acquaintances at every siding. . . . The O. P. is a different country. Have no confidants." [10] Even Jennings himself was not taken fully into Porter's confidence. Although as a post office clerk he smuggled through the prison censorship many letters to Margaret, never once was the child mentioned in their talk. Dr. Thomas, likewise, did not know until long afterward that Porter had a daughter. In planning for the future, Porter made a firm resolve that "I will bury the name of Bill Porter in the depths of oblivion. No one shall know that the Ohio Penitentiary ever furnished me with board and bread." He could only laugh incredulously when Jennings (serving a life sentence, though later pardoned) announced his plan if and when he ever got out. "I will walk up to the first man I see on the street and I will say to him, 'I'm an ex-con—just got out of the pen. If you don't like it, go to hell." All Porter could say to this was: "I would give a great deal for your arrogant independence." [11]

The realities of prison life in 1898 were such that even Porter could ignore them only up to a point. Although he slept not in a cell but on a cot in the hospital, and although he never had to work and eat with the other prisoners, nevertheless as a drug clerk he saw more than the less privileged inmate did of these grim realities. Writing to Roach about the medical treatment provided for the sick, he explained:

I never imagined human life was held as cheap as it is here. The men are regarded as animals without soul or feeling. . . . The hospital wards have from one hundred to two hundred patients in them all the time. They have all kinds of diseases—at present typhus fever and measles are the fashion. Consumption here is more common than bad colds at home. There are about thirty hopeless cases of it in the hospital just now and nearly all the nurses and attendants are contracting it. There are hundreds of other cases of it among the men who are working in the shops and foundries. Twice a day they have a sick call at the hospital, and from two hundred to three hundred men are marched in each day suffering from various disorders. They march in single file past the doctor and he prescribes for each one "on the fly." The procession passes the drug counter and the medicines are handed out to each one as they march without stopping the line. [12]

And writing to Mrs. Roach a few weeks later, after some further experience, he added graphic details:

I have gotten quite expert at practicing medicine. It's a melancholy place, however—misery and death and all kinds of suffering around one all the time. We sometimes have a death every night for a week or so. Very little time is wasted on such an occasion. One of the nurses will come from a ward and say—"Well, So and So has croaked." Ten minutes later they tramp out with So and So on a stretcher and take him to the dead house. If he has no friends to claim him—which is generally the case—the next day the doctors have a dissecting bee and that ends it. Suicides are as common as picnics here. Every few nights the doctor and I have to strike out at a trot to see some unfortunate who has tried to get rid of his troubles. They cut their throats and hang themselves and stop up their cells and turn on the gas and try all kinds of ways. Most of them plan it well enough to succeed. Night before last a professional pugilist went crazy in his cell and the doctor and I, of course, were sent for. The man was in good training and it took eight of us to tie him. Seven held him down while the doctor climbed on top and got his hypodermic syringe into him. These little things are our only amusements.[13]

Nor was it only a matter of sickness and death and suicide. There were darker doings as well, to which Porter alludes briefly in his first letter to Roach: "If a man gets sick and can't work, they take him into a cellar and turn a powerful stream of water on him from a hose that knocks the breath out of him. Then a doctor revives him and they hang him up by his hands with his feet off the floor for an hour or so. This generally makes him go to work again." A somewhat more graphic account of the water treatment is given by Jennings: "A hose with a nozzle, one-quarter of an inch in diameter, sixty pounds pressure behind it, sends a stream of terrific force at the prisoner. His head is held strapped, the stream that is as hard as steel is turned full force in the man's face, his eyes, his nostrils."[14] For more serious offenders, "seventy-five" could be prescribed. Jennings saw a man get this punishment for assaulting a fellow prisoner. "I walked out from the transfer office and looked down the stairs into the basement. The robber, strapped across the trough, his ankles drawn under it, his arms across the top, was already a mass of blood. . . . The robber was beaten to the bone. Long after he was unconscious, the merciless flaying went on."[15]

On one occasion Porter—in a daringly experimental moment—said he wanted to talk with a man who knew he was facing death. "I wonder," he remarked, "if that's the reason Christ called Lazarus

136

back—sort of wanted to know what the big jump might be like."
Jennings arranged for him to walk around the yard with a seven-
teen-year-old boy condemned to be electrocuted for murder.
"When Porter came back to me, his face was sickish yellow. . . .
The sweat stood out like heavy white pearls. . . . 'He hasn't looked
at death,' [Porter said]. 'He's too young. Something should be done
about it.' " [16]

Instead of trying to do anything about such conditions Porter
retired into the world of fiction. After midnight, by which time
most of his medical work was done, he settled down to write. "He
seemed," one of the night guards later wrote, "oblivious of the
world of sleeping convicts about him, hearing not even the occasional sigh or groan from the beds which were stretched before
him in the hospital ward or the tramp of the passing guards. After
he had written for perhaps two hours he would rise, make a
round of the hospital, and then come back to his work again." [17]
Perhaps part of his incentive to begin writing again was a sense,
at last, of his heavy obligation to the Roaches. On December 16,
1898, he wrote Mrs. Roach that he was beginning to submit manuscripts to magazines and that he would send her any money he was
able to make with his writing.[18] At any rate, in what Jennings
called "the raw heart of chill depression," Porter turned out, during
his reduced sentence of three years, fourteen of his best-known
stories.* Not one of them deals directly with the experiences of his
trial and imprisonment. Of the three published while he was still
in prison (signed O. Henry and marketed, it is said, through the
sister of a New Orleans banker who was a fellow prisoner),
"Whistling Dick's Christmas Stocking" is a sentimental story about
a hobo who has not lost his capacity for loyalty and honor;
"Georgia's Ruling" is an even more sentimental story about the
ennobling influence of a dead child; and "Money Maze" is the story
containing the plot structure later elaborated into *Cabbages and*

---

* "Whistling Dick's Christmas Stocking," "Georgia's Ruling," "An Afternoon
Miracle" (a rewrite of "The Miracle of Lava Canyon"), "A Medley of Moods"
(or as first published, "Blind Man's Holiday"), "Money Maze," "No Story,"
"A Fog in Santone," "A Blackjack Bargainer," "The Enchanted Kiss," "Hygeia
at the Solito," "Rouge et Noir," "The Duplicity of Hargraves," "The Marionettes," and (according to Jennings) "A Chaparral Christmas Gift."

Kings. For the setting of the first story Porter returned to New Orleans, for the second to the Land Office in Austin, and for the third to Honduras.[19]

This was the era of muckraking, of on-the-spot reporting of unusual and hitherto unexploited milieux, both in stories and in articles. "Whistling Dick's Christmas Stocking" attracted the editors of *McClure's* because of its first-hand account of the seasonal migration of hoboes, and other early O. Henry stories attracted attention first as the authentic reporting of one who had lived among cowboys in Texas and among fugitives from justice in Central America. Considering the success he had with these sentimentalized stories, it is ironic to think of the sensation he might have caused in literary circles if he had been willing to exploit his prison experience. With prison reform already in the making, he could have done, with much greater impact, the kind of job which Jack London in *The People of the Abyss* (1903) did on slum life in the city of London.

To shield Margaret, as well as themselves, from the talk that was inevitable after Porter's conviction, the Roaches soon arranged to move away from Austin. On July 8, 1898, Porter wrote to Margaret: "I'm so glad you and Mummy are going to Nashville. . . . When you get there I'll write you a letter every week, for you will be much nearer to the town I am in than Austin is." And on August 16 he wrote: "I got your letter yesterday, and was mighty glad to hear from you. I think you must have forgotten where you were when you wrote it, for you wrote 'Austin, Texas' at the top of it. Did you forget you had gone to Tennessee?"[20]

Mrs. Roach and Margaret stayed on the stock farm of Mrs. Roach's brother, near Colesburg, about forty miles from Nashville, until Mr. Roach wound up his affairs in Austin and returned to his home town of Pittsburgh to establish himself in the hotel business. On January 2, 1899, writing to Mrs. Roach, Porter expressed his deep concern over Margaret's state of mind and his hope that she was not homesick for Austin.[21] Sometime before May 17, 1900 (when Porter mentioned the fact in a letter), the Roaches and Margaret were settled in Pittsburgh. Margaret had been told at

first that her father was working in a drugstore in Columbus, and
later that he was a traveling salesman—a story which Porter
backed up by sending stamped, addressed letters in covering envelopes to the postmasters in various cities, to be remailed by
them.[22] He not only wrote to Margaret regularly, but drew
valentines, Easter cards and Christmas cards for her to send to
her playmates. Betty Hall said Porter was "supremely devoted" to
his daughter, and his letters make clear how true this was. "Hello,
Margaret:" he began his first letter, only a few weeks after entering
the penitentiary, "Don't you remember me? I'm a Brownie, and
my name is Aldibirontiphostiphornikophokos. If you see a star shoot
and say my name seventeen times before it goes out, you will find
a diamond ring in the track of the first cow's foot you see go down
the road in a snowstorm while the red roses are blooming on the
tomato vines. Try it some time." [23] Again he told her: "Now, Margaret, don't you worry about me, for I'm well and fat as a pig and
I'll have to be away from home a while yet. . . . I think about you
every day and wonder what you are doing. Well, I will see you
again before very long." [24] When he wrote these letters, during the
summer of 1898, Porter had no way of knowing that his sentence
would be shortened for good behavior, and the prospect of five years
must have seemed almost a permanent separation.

Beginning a valentine letter (dated February 14, 1900), he wrote:
"It has been quite a long time since I heard from you. I got a letter
from you in the last century, and a letter once every hundred years
is not very often. I have been waiting from day to day, putting off
writing to you, as I have been expecting to have something to send
you, but it hasn't come yet, and I thought I would write anyhow."
In the same letter he hoped that "your watch runs all right. When
you write again be sure and look at it and tell me what time it is,
so I won't have to get up and look at the clock." [25] By this time
Porter had sold "Whistling Dick's Christmas Stocking" (which
appeared in *McClure's* for December, 1899), as well perhaps as
some verses and smaller items too, and the watch may well have
been his Christmas present to his daughter; from this time on he did
send her presents from time to time. Two months after his valentine
letter he wrote (on May 17, 1900):

DEAR MARGARET:

It has been so long since I heard from you that I'm getting real anxious to know what is the matter. Whenever you don't answer my letters I'm afraid you are sick, so please write right away when you get this. Tell me something about Pittsburg and what you have seen of it. Have they any nice parks where you can go or is it all made of houses and bricks? I send you twenty nickles to spend for anything you want.

Now, if you will write me a nice letter real soon I will promise to answer it the same day and put another dollar in it. I am very well and so anxious to be with you again, which I hope won't be very long now.

With much love, as ever,

PAPA.[26]

In October—speaking quite clearly out of his own immediate experience—he wrote: "I suppose you have started to school again some time ago. I hope you like to go, and don't have to study too hard. When one grows up, a thing they never regret is that they went to school long enough to learn all they could. It makes everything easier for them, and if they like books and study they can always content themselves that way even if other people are cross and tiresome, and the world doesn't go to suit them." He hastened to add, "You mustn't think I've forgotten somebody's birthday. I couldn't find just the thing I wanted to send, but I know where it can be had, and it will reach you in a few days. So, when it comes you'll know it is for a birthday remembrance." And although in the fall of 1900 he could not have been hoping for an early release, he pacified Margaret and himself by toying with the idea: "I am busy all the time writing for the papers and magazines all over the country, so I don't have a chance to come home, but I'm going to try to come this winter. If I don't I will by summer sure, and then you'll have somebody to boss and make trot around with you." [27]

During the course of the following year and a half Porter continued his faithful monologue by mail:

When I come home I want to find you big and strong enough to pull me all about town on a sled when we have a snow storm. Won't that be nice? . . .[28]

You don't want to go to work and forget your old Pop just because you don't see much of him just now, for he'll come in mighty handy some day to read Uncle Remus to you again and make kites that a cyclone wouldn't raise off the ground. So write soon. . . .[29]

Well, old Christmas is about to come around again. I wish I could come and light up the candles on the Christmas tree like we used to. I wouldn't be surprised if you haven't gotten bigger than I am by now, and when I come back and don't want to read Uncle Remus of nights, you can get a stick and make me do it. I saw some new Uncle Remus books a few days ago and when I come back I'll bring a new one, and you'll say, "thankydoo, thankydoo." I'm getting mighty anxious to see you again, and for us to have some more fun like we used to. I guess it won't be much longer now till I do, and I want to hear you tell all about what times you've had. I'll bet you haven't learned to button your own dress in back yet, have you? . . .[30]

Here it is summertime, and the bees are blooming and the flowers are singing and the birds making honey, and we haven't been fishing yet. Well, there's only one more month till July, and then we'll go, and no mistake. . . . I would like very much to hear from you oftener; it has been more than a month since you wrote. Write soon and tell me how you are, and when school will be out, for we want plenty of holidays in July so we can have a good time. I am going to send you something nice the last of this week. What do you guess it will be? [31]

During the slow passage of the three years during which Porter continued to address Margaret as if she were an eight-year-old, he seems increasingly to have reconciled himself to his lot, and, as in the past, to have become the center of a small group of admiring and helpful friends. By December, 1898, he had come to realize that the appeal of his case might well come to nothing. Writing to Mrs. Roach on December 16, he apologized for not writing sooner; he had used the last stamp she had sent him to write to John Maddox. (Maddox later told Rollins that Porter wrote him "constantly" at the time in question, asking help either in the appeal of his case or in the securing of a pardon.) He had had no reply from Maddox, he wrote Mrs. Roach, and had given up concerning himself over the appeal.[32]

On December 13 the Circuit Court of Appeals considered and rejected the argument that the lower-court judge had refused to submit to the jury the question of whether Porter had actually been a fugitive from justice. "An entirely different case," ran the verdict, "would be presented if the plaintiff in error had requested the trial judge to submit the question of flight to the jury, and if, upon the judge's refusal to do so, the point had been presented for review by us. . . . If this statement were sustained by the record, a serious question would be presented; but we find nothing in the bills of exception to sustain the statement." [33] Obviously the defense attorneys knew, as did everyone else, that Porter had very clearly been a fugitive from justice; they knew it so well, in fact, that they had not risked doing in Judge Maxey's court what they now tried to claim that they had done. The technicalities they raised in the brief which they prepared for the appeal amounted to no more than a futile gesture, as they must have known.

Even after the failure of his appeal, Porter tried to think that there was a chance of his being pardoned. He wrote to Mrs. Roach on January 2, 1899, that through his lawyers or through Maddox he hoped to have some action taken within the next few months.[34] Apparently the hope was a perfunctory one, and we hear no more about it. In his next surviving letter to Mrs. Roach, three months later, he was concerned entirely with immediate problems. Dr. Reinert, the night physician (who "has been my best friend"), was leaving to accept a better position.

You can still address in his care until May 1st, and in the meantime I will make other arrangements. I believe, though, that I will be able to hold my own after he leaves, as I have the confidence and good will of all the officers. Still we never can tell here, as everything is run on political and financial lines. Of course, all the easy positions are greatly in demand, and every variety of wire-pulling and scheming is used to secure them. As much as a thousand dollars have been offered by men here for such places as the one I hold, and as I hold mine simply on my own merits I have to be on the lookout all the time against undermining.

I have abundant leisure time at night and I have been putting it to the best advantage studying and accumulating manuscript to use later.[35]

Porter's fears proved groundless, for Dr. Reinert's successor, Dr. George W. Williard, afterward stated: "I respected him for his strict attention to business, his blameless conduct, and his refusal to mix in the affairs of other prisoners. He seemed to like me personally because I did not ask him personal questions and because I showed that I felt as one intelligent man must feel toward another under such circumstances. So we grew to be friends." [36] On one occasion, during the momentary absence of a guard, a Negro prisoner who had been refused some medicine became so enraged that he began cursing Dr. Williard viciously. So automatic was Porter's loyalty that "my drug clerk went over his counter like a panther. All of his hundred and seventy or eighty pounds were behind the blow he sent into the negro's jaw. The negro came down like a ton of brick. Instantly Porter was behind his counter again. He did not utter a word." On another occasion some equipment had been stolen for which Dr. Williard was to be held responsible. Porter told him who the culprit was—a prison official instead of a convict—and by reporting the matter to the warden the doctor was able to recover the theft.

Porter seems to have succeeded in winning the favor of other officials as well as that of his immediate supervisor. Soon after his arrival, while he was apparently working as a nurse in the hospital, Warden E. G. Coffin was, through some error, given a dose of arsenic. A doctor and various nurses and prison officials were standing around the poisoned man, all of them helplessly panic-stricken. When Porter happened to arrive on the scene, he reportedly concocted an antidote the effect of which put the helpless doctor to shame. "In an hour," as a fellow attendant recounted the incident, "the warden was out of danger and the next day Mr. Porter was made night drug clerk." [37]

His main benefactor in prison was Dr. John M. Thomas, chief physician, whose recommendation won for him the position of secretary to the steward. On November 5, 1900, a letter to Mrs. Roach explained the matter:

About two weeks ago I was given what I consider the best position connected with this place. I am now in the steward's office keeping books, and am very comfortably situated. The office is entirely outside and separate from the rest of the institution. It is on the same street, but quite a distance away. I am about as near free as possible. I don't have to go near the other buildings except sometimes when I have business with some of the departments inside. I sleep outside at the office and am absolutely without supervision of any kind. I go in and out as I please. At night I take walks on the streets or go down to the river and walk along the paths there. The steward's office is a two-story building containing stores and provisions. There are two handsomely furnished office rooms with up-to-date fixtures—natural gas, electric lights, 'phones, etc. I have a big fine desk with worlds of stationery and everything I need. We have a fine cook out here and set a table as good as a good hotel. The steward and the storekeeper—very agreeable gentlemen both of them— leave about four P.M. and I am my own boss till next morning. In fact, I have my duties and attend to them, and am much more independent than an employer would be. I take my hat and go out on the street whenever I please. I have a good wire cot which I rig up in the office at night, and altogether no one could ask for anything better under the circumstances.[38]

Although Porter avoided entangling alliances with most of his fellow prisoners, he made a few close friends—chiefly the five other members of an exclusive group known as the Recluse Club, which met secretly, since it was against prison rules, on Sundays in an office not used apparently by prison officials. "A false wall had been built," according to Jennings, "and the kitchenette with full equipment was hidden like a long telephone booth behind it. It was stocked with silverware, napkins, flavoring extracts, flour and every necessity, enough in fact, for a small hotel. All had been stolen or bargained from the head clerks in other shops or from the chief cook in the kitchen. At a moment's notice the whole kitchenette could be shut away from sight."[39] For their weekly banquets the three embezzlers, two train robbers, and one forger wore clothing wangled from the clerk in charge of supplies—the finest grade of underwear and white shirts, with only the black stripe on the trousers to mar the effect. Even while a convict, Porter was fastidious in his tastes.

One of the embezzlers, a banker of French descent, was the club chef, who had done himself proud on the Sunday on which Jennings first became a member of the club. The flower-decorated table was set formally, and the meal included tomato soup, corn, green peas, roast potatoes, mince pie, and cold bread pudding, all prepared with such skill that Jennings pronounced it the first good meal he had had since getting into jail three years earlier. At each place was a copy of the club rules, written by Porter, and an appropriately illustrated place card; since four of the six men claimed to be innocent of their alleged crimes, Porter decorated the cards with cherubs or friars or pristine lilies.

On a later Sunday, just before arriving at the club, Jennings had heard about the death of an Indian prisoner who had been pronounced dead once before, only to revive before being taken to the morgue. On this second occasion, after the man had actually been placed in the ice-filled trough in the morgue, he had revived again. "He had tried to climb out. His clawing, terrible, long arms were flung forward. His body hung over the board, his head resting on the cement, as though he had lost his balance and half toppled out. The face, one cheek pressed against the ground, was twisted toward us—the mouth agape, the eyes staring." [40] Jennings told the club members the grisly story. One of them cried indignantly: "We should write to the President of the United States about it. It's an outrage." Porter, after leaving the table in a first horrified reaction, returned to remark, according to Jennings, "I think the summer will be quite warm." But Carnot, a pompous former banker, persisted. "Mr. Porter, you should exercise your best ability as a writer on this subject. You should enkindle the world about it. You should put it in an article and send it broadcast." Porter is said to have answered: "I do not understand you, sir. I am not here as a reporter. I shall not take upon myself the burden or responsibility. This prison and its shame is nothing to me." [41] (Fictitious though the actual words may be, clearly Jennings is accurate in his presentation of Porter's attitude in this and in other comparable episodes.)

There were other things, too, about which it was hard not to feel indignation—the way contracts for supplies, for example, were awarded not to the lowest bidders but to friends of the officials, so that inferior goods were often bought at extravagant prices. "It means," Jennings quotes Porter as saying, "that the taxpayers of this community are deliberately robbed of thousands and thousands of dollars on this one contract alone. And a convict who is here on a charge of taking a paltry $5000 [roughly the amount which the bank examiner had accused Porter of embezzling] not one cent of which he ever got, must be a party to the scandal. . . . Why, the convicts doing life here are stainless compared to these highwaymen." [42]

But in the main Porter continued apathetic. To one of Jennings's

145

outbursts against the system whereby police officials "throw men in a hog pen and expect them to come out cleaner than they went in," Porter replied merely, "The world is very illogical," and started to read a magazine. Jennings insisted that he should use his writing talent to attack such a system, an argument to which Porter retorted: "I shall never speak of crime and punishment. I tell you I will not attempt to bring a remedy to the diseased soul of society. I will forget that I ever breathed behind these walls." [43]

Yet Porter was not really callous and self-centered. As at every other stage of his life, all those who knew him were genuinely fond of him, as was illustrated most clearly of all when, after maximum reduction for good behavior, his sentence expired on July 24, 1901, and he prepared to face the world again. He wanted to have returned to him the tweed suit he had worn when he entered the prison, and when it could not be found he wanted something better than the customary going-away suit of cheap, badly cut cloth. "The superintendents of all the shops knew the secretary of the steward's office. They were all fond of the nimble-tongued, amiable dignity that was Bill Porter's. Everyone wanted to make him a present as he was leaving." Not only did he get a suit of fine brown worsted, but a black derby and a pair of yellow gloves.

Even the warden was nervous when Porter came into the office for his discharge [wrote Jennings, who by this time had become the warden's secretary]. . . . Porter's face was slightly lined. He looked older for his thirty-nine months in prison, but even so, his was a head and a bearing to attract attention anywhere. There was about him an attitude of confidence, of self-sufficiency, of dignity. He looked more like a well-educated, cultured business man than like an ex-convict.

There were visitors in the outer office. The warden stepped outside, telling me to give Bill his discharge papers. As soon as we were alone the intense strain became unbearable. I wanted to cram everything into those last moments. I wanted to say: "Good luck—God bless you—Go to hell." . . .

The coaxing smile on his lips, he put out his strong, short hand to me. "Al, here's a book, I sent to town for it for you." It was a copy of "Omar Khayyam." I handed him the discharge and his $5. Porter had at least $60 or $70—the proceeds from his last story. He took the $5.

"Here, colonel, give this to Billy—he can buy alcohol for his locomotor ataxia."

146

That was all. He went toward the door and then he came back, the old drollery in his eye.

"I'll meet you in New York, colonel. You might beat the brakes there before me. I'll be on the watch. Goodby, Al."

Porter's voice lapsed into a low whisper at the end. He went to the door, and, without looking back, went out. I felt as though something young and bonny—something lovable and magnetic—was gone forever.[44]

On November 5, 1900, Porter had written Mrs. Roach that he was sending her a copy of the magazine *Outlook* for June 30, 1900, containing his story "Georgia's Ruling," for which he had been paid $45. ("I am going," he added, "to send $25 to John Maddox,"[45] his first employer in Austin and presumably one of those who had advanced him money in his trouble.) He had, of course, been writing and gathering story material almost from the beginning. Dr. Thomas stated, for example, that the yarns in the volume *The Gentle Grafter* were told to Porter on his night rounds of the tiers of cells, and that many of the other O. Henry stories had their origin in tales told to him by the Western outlaws in the prison.

The most famous of the stories which derived from these days is "A Retrieved Reformation," the story of Jimmy Connors, according to Dr. Williard, or Dick Price as Jennings disguised him, the convict who opened the safe of the Columbus Press-Post Publishing Company after the treasurer had locked up the books and fled to avoid arrest for larceny. Instead of the tools which Porter's Jimmy Valentine used to open the safe, the man who actually did the job filed his nails (according to Jennings) "until the lower half of the nail was separated from the upper by a thin red mark. He filed to the quick. Soon only the lower half of the nail remained." With his fingers thus sensitized to the slightest jar of the mechanism within the steel door, he "kneeled before the safe, put his bruised fingers across the dial, waited a moment, and then turned the combination. . . . There was the slightest pause, his right hand went backward. He turned the dial again, pulled the knob gently toward him. The safe was opened." For Porter, however, the actual details were too unpleasant. "It chills my teeth to think of that gritting operation," he said later in commenting on his story. "I prefer the set of tools. I don't like to make my victims suffer."[46]

While in prison and for a time afterward, Porter kept in a small

147

pocket notebook a record of the stories he was trying to sell. It is an interesting record because it shows so graphically the disappointment and dogged persistence which were required before the most popular short-story writer of the era was able to find an audience. Porter later remarked that one of his stories, "The Emancipation of Billy," was rejected thirteen times before it landed in 1904, and for "An Afternoon Miracle," for instance, the notebook shows five rejections.[47] "A Blackjack Bargainer" was rejected only once before *Munsey's* accepted it, but "A Fog in Santone" (not published until 1910) had accumulated ten rejections by 1902. "Money Maze" found a market after only one rejection, and "The Duplicity of Hargraves" and "Rouge et Noir" clicked on the first trip out, but "No Story" shows six rejections, and "The Enchanted Kiss" shows seven rejections. (Since these two stories were not published until 1903 and 1904, respectively, there may also have been later rejections not shown in the notebook.) Several stories never did make the grade apparently. "No Political Significance," for example, went without success to eight magazines, as "A Trained Nurse" did to five and "Bar to Presidency" also to five. In addition to short stories, Porter sent out from prison such items as "Select Humor" and "6 Jokes" to the Detroit *Free Press,* and similar offerings to *Life.*

While still in the Travis County jail in Austin, Porter had changed his literary name to Sydney Porter (which he signed to some seven stories written in 1901 and later).[48] While in prison he also used the name John Arbuthnott for the three poems which appeared in *Ainslee's* (for the nine poems in the same magazine in 1901 and 1903 he repeated the same name four times and used the names Howard Clark, T. B. Dowd, and S. H. Peters).[49] In the main, however, beginning with his first prison story he concealed his identity behind the name O. Henry (changing it temporarily to Olivier Henry when *Ainslee's* demanded a fuller signature).[50]

The origin of this, after Mark Twain the most famous pen name in American literature, has been much debated. As Stephen Leacock pointed out not long after Porter's death, the name originally must have seemed a very poor choice, one which was evidently adopted "in a whimsical moment, with no great thought as to its aptness." [51] Porter himself once facetiously told an interviewer that he picked the name Henry out of the society columns of a New Orleans newspaper, and the initial O. out of the air as "about the easiest letter written." [52] Of the various explanations as to what started him signing this particular name to his stories, probably no one is the solely correct one, but rather the name stuck in his mind through a series of coincidental recurrences in his experience.

As early as 1886 Porter had signed himself O. Henry in the autograph book of Lollie Cave Wilson. Even before that, while in La Salle County, he had known a Negro ranchman (a rarity in those parts in those days) called Old Henry, or sometimes just O. Henry, who was something of a yarn teller himself.[53] Also in La Salle County, Porter probably became familiar with a cowboy song called "Root, Hog, or Die," in which occurs the passage:

> Along came my true love about twelve o'clock
> Saying Henry, O, Henry, what sentence have you got?

In the First National Bank in Austin, according to one story, there was a Negro porter to whom Dr. Brackenridge was constantly calling out, "Oh, Henry, come here!" [54] Another story has it that the "Oh, Henry!" was addressed to a somewhat deaf, elderly patron of the bank who kept leaving and being called back to listen to one more anecdote.[55] Later, in Honduras, according to Porter's brother, while working as a longshoreman Porter knew a wharf master named Hennery, to whom the men were constantly shouting, "Hennery, oh, Hennery!" [56] In the Ohio Penitentiary, some years earlier, there had worked a captain of the night watch named Orrin Henry, who commonly signed himself O. Henry for short, and Porter may well have noticed the signature on some of the prison records.[57] While in the prison drugstore (as perhaps earlier in Greensboro), Porter, in filling prescriptions, undoubtedly made frequent use of *The United States Dispensatory,* in which several references were made to a European chemist named Etienne-Ossian Henry, abbreviated in the text to O. Henry.[58] There have been other suggestions: that the name was found in Balzac's story "Ferragus," that the jailer in Austin was a man named Henry, whose wife often called to him; that one of the members of the Recluse Club in the prison could not remember names and kept calling Porter not Bill but Henry. Without multiplying such gratuitous stories, it is evident that the name was one which Porter must have encountered more than once, and when

149

he felt that he could no longer sign his work with his own name, he signed himself O. Henry because, as he later said to his editor-friend Robert H. Davis, "Oh, it looked good in print, and is easy for the lips." [59]

The earliest O. Henry stories, written in prison during the years 1898–1901, are not conspicuously more professional in style than his Austin and Houston work, nor conspicuously less so than his later New York work. They do testify, however, to the results of a remarkably thorough self-discipline in a form which previously he had attempted only casually or spasmodically—the short story proper, or rather the short story as it was to flourish through his influence. The fourteen prison stories show almost the full range of O. Henry, all the way from the unredeemed sentimentality of "Georgia's Ruling" to the frothy lightness of "The Enchanted Kiss," all the way from the Honduran adventure of "Money Maze" to the authentic New York setting of "No Story" (written before Porter had ever seen New York), and all the way from the jejune twist that ends "An Afternoon Miracle" to the irony of the reversal in "The Marionettes."

The point of immediate interest is the autobiographical element in the group. Eight of the fourteen have to do with one basic idea: the vindication of a character who has in some way forfeited his claim to respectability or even integrity. Whistling Dick has fallen to the level of professional tramp; Lorison of "Blind Man's Holiday" bears the burden of the knowledge that "from the moment I staked the first dollar of the firm's money I was a criminal"; [60] Tripp of "No Story" has become a fawning alcoholic who thinks himself unworthy of the girl he loves; Miss Rosa of "A Fog in Santone" is a prostitute instead of the pure young girl her admirer imagines her to be; Goree of "A Blackjack Bargainer" has quite literally sold his birthright for whisky; Dr. James of "The Marionettes" has become a part-time thief; the Frio Kid of "A Chaparral Christmas Gift" has allowed the frustration of his love to turn him into a heartless-seeming "bad man"; and, in lighter vein, even Hargraves feels that his duplicity requires that he attempt some kind of amends. For a man who had claimed to be innocent of wrongdoing in the matter of the bank charges, the idea of a lapse from integrity was much on Porter's mind. The idea seems to have become almost a compulsive one, and the plot invariably turns on the regeneration of an admitted delinquent, not on the vindication of a character who is blameless. Is it reading too much into the stories to interpret them as an oblique attempt at confession, even at self-abnegation? From this time forward, Porter's personality seems always to have included an element of bewilderment, as if the wrong he had done seemed to him less a decision of his own than the next, inevitable position into which he had been moved in a game in which he was merely one of the pawns on the board.

CHAPTER NINE

· ⟨∞⟩ ·

Porter emerged from prison on July 24, 1901, to find people singing such new songs as "Absence Makes the Heart Grow Fonder," "A Bird in a Gilded Cage," and "Beautiful Isle of Somewhere." He confronted a literary scene in which a sharp eye could have picked out unmistakable signs of upheaval soon to come. In 1899 Frank Norris had published *McTeague;* in 1900 there had appeared Conrad's *Lord Jim,* Jack London's *The Son of the Wolf,* and Dreiser's *Sister Carrie* (although the edition of Dreiser's book had been withdrawn almost on publication, after the publisher had canvassed the opinions of a group of selected critics); in 1901 another book by Norris, *The Octopus,* was published. The seeds sown by Zola, Flaubert, Ibsen, and other European realists were beginning to sprout in earnest after the appearance as early as 1893 of Stephen Crane's *Maggie: A Girl of the Streets.* Moreover, in August, 1901—less than a month after Porter's release—came the birth of the Socialist Party of the United States under the leadership of Eugene V. Debs, Victor Berger, and Morris Hillquit, and in September of the same year, upon the assassination of McKinley, began the administration of Theodore Roosevelt and the era of *The Strenuous Life.* It was indeed a new century into which Porter emerged within two months of his thirty-ninth birthday.

He went to Pittsburgh, where the process of becoming acquainted with his nearly twelve-year-old daughter must have been an ordeal as well as a long-anticipated joy. The sedentary life in prison had put a good deal of weight on him, which along with a three-year absence made him almost a complete stranger to Margaret. Concerning this and later meetings after later separations, she was to remember how "we would just begin to emerge from an ever-increasing reserve that seemed to beset us both," [1] when the time would come to part again. On this first occasion, however, their reunion was to last some eight or nine months. Roach was now manager of the second-class Iron Front Hotel, where Porter found a room waiting for him and the same steadfast loyalty from the Roaches as if he had actually—as Margaret thought—been absent for three years on business. The loyalty of the Roaches Porter was to retain to the end of his life, and although he never did anything about his heavy financial indebtedness to them, his father-in-law expressed after his death the firm conviction that if Porter had lived he would have repaid every cent of the money they had advanced him through the years.

Without interruption Porter continued in Pittsburgh the writing career which he seems to have regarded as the only means of livelihood open to him now that he had a prison record to conceal. During the eight or nine months before he left for New York in the spring of 1902—in May, probably—he published nine stories,[2] not to mention perhaps half a dozen others which were accepted during this time and published during the next few months. These stories add little or nothing to the scanty records of his stay in Pittsburgh—"the City of Diurnal Night," as he called it in the story "Best Seller." He waxed somewhat more eloquent in "The Making of a New Yorker":

Pittsburg impressed him as the play "Othello" performed in the Russian language in a railroad station by Dockstader's minstrels. A royal and generous lady this Pittsburg, though—homely, hearty, with flushed face, washing the dishes in a silk dress and white kid slippers, and bidding Raggles sit before the roaring fireplace and drink champagne with his pigs' feet and fried potatoes.[3]

Porter did not like Pittsburgh and had no intention of settling there permanently, for only "a month and a half to the day" after leaving prison he wrote Jennings that he was very comfortably situated "but expect to leave in a couple of weeks anyhow." Pittsburgh people, he went on, were "the most ignorant, ill-bred, contemptible, boorish, degraded, insulting, sordid, vile, foul-mouthed, indecent, profane, drunken, dirty, mean, depraved curs" that he had ever imagined could exist, and "I shall linger here no longer than necessary." In a later letter to Jennings he put the matter more succinctly: "The only difference between P. and O. P. is that they are allowed to talk at dinner here." [4]

In the first letter he told Jennings that he had interested the editor of *Everybody's* in an article on "The Art and Humor of Holding Up a Train," to be written by an expert in the business. "My idea," he explained, "would be a chatty sort of article—just about the way you usually talk, treating it descriptively and trying out the little points and details, just as a man would talk of his chicken farm or his hog ranch." On September 21, in answer to some questions from Jennings, he wrote cannily:

DEAR PARD:

In regard to that article—I will give you my idea of what is wanted. Say we take for a title "The Art and Humor of the Hold-Up"—or something like that. I would suggest that in writing you assume a character. We have got to respect the conventions and delusions of the public to a certain extent. An article written as you would naturally write it would be regarded as a fake and an imposition. Remember that the traditions must be preserved whenever they will not interfere with the truth. Write in as simple, plain, and unembellished a style as you know how. Make your sentences short. Put in as much realism and as many facts as possible. . . . I thought I would, when I get your story, put it into the shape my judgment decides upon, and then send both your MS. and mine to the magazine. If he uses mine, we'll whack up shares on the proceeds. If he uses yours, you get the check direct. If he uses neither, we are out only a few stamps.[5]

The project succeeded with surprising speed. A month later (October 24) Porter wrote: "I enclose pubrs letter which explains itself. When you see your baby in print don't blame me if you find strange ear marks and brands on it. I slashed it and cut it and added lots of stuff that never happened, but I followed your facts and ideas, and that is what made it valuable. I'll think up some other idea for an article and we'll collaborate again some time, eh?" [6]

Probably Porter would not have left Pittsburgh "in a couple of weeks" even if he could have managed it financially. He could hardly have been ready so soon for another long separation from his daughter. He seems, however, to have developed an uncomfortable feeling of dependence on the Roaches, for he shortly moved from the Iron Front Hotel to share with a young druggist named Jamison a second-floor room at the corner of Wylie and Fullerton streets. The two men shared the high old double bed, and—as Jamison put it—"together when necessary fought the insect life." According to Jamison, Porter was now working off and on for the Pittsburgh *Dispatch,* and he limited his activities to his work and an occasional game of poker with a five-cent limit.

At that time there was a saloon at 79 Fulton Street, known as Angloch's, and there one could get a fine sandwich for five cents. Beer was also a nickel and they threw in a bowl of soup. That's where O. Henry ate most of the time he was here. He was fastidious about his dress and tried to look as English as possible. He liked yellow kid gloves, carried a cane and wore spats, which in those days were somewhat of a rarity. We used to kid him about his clothes, but he didn't mind.[7]

Porter wrote Jennings on October 24 that, since August 1, he had been averaging $150 a month, which would mean two story sales a month, since Gilman Hall later said that *Ainslee's* paid him at this time about $75 per story.[8] Nevertheless, he seems to have been chronically broke. In view of the capacity he had developed by the time he was launched on his New York career, he must already have been spending a considerable amount on whisky. In addition he must have felt, as no doubt the Roaches did, that he should assume financial responsibility for his daughter. Even so, he was clearly as improvident as ever. Reportedly he once wrote to Dr. Williard back in the Ohio Penitentiary, asking for an emergency loan of five dollars, which, reportedly, he never repaid.[9] Jamison helped out too, when the time came for Porter's move to New York, by obtaining a railroad pass for his indigent friend. According to another story, it was at this time that Porter first tried to interest the *Dispatch* in his work. He is said to have drifted into the editorial office one day, "somewhat shabbily dressed and . . . a bit shy." He was trying to sell some stories for enough money to get to New York. After the stories had been read, Porter was told that they were too good for the prices the *Dispatch* could pay, that he should send them to a magazine.

"That's very nice, boys," Porter is quoted as having said, "but I need some coin right now. I'm on my way to New York. . . . I could telegraph to some friends in Ohio, if I had a dollar for the Western Union. . . . If I don't sell a story, I'll have to borrow a dollar of somebody, and I don't know anybody that rich."

"You can borrow a dollar right here," said one of the newspaper men, producing a silver dollar and spinning it on the desk.

"Thank you very much, boys," Porter said, pocketing the coin. "You'll get this dollar back as soon as I land somewhere and sell some of these stories." (But again, according to the story, the loan was never repaid.) [10]

Another, better documented story concerning Porter's financial status and his New York aspirations comes from Charles Hanson Towne, then on the staff of the *Smart Set*, to which Porter sold the story "By Courier" early in 1902 (at one cent a word, for the sum of $17):

And when another story came in from this author . . . [Towne remembered] he wished to know if we could send the check immediately, as he wanted to come to New York and settle down to write. He further stated that if we could pay him at once, we might deduct ten dollars for cash, so anxious was he to be on his way to the metropolis. The story ["Madame Bo-Peep of the Ranches"] was six thousand words in length, but we did not deduct anything. We sent him the full amount and asked him to call on us when he arrived in town. But he didn't; it was some months later that I first met him.[11]

Evidently Porter had intended from the beginning to go to New York as soon as such a move became feasible. It seemed to him to be the place he had to go if he was to make a career out of his writing. As he was to write in 1905 to the woman he later married (who herself had literary ambitions): "You ought to come to New York, where you will be *in medias res*. There's nothing like being on the ground. . . . You want to know the dealers." [12] From another point of view also, New York was the logical destination for Porter. In prison his one overriding impulse had been the determination to bury his past—to change not only his place of residence but even his name, and so to make a new life for himself. In Pittsburgh, far as it was from Austin, he could not entirely succeed. Not only must the Roaches themselves have constantly kept the past alive in his mind, but they must have had friends who wondered about the past history of their uncommunicative son-in-law.

In any event, about the same time he broached the idea to Charles Hanson Towne, he made a bolder proposition to Gilman Hall, of *Ainslee's,* the magazine to which he had already contributed four stories and four poems. The first story, "Money Maze," which had appeared in May, 1901, had attracted considerable attention and aroused the curiosity of several other editors as to the identity of O. Henry. With "Money Maze" and "Rouge et Noir" Porter had successfully invaded the province of Richard Harding Davis, and in the other two stories in *Ainslee's* ("The Passing of Black Eagle" and "Friends in San Rosario") he had furnished glimpses of the Southwest which were as journalistically authentic as the accounts which Jack London was beginning to publish of the sea and of the Northwest. The editors of *Ainslee's* had good reason to encourage their new discovery; in fact, Gilman Hall had suggested that he visit New York to talk things over with them in person. On March 9, 1902, therefore, Porter wrote to Hall explaining his wish to move to New York and asking whether *Ainslee's* would advance him a $100 payment on future stories to make possible such a move.[13]

After consultation with George Smith, one of the owners of *Ainslee's,* Hall sent Porter a check for $100. But the days went by, and Porter did not appear. On March 22 he had still not appeared, for on that date Hall wrote to his sister-in-law, a student of graphology, enclosing Porter's letter and asking if she would examine it "and let me know three or four salient things of his handwriting. The one thing I want to know is whether he is honest and trustworthy. Something intuitive has made me distrustful of this man. . . ." Hall's sister-in-law, who herself judged the writer of the letter to be entirely trustworthy, sent the letter on to her correspondence-course instructor, who in turn replied from Grand Rapids that he would judge the writer to be a good risk, a straightforward, honest man "but with less firmness of will than his capacity for work calls for, i.e., work and speech comes easily to him, but as there are no signs of enduring will . . . , his 'foe to be fought' is his versatility, his tendency to change his work or cease from it in case he runs against snags." [14]

This report reached Hall probably on the last day of March, almost simultaneously with a second letter from Porter containing the news that the $100 advance had somehow "evaporated" and that he would have to have an additional $100 in order to get to New York. It was with some trepidation that Hall took the letter in to Smith, but after they had discussed the inadvisability of sending good money after bad, Smith suddenly exclaimed: "He wants to get out of Pittsburgh, does he? Well, I don't blame him. Send him another hundred."

On the afternoon of the third day following, the long-awaited visitor arrived at the offices of *Ainslee's*. In the words of Richard Duffy, Hall's co-editor: "He wore a dark suit of clothes, I recall, and a four-in-hand tie of bright color. He carried a black derby, high-crowned, and walked with a springy, noiseless step. To meet him for the first time you felt his most notable quality to be reticence, not a reticence of social timidity but a reticence of deliberateness." [15] Porter himself later reported the first incident of this meeting with his editors. "They escorted me, with fear and trembling, to the office of the publisher, Mr. S——, who abruptly dismissed them, closed his office door and motioned me to a chair. Fearing the worst was yet to come, I hastened to thank Mr. S—— for his generosity and assured him that his confidence was not misplaced.

" 'Don't mention it, my dear sir,' he rejoined. 'I was born and brought up in Pittsburgh, and was only too happy to assist in your escape.' " [16]

It was closing time before Porter's visit to the office of *Ainslee's* ended, and Hall and Duffy invited him to accompany them on their customary walk from Duane Street as far uptown as Madison Square. They tried to talk of literary matters, but could not divert Porter's attention from the elevated railroad. Continuing to stare at it, he inquired, "so that we doubted his seriousness, why people were not afraid to ride on such trains, as they might so easily fall into the street." [17] In all their future rambles around the city together, Duffy added, Porter confined himself to the subways and surface cars, never risking his safety on the Elevated. Reportedly he never ceased to affect a provincial, small-town manner, but as Alphonso Smith aptly observed, "If ever in American literature the place and the man met, they met when O. Henry strolled for the first time along the streets of New York." [18]

That first stroll was notable for another reason too. For the first time since leaving prison, Porter was able to merge inconspicuously into endless, anonymous crowds, in which he was to become quite literally a man in hiding. After spending his first night or two in an unnamed cheap hotel, he moved (apparently without giving his address even to Hall and Duffy) to the Hotel Marty, a French table-d'hôte hotel on West Twenty-fourth Street, where he took up an existence suggestive of Dostoevski's man from the underground. Something over a year later Robert H. Davis, sent by the *Sunday World* to seek him out, found that no one seemed to have any information more definite than the fact that he lived over a restaurant somewhere around Madison Square.[19] To the end of his life, Davis comments, "Porter fled from publicity like mist before the gale. He shrank from the extended hands of strangers . . . and avoided conversations about himself." [20] Gilman Hall, who became his closest friend in New York, spoke after his death of the way Porter would glance behind him when they were eating together in a restaurant. The "furtive manner" made Hall wonder whether Porter had killed somebody.[21] To Jennings, who later stayed for some time in New York, Porter confided the truth: "Colonel, every time I step into a public cafe I have the horrible fear that some ex-con will come up and say to me 'Hello, Bill; when did you get out of the O. P.?' " And while still in Pittsburgh, he had written Jennings: "By the way, please keep my *nom de plume* strictly to yourself. I don't want anyone to know just yet." [22]

Things were not always easy after the move to New York. According to Anne Partlan, he was entirely penniless on at least one occasion. He was so hungry, in fact, that he could not continue writing, especially after the smell of cooking began to emanate from a nearby room. He had begun to pace up and down the hall when the door in question opened and a girl looked out and said: "Have you had your supper? I've made a hazlett stew and it's too much for me. It won't keep, so come and help me eat it." Some time afterward, when he had been paid for a story, Porter knocked at the girl's door to invite her to dinner with him, but she had moved.[23] For his first year in New York, Porter had no known associates except for

Hall and Duffy, with one or both of whom he frequently dined or went out on the town at night. He avoided any open alliances with women, being interested (in Hall's words) "only in girls of a certain class," so that when Mrs. Hall once said to him, "Please write about a higher class of women," he replied, "I don't know any others." [24] Already, too, he had begun to depend on alcohol to complete the withdrawal he had undertaken. According to Hall's later statement, he began drinking before breakfast and had such an "infinite" capacity that he never seemed drunk. Another close friend, Robert H. Davis, has written: "He was a two-bottle man; that is, his average daily consumption in the years of his caliphing in New York was two quarts of whisky. Porter could consume a vast amount of strong spirits and not show it. His bibulous habits rarely affected his deportment, swayed his gait, or altered the tenor of his low, even voice." [25]

Drinking to any such extent as this obviously had a bearing on Porter's work—on its nature and quality—but for the first three or four years in New York his work was certainly not hampered from a quantitative standpoint, and recognition came quickly once he was launched. Witter Bynner, at that time a first reader on the staff of *McClure's*, was so excited about a manuscript entitled "Tobin's Palm" that when the head reader rejected it in spite of his recommendation, he went to S. S. McClure himself to protest. Convinced by his young employee's enthusiasm, McClure sent him on a recovery mission, authorized to accept the story on the spot. Fortunately, Bynner remembered the address on the manuscript. He found Porter at the Marty in a room furnished with a bed, a chair, and a trunk; on the trunk lay the envelope in question.

" 'Tobin's Palm'?" Bynner asked unceremoniously, pointing. Porter indicated it was, and Bynner announced, "It's sold."

"Good," Porter replied. "I'm flat broke."

So the story was brought to the personal attention of McClure, who liked it so much that he paid $100 for it, the highest price which Porter had yet been paid. [26]

About the time that *McClure's* was accepting "Tobin's Palm," a lighthearted story with a strong flavor of New York Irish, *Ainslee's* published (in May, 1903) a story with a New York setting, "While the Auto Waits" (signed James L. Bliss because of the number of stories *Ainslee's* had been publishing by O. Henry, or Olivier Henry as they preferred to call him at this early stage). A few days afterward, in an editorial comment on two current short stories which it recommended to its readers, the New York *Times* observed: "We do not know who James L. Bliss is. The name is a new one to us. But we defy any one to produce a French short-story writer of the present day who is capable of producing anything finer than 'While the Auto Waits.'" [27]

Porter published seventeen stories in 1902, and a dozen more in the first four months of 1903, including such titles as "The Duplicity of Hargraves," "A Retrieved Reformation," and "Roads of Destiny." As a result magazine editors began to seek him out, "which," as Duffy put it, "was a job somewhat akin to tracing a lost person." [28] At about this time, apparently, the mystery of O. Henry led to an amusing situation. A student at Harvard (an orphan being educated by his uncle and aunt) was not taking the fullest advantages of his opportunity. Upbraided by his benefactors, who suggested that anyone who seemed to be learning so little in college might better find himself a job, the boy was in a difficult situation until his eye happened to fall on a current magazine lying on a table, a magazine carrying a story by O. Henry. He had a sudden inspiration. The truth, he said, was that he had been working harder than his grades showed; he had been publishing short stories under the name O. Henry. The uncle read the story and was so impressed that he sent it to one of the boy's professors, who in turn was so impressed that he made an announcement to the class about their fellow student's remarkable achievement. Evidently the class had a wide geographical representation, for the news spread as far as Minneapolis, where one of the newspapers broke the story that the widely read author O. Henry was, astonishingly enough, not a former cowboy or soldier of fortune, but a Harvard sophomore. The upshot of the matter was that *Ainslee's* had a visit one day from a representative of another publisher, who had been in communication with the student and wished to have a courteous understanding with the boy's other publishers. Only then was the bubble pricked. Porter's own attitude in the matter was a characteristic one. His only concern was to caution Hall and Duffy "to be sure and send all O. Henry checks to him." [29] And when the boy wrote him a remorseful letter, Porter replied: "Of course, I know it was only a prank. Come down to New York some time and we'll do the town together. It was generous of you to stand for all that stuff." [30]

By the end of a year in New York, Porter's self-confidence must have been higher than at any time since his early years in Austin. The loneliness of his underground life must have begun to tell on him, too. On both counts a good deal is revealed by his reaction to a letter from Mabel Wagnalls, daughter of the publisher. On June 9 he answered her letter:

The "Cosmopolitan Magazine" forwarded me yesterday the little note you wrote on May 9th. . . . Since you have been so good as to speak nicely of my poor wares I will set down my autobiography. Here goes. Texas cowboy. Lazy. Thought writing stories might be easier than "busting" bronchos. Came to New York one year ago to earn bread, butter, jam, and possibly asparagus that way. . . . I don't like to talk about literature. Did you notice that teentsy-weentsy little "1"? That's the way I spell it. I have much more respect for a man who brands cattle than for one who writes pieces for the printer. . . . There are one or two stories that I think you have not seen that I would like to have your opinion of if you would let me submit them to you some time. I think the judgment of a normal, intelligent woman is superior to that of an editor in a great many instances.

Although he signed the letter "O. Henry," he gave his address: 47 West Twenty-fourth Street.[31]

Miss Wagnalls, who was visiting her grandmother in Lithopolis, Ohio (a town of 350 inhabitants), evidently replied at once and in just the terms Porter had hoped she would, for two weeks later he was writing again:

Your pleasant little note from the metropolis Lithopolis was received and appreciated, although some envy was stirred up at the sight of your postmark. Just think!—you are out in the wilds of Ohio where you can pick daisies and winners at the county racetrack, wear kimonas and shoes large enough for you and run either for exercise or office as often as you please. Me—I'm in my garret nibbling at my crust (softened by a little dry Sauterne) and battling with the wolf at the door (he's trying to get out—don't like it inside).[32]

To Miss Wagnalls's inquiry as to whether he liked music, Porter replied with an account of how he once gained a reputation for musical knowledge by his adeptness in turning the pages for a young lady pianist. "No one," he confided, "ever found out that she gave me the signal by moving her right ear." He mailed separately "two or three recent stories" and promised to send in a day or two the July issue of *McClure's* (which carried "The Fourth in Salvador"), remarking, "I don't think that anybody but you reads them, and I don't want my audience to get away."

The acquaintance by mail continued through the summer and fall, with Porter becoming more and more candid. In reply to his correspondent's praise of the stories he had sent her, he affected the awkward modesty of a cowhand. He was "awfully obliged," he said, but "I don't think very much of 'em myself. . . . The whole business—life, literature, operas, philosophy, & shirt waists—is a kind of joke, isn't it? I reckon that riding around on a pony on the Texas prairies thinking about the beans and barbecued beef we're going to have for supper is about as good as anything." [33] In September he protested: "You must know I haven't nearly 'arrived' yet. I'm only on the road, and the 'meteor' and 'comet' & 'fixed star' that you make believe you see is only the milky way, and very skim-milky at that." But Miss Wagnalls's praise had drawn him out enough so that he sent her his photograph, asking for one of her in return. "I enjoy your letters very much," he wrote with obvious sincerity, "only they are too brief." [34] In October, by way of answering her question about his name, he sent her a clipping of a recent article in a magazine called the *Reader,* in which "the new luminary in fiction's firmament" was for the first time publicly identified as Sydney Porter. And in the same letter, waxing even bolder, he wrote: "I would be very glad and pleased to call at your home as you have so graciously extended permission." Miss Wagnalls was by now back in New York. She had written something about needing a new frock before seeing him, to which he replied (with obvious pride in his esoteric knowledge): "Please don't do it. I'm only a lone cowpuncher. . . . I shy like a broncho at anything with passementerie or ruching on the flounces." He was not so busy as she imagined, he said, and he would "esteem it a great favor to be allowed to call any evening—say Thursday or Friday this week or any evening next week." [35]

Porter duly made his call, Miss Wagnalls later reported. She served tea and cakes, and they talked casually on random topics. Porter himself referred to the occasion in the inscription to one of his books which he afterward sent her: "To Miss Mabel Wagnalls —with pleasant recollections of a certain little tea party where there were such nice little cakes and kind hospitality to a timid stranger." The phrase "timid stranger," Miss Wagnalls wrote, exactly described him, although on one topic, it seems, he lost his reticence. Speaking of poverty, he said: "That is something you cannot imagine. No one who has not known it can imagine the misery of poverty." His voice struck her as almost tragic as he said with deep feeling: "Poverty is so terrible and so common, we should all do more than we do—much more—to relieve it. You ought to do more, so ought I, right now. I ought to give $50, but I don't." [36]

Whatever the cause, no further meetings are recorded; and when Miss Wagnalls soon afterward left with her mother for a trip to Europe, the wistful little platonic affair came to an end.

Several months earlier Porter had received his most gratifying and lucrative recognition thus far. The *Sunday World* had sought him out to write brief introductions to special feature stories. Robert H. Davis was sent to search for Porter, with the instruction: "Offer him forty dollars a week. If he balks jump to fifty dollars. The third and last call is sixty dollars." Able to learn only that his man's name was Sydney Porter and that he lived over a restaurant in the neighborhood of Madison Square, Davis began to comb the area. After working his way through four buildings, he came about noon to the Hotel Marty, a pair of brownstone fronts combined into an establishment presided over by a Frenchman who apparently had never heard of either Sydney Porter or O. Henry but who was agreeable to a search of the premises. Davis began at the top floor. On the next floor down, the fourth, from Room Number Seven he received a "cheerful invitation to enter." He opened the door of a small, darkish room where he confronted "a rather corpulent figure in his shirt sleeves and with his suspenders down, seated beside a washstand upon which reposed a huge bowl containing perhaps five pounds of cracked ice in which nestled a half dozen fine Bartlett pears. The fat man arose with considerable dignity and bowed. 'Come in, mister,' said he," and when told who was being sought, he admitted his identity, adding, "Have a chair. Have some fruit. It is nice and cool. I suffer like hell from the heat. What can I do for you?" [37]

On being informed that his visitor had business to discuss, he "wiped the perspiration from his brow and cupped his left ear with his hand." Davis, liking him immediately, made his last offer first. It was accepted just as expeditiously, after which Porter insisted on sealing the bargain by taking Davis to the restaurant downstairs and ordering a full-course dinner, complete with enough wine to prolong the meal until three o'clock in the afternoon.

This particular contract with the *Sunday World* lasted for only two or three months. After the retirement of F. L. H. Noble, the editor who had arranged it, the contract was terminated by his successor, Caleb Van Hamm, who evidently stayed with the paper only briefly. Davis himself soon left the *Sunday World* to become fiction editor of *Munsey's*. Exactly how the fact of Porter's first employment by the paper could have been entirely forgotten is incomprehensible, but apparently something of the sort must have happened. According to Davis's account, Porter afterward signed a contract to write a weekly short story for the *Evening World*.[38] The famous two-year series in fact appeared in the *Sunday World*. In later years William Wash Williams had his own story of being, in his turn, sent by the *Sunday World* to search out Porter "in the fall of 1902." [39] (Clearly the dating is a year off, for the stories began to appear in December, 1903.)

On this occasion, when Williams found his way at last to the Hotel Marty, the generously proportioned Frenchwoman at the desk recognized the name Porter and, after a shouted consultation with an employee somewhere upstairs—who evidently conferred with Porter—she allowed Williams to go up. He found a man who looked about thirty-five years old (Williams himself was a very young reporter at the time), a man "broadly built, possibly five feet seven inches tall and particularly heavy about the shoulders and chest. . . . His features . . . were rather coarse and heavy; the nose short and fat, the lips thick, the cheeks broad and full, the undershot

jaw ponderous . . . and when he pulled [his chin] back hard between the batwings of his collar—as was his habit—a roll of fat
swelled beneath it." [40] The impression which Williams received was
of a relaxing tension after a first moment of trepidation or anxiety
on Porter's part. It was puzzling, too, "why a man who had made
a sufficient hit in the short story game to be sought after by editors,
would hide himself away, to be startled by discovery and then very
calmly, with an embarrassed smile, readily admit his identity and
seem relieved about it."

Porter excused himself long enough to go downstairs and buy
two cigars. "Have a smoke," he said, returning, "and I hope you
find it a good one. I'm going to join you, so if there is anything the
matter with the brand we will suffer together." He listened to
Williams's account of his mission, which was to make an appointment for Porter to talk with Nelson Hersh, now editor of the
Sunday World, about a weekly series of New York stories for the
paper. Porter accepted the invitation, expressing the hope that
Williams would be there to help him out when he arrived.

"You see," he said with a show of embarrassment, "I am not very
thoroughly broken in yet to meeting New York editors . . . so
thought you could kinda put me on and see me through."

It must have been a triumphant occasion for Porter when he
went next day to the sixteen-story Pulitzer Building on Park Row
and ascended to the eleventh floor to the offices of the most influential newspaper in New York. Bill Nye had moved to the city
in 1887 to become a columnist for the *World,* which he had said
at the time was the "largest paper in America with a circulation of
252,000." [41] By now its circulation figure was 400,000 (more than
double that of its nearest competitor among morning papers, while
the *Evening World* ran neck and neck with its rival, Hearst's
Journal). It was on this day that, financially speaking, Porter
"arrived" as a writer. In a little less than an hour he emerged from
Hersh's office with a contract to supply the Sunday magazine section with a weekly story at $100 per story. During 1903, his best
year as a writer up to now, he had never averaged more than $200
a month. Now, in addition to a comfortable income, the value of
his name among editors would steadily increase. From this point on,
all of his stories were signed O. Henry. Clearly Gilman Hall did not

exaggerate when he said that Porter was "jubilant" over his new contract.

Within a short time he moved across Madison Square to a house on East Twenty-fourth Street opposite the Metropolitan Life Building.[42] Here he had roomier quarters—a bedroom and a sitting room —although his window looked out on a sunless back yard adorned with a lone ailanthus tree. He had visited Pittsburgh in September (encountering "Smoke, soot, gloom, rain, hordes of philistines and money-changers in all the temples"),[43] and he was regularly sending the Roaches money for Margaret's upkeep. (After she entered Belmont College in 1905 he sent her more than $1,000 a year.) [44] At this time he began to expand his social life. To the end of his life he moved only in a small and grudgingly enlarged circle, but it was not until the end of 1903 that he had even a small circle of friends. It was at this time that he met Anne Partlan, a woman who became one of the three or four close friends he made in New York. To Miss Partlan, a thirty-year-old career woman who in addition to her job in advertising had published short stories about the laboring class, Porter remarked on being introduced: "When I read 'Among Themselves,' I resolved some day to camp on your territory." [45]

Once Anne invited Porter to a dinner she was giving for a group of department-store employees. "He leavened their shop talk," she remembered, "with genial, simple expressions of mirth as they told their tales of petty intrigue and strife for place amid the antagonism and pressure which pervades the atmosphere of every big organization. On leaving he remarked to me, 'If Henry James had gone to work in one of those places, he would have turned out the great American novel.'" On another occasion Porter accompanied Anne and her father (a mechanic and inventor of blacksmith's tools) to a convention of master workmen, where he listened respectfully to speeches about side-hill plows, bolt cutters, rock chisels, and the like. After Anne's father had made a talk explaining how he had perfected a hammer for forge use, the audience applauded and Porter shook hands with him, saying, "Tom, I would give anything if I were as valuable a man as you are." Relaxing completely in such an atmosphere, where nothing was expected of him or known about him, he joined in the dancing that followed the speeches. In Anne's words, he "threw himself into the spirit like a boy. He danced and whistled and called out numbers, laughing heartily when in the maze of a wrong turn. No one there dreamed he was other than a fellow-working man." [46]

Among people of his own walk of life Porter kept up his guard, only relaxing up to a point under the influence of alcohol. A typical reminiscence is that of John Seymour Wood, who described the evening on which he met Porter in the popular German restaurant known as Allaire's or Scheffel Hall (the establishment which Porter was to call the Old Munich in his story "The Halberdier of the Little Rheinschloss"):

I recall that . . . he was very retiring and reticent and almost morose, until the third or fourth stein [presumably not unaccompanied by something stronger], when he became jovial, and, I may say, vaude-villian. He seemed to me like a star artist from the Varieties. . . . He made puns. He used slang, localisms; he seemed the very opposite of Whiteing [Robert Rudd Whiteing, who had introduced Porter to Wood and his friends], who preserved the tone of a cultivated college man. . . . He was well-bred—country well-bred. He had the polish of rusticity— perhaps he assumed it as did Artemus Ward. [47]

This last quality was commented on by another acquaintance too, H. C. Greening, who remembered Porter as a man who "always looked and acted 'small town' and would have been at home in a town. The part where he lived is like a small town, anyway." [48]

The section Greening meant was Irving Place, to which Porter moved after a few months on East Twenty-fourth Street. He moved, he told Duffy, because the man of the house did most of the housework—a species he was to caricature in "Ulysses and the Dogman"—and he had seen enough of such men without living under the same roof with one.[49] Irving Place, which runs from Fourteenth Street to Gramercy Park at Twentieth Street, in those days had a secluded, tranquil air which made its name appropriate. At Number 55—a narrow brown front of four stories presided over by an efficient Hungarian landlady named Jaffe, whose husband ran a neighborhood laundry in the basement—Porter rented the front parlor, with its wide bay-window and marble mantel and glass-beaded chandelier; there was also a rear alcove, in which a bathtub was installed at Porter's expense.

It had been on Williams's recommendation that Porter moved to Irving Place, and it was Williams who introduced him to the neighborhood, beginning with Gramercy Park, which with its high iron fence and locked gates was the resort by day of nurse-maids with small children, and by night of privacy-seeking young couples. At Seventeenth Street and Third Avenue was Scheffel Hall, a high-vaulted, smoky-raftered family resort famous all over the city for good food and drink. At Seventeenth Street stood the reputed city home of Washington Irving, before which Porter is quoted by Williams as having commented, "A fellow kinda feels like wearing his hat in his hand when he stands here, doesn't he?" [50] At Sixteenth Street the staid Westminster Hotel, with its quiet, unfrequented bar, had been one of the stopping places of Dickens in New York. On Fifteenth Street the Hotel America was a gathering place for Latin Americans (Porter described them in "The Gold That Glittered," in which the hotel is called El Refugio), who congregated here "to lay counterplots, to bide their time, to solicit funds, to enlist filibusters, to smuggle out arms and ammunitions, to play the game at long taw. In El Refugio they find the atmosphere in which they thrive." [51] Irving Place came to an end amid the tawdry honky-tonks of Fourteenth Street, including such attractions as Billy McGlory's famous bawdy house, Tony Pastor's vaudeville theater, and Tom Sharkey's saloon with its sign-painter's wall-sized rendering of the Sharkey-Jeffries fight (an object of art about which Porter wondered "whether it was the work of one of the crews which did the 'Battle Axe Plug' posters through the Southwest during the early Nineties").[52]

It was while living in Irving Place that Porter became the O. Henry of fact and legend, the O. Henry whose stories suggested to his friends the role in which he is familiarly pictured—that of the Caliph of Bagdad-on-the-Subway. When he set up headquarters in Irving Place, his contract with the *World*—in the words of his friend Robert H. Davis—"enabled him to establish himself in what he called 'the business of caliphing,' and to indulge in the vagaries and extravagances appropriate to the generous-handed role. Figuratively, he was in a position to toss about his 'purses of gold.' In the years from 1904 to 1907, O. Henry was Haroun in his golden prime." [53]

CHAPTER TEN

· ❦ ·

In February, 1904, the *Critic* published an announcement which the editors clearly regarded as something of a scoop and as a matter of considerable interest to their readers:

Less than a year ago the readers of popular magazines began to be startled and delighted by certain fantastic and ingenious tales, mainly dealing with Western life and bearing the strange device "O. Henry" as a signature. In a short time people began to talk to each other about the stories, and very soon they began to ask who the author was. It was then that a new problem fell upon this over-puzzled age,—who is "O. Henry"? No one seemed to know the author's real name, and immediately vague and weird rumors began to be afloat and the *nom de guerre* was soon invested with as much curiosity as surrounds an author after his decease. But, like most mysteries, when it was probed there was no mystery about it. "O. Henry's" real name is Mr. Sydney Porter, a gentleman from Texas, who having seen a great deal of the world with the naked eye, happened to find himself in New York about two years ago and there discovered a market where people would buy stories of his experiences. Being of a lazy disposition he very naturally quitted active life and took to his desk. He signed the name "O. Henry" merely because he did not take his real self seriously as a maker of fiction. He really does shun notoriety—a most unusual characteristic among present-day writers—and he disclaims any intention of having purposely created a mystery about his identity. But he is still not too old to become a professional.[1]

Along with this disclosure—the first in a widely read magazine—appeared a photograph of Porter in his Austin days, with curled-up mustaches.

Presumably it was this magazine which came to the attention of Judge E. P. Hill, owner of the Houston *Post* at the time Porter joined the staff in 1895, the man from whom Porter had borrowed the $200 he needed to engage legal counsel. At any rate, on August 26, 1904, Porter wrote the following reply to a letter from Hill:

MY DEAR JUDGE:

Your very kind letter was delivered to me by "Everybody's Magazine." I haven't neglected to reply; but I have been working day and night to complete a book which McClure's will bring out in the fall, and have actually been unable to find the time.

I haven't acquired success yet, but I am living, and hope to do better a little further along. I am living here very quietly, not mixing with people much, and working hard. The picture of me that you saw in a magazine was inserted without my knowledge or consent. I am not advertising myself. If I were I would not write over a pen name.

I very much appreciate your generous letter, and I am glad to hear from you for another reason. I have reason to believe that my book will bring me in some money, and with the first surplus over my living expenses I intend to settle up some old debts. Yours I have not by any means forgotten, and it comes among the first.

Will you be kind enough to let me know if Fort Davis is your permanent address, so I can reach you when that hoped-for time comes?

Thanks again for your good words and wishes, and for favors in the past.

Yours very truly,
W. S. PORTER.[2]

These two documents point up the dominant aspect of Porter's life in New York. None of those who knew him expressed the matter so succinctly as John D. Barry: "I never knew a writer and a man so different. It seemed, at times, as if, in his case, they could not be one and the same. The only link between them was the wit that flashed both in the printed page and in the everyday speech." [3] Porter was never able to escape or resolve this duality. "Some day," he once remarked to Robert H. Davis, "I'll tell you how I fell heir to enough spare time to take up fiction seriously." This was the closest he ever came—except on one memorable later occasion—to speaking openly about his prison experience. Apparently he started to tell Davis on the spot, but could not quite manage it, saying instead: "Let me write it to you. The story can be told in four lines." A week later Davis received the following communication:

Davis's curiosity was only whetted by the little document,[4] with its fluent upper signature contrasting so pointedly with the crude, anonymous mark of the self he hid from the world. Assuming, however, that Porter had revealed all he felt able to reveal, Davis asked no questions, and neither of them ever mentioned the matter again. All of Porter's friends sensed that there was a line which they must not cross. As Richard Duffy put it, Porter "never wanted a man to think he knew him so well he could slap him on the back." Duffy told of standing one day looking into a bookstore window with Porter when a man stopped beside them and slapped Porter on the back, exclaiming, "Hello, O. Henry!" Porter responded politely enough, but afterward he asked Duffy who the man had been. "Why, don't you know him?" Duffy said. "He's Soandso, the publisher." Sardonically Porter replied, "Oh, is he? I almost said to him, 'Name, please.' "[5] Before the end of Porter's life some of his friends discovered the nature of the barrier which he had set up between himself and others, but they did not know how to break it down. In Will Irwin's words:

Why didn't someone speak out? Why did we all keep up the polite pretense of ignorance? How different it might have been. Why didn't one of us go to him and say, "Bill, we know all about it and it doesn't

172

make the slightest difference. If you ever owed a debt to society you've paid it in full. At that, maybe it was an unjust debt. But that's all past. What counts is that every man in the crowd, every man with whom you go to dinner, or with whom you take a drink at the bar, knows all about the years at Columbus, and no one cares a damn. You're the only person who thinks about it; nobody else does. We like you and we respect you. You're O. Henry. You're doing great work. That's the only thing that counts. Snap out of your mood. Stop trying to hide yourself from strangers for fear of running across someone with a knowledge of a secret that is no secret at all. Stiffen your shoulders and once and for all throw off your Old Man of the Sea.[6]

Just when and how the facts of Porter's past leaked out among some of those who knew him (not all of them by any means, despite Irwin's statement), there is no way of saying. The astonishing thing is that—with his picture and his Texas connections publicized in print by 1904—the truth was not much more widely known. As is indicated in the episode with Davis, he must have longed to have the whole business out in the open and done with. Instead he fabricated for himself a new chronology, which omitted the three prison years and two more years for good measure. In the interview he granted to George MacAdam in 1909, he said that he had been born in 1867, and he omitted all of the events of his Austin residence, saying that after two and a half years on Lee Hall's ranch he had gone to Houston, first to work on the *Post* and afterward to edit the *Rolling Stone* until he went to Central America to try the fruit business with a friend. Back in Texas, he said, he had worked for two weeks in a drugstore in Austin, then gone to New Orleans and begun writing stories. "After drifting about the country," he concluded with strategic vagueness, "I finally came to New York about eight years ago."[7]

Paradoxically, then, Porter was still a man in hiding (who was seriously annoyed when his friends forgot and introduced him to strangers by his real name), although by 1904 he had become a well known writer, whose pseudonym was to become during the next half-dozen years probably the most widely familiar literary name in America. Alphonso Smith tells of meeting on a train a businessman of the type Sinclair Lewis was later to name Babbitt, whose conversation immediately became stiff and unnatural when

173

he learned that Smith was a professor. He remarked, dutifully, that Emerson was a very "elegant" writer, and after a pause, that Prescott was also a very elegant writer, was he not? After another awkward pause, Smith asked, "Did you ever read O. Henry?" The man's manner changed instantly. "Professor," he answered feelingly, "that's literature, *that's literature, that's* REAL LITERATURE." [8] A different level of enthusiasm is illustrated in John S. Reed's anecdote about looking at a volume of O. Henry in a bookstore window one day when he was a Harvard freshman. "A quietly dressed, unimpressive man with a sparse, dark beard came up and stood beside me. Said he suddenly: 'Have you read the new one?' 'No,' I said. 'Neither have I. I've read all the others, though.' 'He's great, don't you think?' 'Bully,' replied the quietly dressed man; 'let's go in and buy this one.'" The man was William James.[9] Still another kind of testimonial came from Theodore Roosevelt, who remarked some years after Porter's death, "It was O. Henry who started me on my campaign for office girls." [10] Summing up the general feeling in 1916, William Lyon Phelps bracketed O. Henry with Irving, Poe, Hawthorne, Bret Harte, Stevenson and Kipling.[11]

The unlikely object of such acclaim was, in person, the self-effacing neighbor on Irving Place of *World* reporter William Wash Williams, who has written a vivid account of their relationship. Though soon to be one of the best-known literary figures in New York, Porter was lonely enough to welcome the friendship of a naïve young man fifteen years his junior, with whom he spent many evenings at "The Club," as the nearby Healy's saloon was called by the group who hung out there at night. (Porter renamed it "Con's," in his story "The Lost Blend," the allusion being to Cornelius Delaney, the night bartender.) Here gathered in the evenings a haphazard group, including one or two idle cabbies from the livery stable across the street, a few small-time actors of middle age, some newspaper men and other young hopefuls still at loose ends in the big city, a shoemaker from Sicily, and the "Professor," a quiet little German who taught his language to a few private pupils and acted as janitor for a small Lutheran church nearby. Amid the aimless talk and moderate drinking which served to occupy

174

an evening in Healy's, Porter sat silent but convivial: "he drank as the Southern gentleman he was," Williams comments, "and carried his liquor as a gentleman does." [12] Whether brooding over his glass in Healy's or walking speculatively about the city with his young friend, Porter talked little (he apparently wanted from the relationship merely the proximity of a fellow human being), and when he did talk there was no sparkle. He clearly made an effort to confine himself to the idiom of his companion.

"Bill," Williams quotes him as saying once, "writing stories is my business . . . , it is my way of getting money to pay room rent, to buy food and clothes and Pilsener. I write for no other reason or purpose. There's nothing in that fame business, Bill. . . . I wouldn't give a plugged nickel for a whole barrel of it." [13] On another occasion he grumbled about some "literary people" with whom he had spent an evening: "When it comes to spending a whole evening discussing literature, I'm stopped, flabbergasted, and ruled off the field. I can't chip in a sentence and have to sit there like a dummy with everything going over my head like a Sixth Avenue elevated train. What do I know about literature, or care!" [14] That these were not Porter's true feelings is fairly obvious. In certain other circles the level of his conversation was somewhat higher than that of the sort of typical remark with which he enlivened his evenings with Williams between periods of "comfortable" silence: "Peanuts," Porter observed while they sat on a park bench one night sharing a bag of them, "are good for you, Bill, if you chew them well. And when a fellow has been drinking a lot of stuff he ought to eat them, for they give the liquor something to work on besides his stomach." [15]

A more perceptive acquaintance thought that "Porter really wanted to mix with men of his own ability," as was evidenced later by his abortive scheme to get together a round table of writers and artists at the Brevoort. Yet Porter never ventured to associate with his equals. "He . . . always acted as if he didn't give a damn if school kept or not," continued the acquaintance, whose own opinion was "that O. Henry's somewhat furtive manner was the result of heavy drinking—it was *exactly* that manner." [16] His seeming refusal to take himself or the world seriously was part of the role he had set himself to play; no doubt it was aided and abetted by his steady intake of alcohol, but it had its origin in the dilemma which produced the need for alcohol.

Stubbornly Porter limited his circle of friends almost exclusively to the series of editors who happened to become involved with his work. Invariably he fled from formal affairs and group activities. Once he was enticed on an all-day picnic on Long Island for staff members of the *World* magazine section. He made the trip, partook of the lunch, and even made retorts-in-kind to the bantering that was the order of the day, but during the ball game which followed lunch he disappeared. When Alexander Black, then *Sunday World* editor, made inquiry some days later, Porter, "with suddenly enkindled embarrassment," explained: "You know, I found a wonderful road." According to Williams, the wonderful road was no doubt the railroad back to the city, and Black's comment on their conversation was: "It would have been cruel and fruitless to ask further. He was always finding wonderful roads—one-man roads." [17] On another occasion—a boat trip up the Hudson to Albany with the Periodical Publishers Association—"he did not share in the festival spirit. Writer after writer was brought up to him for a handshake and a word of greeting. He stood it all, half-bored and half-scared, until the boat reached Poughkeepsie, when he eluded his friends and escaped, to take the next train back to New York." [18] Consistently he declined the invitations he received to out-of-town weekend parties where the guests were distinguished figures in society and the arts. As a protective device he even resorted to an Artemus Ward air of rusticity: a woman who once insisted on introducing him to a friend told him afterward, "You mortified me nearly to death, you were so ungrammatical." [19] Robert H. Davis regarded his fastidiousness in dress—his invariable gloves and gold-headed cane—as a kind of protective armor. Another editor-friend, William Johnston, summed up the matter when he commented that "each time I read some new recollection of an 'intimate friend of O. Henry's,' I always picture his ghost sitting somewhere over a celestial highball—they must have highballs there or it wouldn't be heaven for him—smiling sarcastically. For Sydney Porter, gentle, lovable, talented though he was, had no intimate friends." [20] A vivid impression of Porter the solitary is furnished by Will Irwin:

He had the faculty of sitting perfectly silent and yet of stimulating the talk rather than deadening it. And about once in ten minutes he would throw in a remark, delivered in his low, apologetic Southern voice, which went straight to the heart of the thing.

It was then, I suppose, that a clever stranger would have recognized a big man in this suppressed, middle-aged person who sat so quietly in the corner and was yet the head of every table at which he sat.[21]

The only kind of social life into which he entered without restraint has been described by Art Young, who accompanied his brother, William W. Young, to a casual gathering at 55 Irving Place. When he entered the large front room with its bay window, he identified Porter as the man in shirt sleeves mixing drinks at the sideboard (Mamie Taylors, he called them: a mixture of Scotch and ginger ale). Porter at this time was a man of medium height with a heavy chest and not much neck, slightly florid, with rounded features and no sharp angles anywhere, neat at shirt cuff and collar, with an expression of sad gentleness; he spoke quietly, with a Southern accent and less bass in his voice than would have been expected —"altogether a likeable, extremely modest man, with a natural courtesy and a beautiful wit." [22] In conversation, according to Young, Porter liked to "O. Henryize" the sort of familiar story which was going the rounds—for example, the one about the man in the upstairs room who was too slow about dropping his second shoe on the floor. Unfortunately, Young does not reproduce the story, nor does he enlarge on his statement that Porter was an excellent mimic; instead he describes another evening when Porter took him along on a visit to a Bowery dance hall, where he sat smoking and fingering his glass, "smilingly absorbed in the scene," so that Young surmised he was storing away impressions for a story. His wit has been commented on too frequently to be doubted. Clearly the degree of his taciturnity depended on the company present.

Porter preferred most of all to combine business with pleasure by exploring the city with Williams or one of his editor-friends. As he himself later put it, "I used to walk at all hours of the day and night along the river fronts, through Hell's Kitchen, down the

Bowery, dropping into all manner of places and talking with anyone who would hold converse with me." [23] One of his favorite places was Koster and Bial's, at Sixth Avenue and Twenty-fourth Street, where the cancan dancers showed their frilly drawers and where the better class of prostitutes hung out. Porter liked to gather a group of these girls at his table and play the chivalrous host to them, so that one night when Williams was alone in the café one of the girls inquired of him, "Where's your nut friend this evening?" When Williams protested at the word, the girl explained: "Well, you know he never offers to take one of us girls out—simply wants to talk to us here and buys us drinks—but he pays us just the same. He always slips each girl around the table a bill before he leaves." [24]

Another hangout was the notorious Haymarket, a place run on somewhat freer lines than Koster and Bial's: women did not have to wait to be invited to a man's table but could seek out their companions openly. It was to the Haymarket that Porter and Williams once took a young innocent from the Midwest, who ordered lemonade and settled down to study (a bit overzealously) the ways of sin in the big city. Finally, seeing nothing to shock him on the dance floor or among the groups at the surrounding tables, he inquired with some disappointment, "Is this all there is to it?" Entering into the spirit of the occasion, Porter invited several unattached women over to their table, one of whom the young man singled out for an inquisition. "You don't look like the kind of a girl that belongs in a place like this," he told her. "Have you been coming here long?" His blunt questioning—asked in the spirit of a curious visitor at a zoo—became too much for Porter, who leaned over to whisper to Williams: "Let's get out of here, Bill. The fellow is not only a simpleton, but an ass." [25] To women of whatever class Porter was unfailingly courteous. And, it might be added, he had learned the hard way to respect the dignity and the privacy of his fellow human beings, whatever their outward circumstances might be.

The first decade of the century was the heyday of vaudeville and musical comedy, of which Porter studied all levels, from the clean bill offered at Tony Pastor's or Keith and Proctor's, to the burlesque shows at the Dewey. One of the most notorious performances of the time was that of the "Girl in Blue," who in her strip act on a trapeze (stripping went down only to tights in those days) removed her fancy garters and tossed them down to the men in the audience: a performance Porter commemorated in his story "The Memento." Nor was his knowledge confined to that of a spectator. The garter girl in his story speaks very convincingly of "the kind of men we stage people have to be up against. You know what the game is to us—it's a fight against 'em all the way down the line from the manager who wants us to try his new motor-car to the bill-posters who want to call us by our front names. . . . *When you know one man you know 'em all!*" [26] Despite his familiarity with such matters, Porter was said by all of his friends never to have told an off-color joke. As Williams put it: "He wouldn't tolerate a story which wasn't clean or lend an ear for a minute to any stag discussion of women. He would walk out on the party the instant it took such a turn; and all of the regulars in Healy's knew it and respected him the more." [27]

The midtown bowling alleys and shooting galleries were also familiar haunts of Porter's. One friend has told of being taken to one of the Seventh Avenue underground ranges for a contest of skill after he had won a rifle competition which had been written up in the newspapers. Porter watched his friend's shooting, praised it, then put on a memorable exhibition of "string shooting" with a revolver (cutting a string on which was tied a weight to be swung back and forth). Expert shot though he was (the proprietor of the range said he was one of the best pistol shots he had ever seen), Porter always visited the shooting galleries at a late enough hour to avoid witnesses; and once, after the same friend had talked about his prowess, he protested jokingly but in clear earnest: "Please don't tell folks I can shoot. My reputation's bad enough as it is, and besides somebody might try to get me on the police force." [28]

Wherever he went, Porter paid his way with the lavishness of a man not sure of his position. It would not be fair, of course, to deny Porter's very real kindness and generosity, but his handling of money at this stage of his life calls for explanation. He had heavy obligations both to Margaret and to the Roaches, not to mention all the Texas friends who had advanced him money at various times, but such claims weighed lightly on his mind. After Porter's death

179

his father-in-law said that he had recognized his indebtedness and "was going to pay," that in fact he once offered to send $200. His father-in-law told him to wait until he could send $700—apparently needed by the Roaches for some purpose—and that was the last they heard of the matter.[29] As always, his intentions were the best in the world, but his sense of the value of money was still that of a child. Instead of making payments on his debts, he gave away money so freely that he was chronically in need of advance payments from his various publishers. His tips were proverbial—often larger than the amounts of the bills—and the extent of his charities would be hard to estimate. There is the familiar story, for example, about the tramp into whose hand he slipped a bill one evening while walking with a friend on the East Side. After a moment the tramp caught up with them again to hold out the money with an apologetic explanation: "You made a mistake. You gave me twenty dollars." Porter pushed the man aside with the brusque retort: "Who told you I made a mistake. Be off." [30] Such episodes are plentiful in the reminiscences of his friends, and Williams reports a standing account which Porter maintained with a neighborhood doctor for the indigent patients he sent to him.

He would send them around to my office [the doctor is quoted as explaining] with his card, on which was written a request that I take care of them, in that whimsical style of his. . . . Then every once in a while he would appear and hand me ten or twenty dollars without a question as to how our account stood. . . . I saw him only a short time before his death and he handed me twenty dollars. I told him, at the time, that I didn't believe he owed me anything and was loath to take the money. "Never mind, Doctor," he said, "if I don't owe it to you now, I will." [31]

On one occasion, Williams reports, Porter expressed indignation over the deceit which had been practiced on him by "a girl I've known for some little time," who had told him an elaborate story about a sick mother in order to get fifty dollars from him. "Anybody can have my money any time," he said to Williams. "They don't have to lie to me to get it; just say they want it, that's enough. I'm an easy mark and I know it, but that's my own business." [32] On another occasion he insisted on lending Williams money to pay

180

his room rent, saying, ". . . when one of us is up against it and the other is making money, the fellow who needs a lift has a right to go to his flush friend and *demand* that he help him out—not ask but demand. . . . Bill, if friendship doesn't mean that, it doesn't mean anything." [33] One of Porter's favorite charities in the Irving Place days was the bed line which he described in "The Fifth Wheel":

The ranks of the Bed Line moved closer together; for it was cold, cold. They were alluvial deposit of the stream of life lodged in the delta of Fifth Avenue and Broadway. The Bed Liners stamped their freezing feet, looked at the empty benches in Madison Square whence Jack Frost had evicted them, and muttered to one another in a confusion of tongues. . . .

Standing on a pine box a head higher than his flock of goats, the Preacher exhorted whatever transient and shifting audience the north wind doled out to him. It was a slave market. Fifteen cents bought you a man. You deeded him to Morpheus; and the recording angel gave you credit.

. . . Now and then, shyly, ostentatiously, carelessly, or with conscientious exactness one would step forward and bestow upon the Preacher small bills or silver. Then a lieutenant of Scandinavian coloring and enthusiasm would march away to a lodging with a squad of the redeemed. All the while the Preacher exhorted the crowd in terms beautifully devoid of eloquence—splendid with the deadly, accusive monotony of truth.[34]

According to Williams, after they had listened awhile, Porter would say: "Well, got enough? Let's be going." And unobtrusively he would hand the preacher some money—enough, Williams surmised, for the entire line to have lodging on that particular night.[35] Among many other statements, one by Anne Partlan (who, with the possible exception of Gilman Hall, was Porter's closest confidant at this time) deserves quotation. Porter, she said, "had the compassion of Christ for the suffering. . . . He used to say, 'I know how it is.' That was his gift." [36]

Porter seems paradoxical from almost any angle of approach. Just as he gave away money freely, even recklessly, in the face of debts which he never paid, so his well known concern for the underpaid shopgirl seems to have contained contradictory elements.

In perhaps the best known of his many stories on the subject ("An Unfinished Story"), the narrator finds himself, on judgment day, standing near a prosperous-looking group of spirits.

> "Who are they?" I asked [of a celestial policeman].
> "Why," said he, "they are the men who hired working-girls, and paid 'em five or six dollars a week to live on. Are you one of the bunch?"
> "Not on your immortality," said I. "I'm only a fellow that set fire to an orphan asylum, and murdered a blind man for his pennies." [37]

On the other hand, in one of his rare moments of complete candor Porter remarked about the same story, "The real Dulcie was a shop girl in Wanamaker's and she did turn Piggy down. And Piggy—I was Piggy." [38] In the story Dulcie is temporarily rescued from a dinner date with Piggy, a character who

> needs but a word. When the girls named him, an undeserving stigma was cast upon the noble family of swine. The words-of-three-letters lesson in the old blue back spelling book begins with Piggy's biography. He was fat; he had the soul of a rat, the habits of a bat, and the magnanimity of a cat. . . . He wore expensive clothes; and he was a connoisseur in starvation. He could look at a shop-girl and tell you to an hour how long it had been since she had eaten anything more nourishing than marshmallows and tea. He hung about the shopping districts, and prowled around in department stores with his invitations to dinner.

Porter is said to have had many light affairs with girls of easier virtue than Dulcie, and evidently he despised himself for being reduced in matters of sex to a social level where his conquests could be construed as preying on the underprivileged.

Another of his contradictions was between what Gilman Hall called his "two antagonistic strains, aristocratic and common. I could tell at a glance whether he had money. If so, he had the manner of a patrician." [39] Without money, he was without self-confidence: he was the man with a past, the disreputable pretender, whose almost histrionic "commonness" was a gesture of his defiance. Jennings once remarked that Porter served two masters, Bohemianism and Convention: he seemed irresponsible and aimless, while at the same time he was grimly purposeful.[40] What is one to say of a personality as paradoxical as Porter's? Surely, in part at least, it was a matter of his inability to face the truth of his past, to take off his mask and show himself to the world as he was. Not daring to undertake anything so drastic, he was hopelessly caught in the toils of his own inconsistencies.

In the words of one friend, Porter's secret "became a prison quite as limiting as the walls of the penitentiary." [41] His inescapable loneliness, as much as the quest for story material, explains his roaming of the highways and byways of New York: he had both a craving to mix with his fellows and a fear of the scrutiny of individual friends. He walked the streets and sat in parks because to return home was to return to a "furnished room," which

received its latest guest with a first glow of pseudo-hospitality, a hectic, haggard, perfunctory welcome like the specious smile of a demirep. The sophistical comfort came in reflected gleams from the decayed furniture, the ragged brocade upholstery of a couch and two chairs, a foot-wide cheap pier glass between the two windows, from one or two gilt picture frames and a brass bedstead in a corner. . . . It seemed that the succession of dwellers in the furnished room had turned in fury—perhaps tempted beyond forbearance by its garish coldness—and wreaked upon it their passions. The furniture was chipped and bruised; the couch, distorted by bursting springs, seemed a horrible monster that had been slain during the stress of some grotesque convulsion. . . . Each plank in the floor owned its particular cant and shriek as from a separate and individual agony. It seemed incredible that all this malice and injury had been wrought upon the room by those who had called it for a time their home; and yet it may have been the cheated home instinct surviving blindly, the resentful rage at false household gods that had kindled their wrath. A hut that is our own we can sweep and adorn and cherish.[42]

Porter's poignant loneliness was sharply felt by Williams, who quotes him as remarking one evening: "I shouldn't be standing here talking to you, Bill. I ought to be in my room right now working like the dickens. . . . But I don't want to go there alone tonight. Come along and sit with me a while, Bill." [43] Even more revealing is the comment of Porter's second wife on his dislike of solitude and of darkness: it was a long-standing habit of his to burn a light all night, dimming it by tying a handkerchief around it (so that many of his handkerchiefs were scorched and had holes in them).[44] A great deal is suggested, too, by Gilman Hall's statement that Porter "was obsessed with the idea of [his story] 'The World and the Door.' They would do anything (throw away love) to get back to civilization. He talked for hours about this theme." [45] The story in question concerns a man and a woman, each supposedly a person with a past, who have taken refuge in Central America. They fall in love, but just before they plan to be married they discover that they are, separately, innocent of the murders which they have thought they committed. Before this startling discovery they have been supremely happy. "They shut the world out and bolted the doors. Each was the other's world. . . . Mrs. Conant was content now for the horizon of that shimmering sea to be the horizon of her life." But after her discovery Mrs. Conant paces the floor of her room for half an hour, after which she calls her maid to inquire whether there is a steamer preparing to leave any point on the coast. On her way to take passage, she stops at the local hotel for a last word with her lover before she abandons him. "But does not the senora know," she is told, "that Senor Merriam sailed on the Pajaro for Panama at three o'clock this afternoon?" [46]

Porter lived in exile from the world, a self-imposed exile from which he never succeeded in escaping and which was the inevitable conclusion to an inner conflict dating back to the family situation of his boyhood. This exile in which he lived had its bearing on his work as well as his life. For all of its emphasis on the facts of life as he saw it around him, in the final analysis his work is never realistic. The surprise endings of his stories are not merely a device: they grew out of a childlike expectation of daily novelty and surprise to break the monotony of adult routine. He could write authentically about a girl who entered Rooney's saloon after midnight, "glanced around with leisurely swiftness, and sat opposite McManus at his table. Her eyes rested upon him for two seconds in the look with which woman reconnoitres all men whom she for the first time confronts." The pair are instantly taken with one another, so much so that when McManus is about to be arrested for knifing a man in a saloon brawl some days before, the girl gives up her pretense of being relatively pure and innocent. She rescues McManus by reminding the policeman of the five-dollar graft which he had accepted from her two hours earlier. "Witnesses saw me give you the money tonight," she informs him, "and last week too. I've been getting fixed for you." [47] But now, after the pair stand exposed to each other for what they really are, McManus walks the girl down the street to a house bearing the name plate "Reverend Jeremiah Jones." Such is the O. Henry portrayal of the course of true love. Consistently marriage is portrayed not as the complicated actuality which Porter himself had experienced, but as a simplified state of sacrificial devotion which might have reflected the mind of a sentimental bachelor. The young couple in "The Gift of the Magi" are O. Henry's archetypal husband and wife. A passage from "The Green Door" sums up the essential spirit of his work:

In the big city the twin spirits Romance and Adventure are always abroad seeking worthy wooers. As we roam the streets they slyly peep at us and challenge us in twenty different guises. Without knowing why, we look up suddenly to see in a window a face that seems to belong to our gallery of intimate portraits; in a sleeping thoroughfare we hear a cry of agony and fear coming from an empty and shuttered house; instead of at our familiar curb a cab-driver deposits us before a strange door, which one, with a smile, opens for us and bids us enter; a slip of paper, written upon, flutters down to our feet from the high lattices of Chance; we exchange glances of instantaneous hate, affection, and fear with hurrying strangers in the passing crowds; a sudden souse of rain—and our umbrella may be sheltering the daughter of the Full Moon and first cousin of the Sidereal System; at every corner handkerchiefs drop, fingers beckon, eyes besiege, and the lost, the lonely, the rapturous, the mysterious, the perilous changing clues of adventure are slipped into our fingers. But few of us are willing to hold and follow them. We are grown stiff with the ramrod of convention down our backs. We pass on; and some day we come, at the end of a very dull life, to reflect that our romance has been a pallid thing of a marriage or two, a satin rosette kept in a safe-deposit drawer, and a lifelong feud with a steam radiator.[48]

For two full years—1904 and 1905—Porter produced a story a week for the *Sunday World*, almost without missing a deadline. The quantity of his output is, in part at least, a measure of his determination to put the past behind him, to transform himself from W. S. Porter into O. Henry. Production in such quantity necessitated writing briefer stories, often merely expanded anecdotes with the characteristic twist at the end: "features," they might almost be called, the weekly assignments of a reporter-at-large sent out to exploit the unexpected ironies of the life familiar to masses of readers who lacked either the time or the inclination for any kind of reading except eyecatching items in their daily newspaper. The elaborately plotted, fully developed stories of Porter's early days gave way to the "typical O. Henry" story. Chattily familiar with the reader, facetiously casual about story structure, always keeping himself in the foreground as the teller of "one more good one," O. Henry became for millions of readers the familiar and eagerly applauded spokesman of the decade.

Counting four stories in 1903 and ten more in 1906, he contributed 113 stories in all to the *World*, which syndicated them all over the country. In addition, he continued to publish in magazines. In 1904, fifteen stories appeared in magazines (making a total of 66 stories published during the year); in 1905, six stories appeared in magazines (making a total of 54 stories for the year). It is an incredible output, not so much from the standpoint of bulk as from the standpoint of inventiveness. In plot making, in mechanical invention—as one of his early critics, O. W. Firkins, rightly observed—O. Henry is not surpassed by any writer in English. Although this is not a faculty of first importance (it was conspicuously lacking in Shakespeare, for example), it is not a matter of the last importance either. "That a half-educated American provincial," Firkins wrote, "should be original in a field in which original men have been copyists is enough of itself to make his personality observable." [49]

The week-to-week routine during these prolific years was no less grueling for Porter's editors than for Porter himself, who was never known to get a story into the hands of an editor until the last possible moment. William Johnston, associate editor of the *World* magazine section and Porter's assigned taskmaster, began each week with a note to his star contributor: "Where is this week's story?" In reply he would receive notice that the story was in progress, with the invariable request, "Can you send me $50 by this messenger?" It did not take Johnston long to learn that he must turn a deaf ear to these requests until at least some portion of the manuscript was in his hands. This fact explains the conspicuous irrelevance of the introductory sections of some of the stories, written as they were to gain an advance payment before an idea for the story had germinated.[50]

Occasionally, when he happened not to be broke, Porter injected variety into his replies to Johnston's weekly reminders. Once he wrote:

What you say? Let's take an evening off and strike the Cafe Francis for a slight refection. I like to be waked up suddenly there by the music and look across at the red-haired woman eating smelts under an original by Glackens.

Another time he wrote:

Being entirely out of tune with the muse, I went out and ameliorated the condition of a shop girl as far as a planked steak could do so.

At one point in their relationship, Johnston, goaded to protest, wrote his contributor a little parable about judgment day, when a weary editor spoke up about a famous author before the bar: "He never kept a promise in his life." In reply Porter wrote:

Guilty, m'lud.
And yet—
Some time ago a magazine editor to whom I had promised a story at a certain minute (and strangely enough didn't get there with it) wrote to me: "I am coming down to-morrow to kick you thoroughly with a pair of heavy-soled shoes. *I* never go back on *my* promises." And I lifted up my voice and said unto him: "It's easy to keep promises that can be pulled off with your feet." [51]

Throughout the period of his *World* contract and afterward, Porter was in similar correspondence with other editors, notably Robert H. Davis, who had become fiction editor of *Munsey's*. (In 1905 *Munsey's* signed with Porter a five-year contract for first reading of all his magazine stories, those accepted to be bought at ten cents a word.) As is indicated in one of his notes to Davis, the pace was already beginning to tell by the end of 1904: "I am taking two kind of dope out of two boxes from old Doc Wildman, a distinguished specialist on 94th St. And I rid up there in a Ridgway-Thayer automobile." He was sleeping well now, Porter went on to report, and would send a story within a few days.

Meanwhile, he wondered: "Got $50 more up there you want to advance to a hypochondriac? Let it be cash if so. I must sell a little part of my soul to buy some bread and sharlot rust. . . . If you ain't got the money let me know, and I will tackle the Philistines."[52]

He continued to communicate his troubles to Davis. "Lend me $15 till Monday? My banker is out of town," he wrote in the spring of 1905, a request which he followed up a couple of weeks later with a manuscript and a further request: "Can you raise the immediate goods for this, and once more rescue little Ruby from certain death?" Early the following year he reported another, increasingly troublesome problem:

My dear Mr. Davis: (ain't that formal?)

It was my intention not to approach you again without the goods; but it is calorified atmosphere once more for yours.

Whereas Justus Files Mormon or any other of the white lights could take a barge for Europe for a month's rest on being proven paretic, I, having no v. m. o. s. (visible means of support) have had to continue treading the winepress, though the exudation of the real juices has been so that you could scarcely notice it at all. . . . I have sat or sot at my desk day after night, and, as Colonel J. W. Riley says, haven't been able to think of a damn word.[53]

Some three months later the familiar tune is played again, in a somewhat graver key:

Listen to the voice of business, with personal regards undiminished, relegated to one side. . . .

I've got to have some money—some to send home and some for expenses. I'm not asking "Munsey's" for it (still less you personally) but I'm going to raise $250 to-day sure. If your magazine doesn't care to advance it I'll have to get it somewhere else, which I won't have the slightest trouble in doing.

Of course I'll have to abandon short story work to do it; but it's a case of "must." I'll have to go up town and make arrangement for a serial right away.

Dropping the short stories will be a big set-back for me, but I've got to have the money; and if your people object to investing it with me I've got to get it where I can.

Please give me a definite final answer at once.[54]

A different approach is illustrated in a note written hardly two months later:

I am a man of dam few words. I want $125 (don't read that a dollar and a quarter). That, in addition to the $150 that I screwed out of the high-browed and esteemed B. Merwin during your absence will make a total of $275 which will be more than covered by the moral and entertaining tale that I agree to have finished and delivered to you all by 10:30 A.M., Aug 27 or perhaps earlier.[55]

The role in which Davis and other editor-friends were cast was the same role which had been filled by the elder Halls in North Carolina, by the younger Halls and the Harrells, Maddoxes, Andersons, and Roaches in Austin, and by Dr. Thomas and others in the Ohio Penitentiary. At no stage in his life was Porter unprovided with benefactor-friends on whose helping hands he could and did lean regularly. Nor did he accept such favors less willingly as he grew older. In his young manhood he had struck Betty Hall as feeling no sense of indebtedness to her family. In New York, as his needs increased and his capacity for work waned, he gradually worked out a pattern of demand. In return for advance payments he promised stories which never got written or, if they did, were sold to other editors for desperately needed additional payments. His situation by 1908 or 1909 is illustrated by the experience of a literary agent, a young woman named Holly. Porter had enlisted her help in 1906 or 1907 when he wanted to sell some stories written by Sara Lindsay Coleman, who in 1907 became his second wife. At the time he had agreed to send Miss Holly one of his own stories sometime. Finally Porter did send her a story, which she eagerly started out to sell. Davis relates the incident vividly:

In the course of the next few hours the bright dreams dissolved. Bob Davis was the first editor to be approached. Eloquently he tossed his hands to high heaven. "He owes me four stories already. Not another cent until he delivers the copy for which he has been paid." In turn other editors were visited; the entire round of the New York magazine offices made. Everywhere the experience was the same; everywhere the suggestion was met by outraged expostulation and reference to debts already incurred. It was late in the afternoon, after having tried every possible market, that Miss Holly returned to her office. There, according to the agreement of the morning, O. Henry called her up. "I couldn't do it, Mr. Porter," she explained unhappily. "I've tried everywhere and it's no use." Reassuring, comforting, came back the gentle suave voice: "Don't let that worry you in the least. You see I made it into a Christmas story, and I've just sold it myself to the New York *Herald*." [56]

Porter's attitude toward money was precisely the same as it had been in the days when he "borrowed" bank funds in Austin. Now, as then, he intended no dishonesty: he simply never learned that money is something to be earned and husbanded, not something to be found growing on trees spaced out providentially but always just short of sufficiently along the road.

During the year 1904, in addition to his $400 a month from the *World*, Porter averaged more than one story a month for the magazines, which by now were paying him at least $100 per story. Even in New York a monthly income of $500 was an ample one in 1904, and the following year the sum must have increased to more than $600. How did Porter run through that much money so consistently that he had a chronic need for fifty-dollar advances for unwritten stories? Fastidious in his dress though he was, moderately extravagant though he may have been about food, steady drinker though he certainly was, still the conclusion seems obvious that he did not spend most of his income on himself.

In the years just before and after his death there were rumors that he had been bled by blackmailers who threatened to tell his daughter of his prison record. Jennings later wrote that Porter told him about being blackmailed at one time by the wife of a prominent broker in New York. "Not a former convict at the penitentiary— none of these, so far as I know, ever bothered him—but a woman of high social class, a woman who had lived in Austin and flirted with Bill Porter in his troubadour days." Porter finally called her bluff, according to Jennings, who added, "Not blackmail, but fantastic liberality kept his pockets empty." [57] Alphonso Smith, after a thorough investigation, came to the same conclusion: "Those who knew him best . . . discredit the theory." [58]

In addition to what Jennings called his "fantastic liberality," Porter's daughter would have accounted for a sizable portion of his income. After Margaret entered a Nashville finishing school called Belmont College (later Ward-Belmont) in 1905, Porter spent more than $1,000 a year on her schooling,[59] in addition to frequent gifts of clothing, and no doubt he spent lavishly on his trips to see her each summer in Pittsburgh. At least once during the Irving Place days Margaret visited him in New York. William Wash Williams remembered being told once that Porter would be out of circulation for a few days, and later being shown a photograph of a sightseeing bus with Porter and his daughter sitting in a rear seat. In an attempt to make up for the orphan's life she had led, he "tried to fulfill Margaret's slightest wish" (according to one of Roach's daughters),[60] and Porter himself once remarked to a friend, "The one purpose of my life is to give my child every possible educational advantage, so she will be well equipped for the battle when her time comes."[61]

Faced with the endless series of deadlines to be met if he was to continue spending on the scale to which he had accustomed himself, Porter kept a small pocket notebook in which he jotted down ideas for stories whenever and wherever they occurred to him. For example, "The Venturers" grew out of the following entry in the notebook:

> Followers of
> Chance—Two
> "Knights errant"
> one leaves girl
> and other marries
> her for what
> may be "around
> the corner"

"The Duplicity of Hargraves" had its origin in this entry:

> Old darkey—dif-
> ference between Yankee
> and Southerner— N.Y.[62]

Many others stories were suggested by experiences in Porter's wanderings about the city. Once, for example, an acquaintance described "the most picturesque bit of rear tenement that remains in New York." Having aroused Porter's interest, he led him down to Greenwich Village, where at the end of Grove Street they found the spot in question. Porter's guide quoted him as remarking, "There is a story there, a story that reminds me of an episode that I was reading a little while ago in Murger's *Vie de Bohème*. . . . It is where the *grisette*, at night, waters the flowers to keep them alive. The lifetime of the flowers, you remember, was to be the lifetime of that transient love." [63] This excursion led to "The Last Leaf." Again, during a dinner at Mouquin's, there was some talk about where and how Porter found his ideas. "I think I'll make a story out of this table," he remarked, singling out the menu for his attention. "Here it is, Colonel," he said after some thought, and he gave his dinner companions a résumé of the story which was to be called "Springtime a la Carte" (1905). An even more familiar story, "The Halberdier of the Little Rheinschloss" (1907), grew out of an alcoholic evening at Scheffel Hall.

Of the most famous story of all, the genesis was haphazard in the extreme. It was to be a Christmas story, and the *World* illustrator was waiting impatiently for copy so that he could begin his work. "I'll tell you what you do, Colonel," Porter told him. "Just draw a picture of a poorly furnished room, the kind you find in a boarding house or rooming house on the West Side. In the room there is only a chair or two, a chest of drawers, a bed, and a trunk. On the bed a man and a girl are sitting side by side. They are talking about Christmas. The man has a watch fob in his hand. He is playing with it while he is thinking. The girl's principal feature is the long beautiful hair that is hanging down her back. That's all I can think of now. But the story is coming." That same day Porter telephoned one of his friends, Lindsey Denison, to come over, and Denison found him busily writing with a needle-sharp pencil on yellow copy paper (the equipment in favor of which he customarily rejected the typewriter). "Lie down there," Porter ordered, pointing to the sofa as he went to the sideboard for refreshment for his guest. "I've got to forget this story and write another one. Have to have it done this afternoon and not a line written. I've thought of an idea for it but I need a living model. . . . I've never met your wife but I think that you two are the kind that would make sacrifices for each other. Now stay on the sofa and don't interrupt." Some three hours later the story was done, and he entitled it, of course, "The Gift of the Magi." [64]

192

Porter's sofa, it seems, was not infrequently occupied by editors come to claim overdue manuscripts on which they had made advance payments. It must have been a nerve-racking procedure to have to finish a story (the beginning of which had sometimes already grown dim in his memory) while the editor grimly waited. Porter had a habit in his *World* days of selling his weekly story to another magazine whenever he managed to get it written ahead of schedule. This meant that a good many of his *World* stories were thought up at the last moment and written in a one-night stint to meet his deadline. Occasionally, in an attempt to get ahead of the game, he would lock his door and write for three or four days straight, having his meals sent in and refusing to see anyone. William Wash Williams, breaking in on him at one of these times, found "a sock-footed laborer, stripped down to undershirt and trousers, like a puddler in a rolling mill, with hair disheveled and face set hard." To Williams's expression of amazement at the speed with which he was able to turn out stories under these conditions, Porter replied: "I have to do it, Bill. I have to get a story off my chest as soon as possible. . . . I have to top it off while my interest is still hot. Once I begin a yarn I must finish it without stopping or it kinda goes dead on me." [65]

But these were the fortunate times. There were others when he chewed his pencil and at the end of hours of work had only a few lines to show. In the main he seems to have written with great facility once he had a story thought out, but (as Gilman Hall told Smith) he often sweated out his plots. He had so much trouble with "The Country of Elusion," for instance, that he allowed Anne Partlan to help him finish it, and on another occasion in the same year (1906) he was reduced to buying from her—for $40—the plot of the story he entitled "The Trimmed Lamp." [66]

In addition to magazine work, Porter was periodically engaged, from 1904 on, in assembling collections of his stories for book publication. Gilman Hall had from the beginning urged him to write a book, and the idea suddenly took fire when in 1904 Witter Bynner, of *McClure's*, suggested that he tie together a series of his Central-American stories with a narrative thread furnished by one of the earliest of them, "Money Maze," so as to make a loose sort of novel out of the collection.

It has been said that about a third of *Cabbages and Kings* was written after Bynner suggested the scheme to Porter.[67] In actual fact, practically the entire book was assembled from stories already in print. The long story "Money Maze" (the chapter bearing the same name in the book has no connection with the earlier story) was broken up into scattered sections which constitute the plot of the book: the theft of the national treasury of Anchuria and the confusion of the absconding President Miraflores with another embezzler, President Wahrfield of the Republic Insurance Company of New York. Of the remaining chapters, only half of "Fox-in-the-Morning," half of "Cupid's Exile Number Two," and all of "Money Maze," "Remnants of the Code," and "The Vitagraphoscope" were written for the book.[68] There was not even much cutting or altering of the previously published stories except for names of persons and places. One of the few passages which were cut for book publication was, characteristically, a pair of sentences from "Rouge et Noir" descriptive of the foreign population of Puerto Rey, mostly "fugitives from some sort of justice—uneasy exiles who watched every incoming steamer with poorly concealed anxiety." [69]

Published by McClure, Phillips, & Co., on November 28, 1904, *Cabbages and Kings* was not the success which Porter and Bynner had hoped for, although there were a number of good reviews. The *Critic* said: "Central America never had a more amusing aspect than in *Cabbages and Kings*." [70] The *Independent*, while feeling that the various episodes did not fuse into a satisfactory whole, assured its readers: "To those to whom this volume comes as an introduction to Mr. Henry, it will prove a delight. . . . Mr. Henry opened up a new province and employed a new manner when he came before the public a few years ago." [71] Most favorable of the reviewers was Stanhope Searles, who wrote in the *Bookman:* "With his stories of life in the Central American republics Mr. Henry is seriously threatening the supremacy of Richard Harding Davis, in a field in which for several years that most widely known writer has been absolutely alone. . . . [The characters] are portrayed with much humour and sympathy and keenness, and behind them you are made to see that wonderful background of white beach and waving palms and sunshine and flowers and fruit and dirt and discomfort. . . . *Cabbages and Kings* is a book of very unusual interest and cleverness." [72] As Searles pointed out, however, the popularity of the book "will necessarily be limited by the fact that it is essentially a man's book—above all the kind of man who at some time of his life has felt the nostalgia strong upon him and yearned to slake his thirst with the drinks of home." And as Gilman Hall later remarked (presumably speaking in financial terms), the book was a "failure."

Even so, by the end of 1904, Porter had not only "arrived" as a writer of fresh and irresistible stories in widely read periodicals. By the publication of *Cabbages and Kings* he was established as an author to be reckoned with by serious reviewers.

CHAPTER ELEVEN

· ᙅᙡᕤ ·

In 1904 a performance of Bernard Shaw's *Mrs. Warren's Profession*
was raided by the police. In 1905 the New York Public Library
discreetly catalogued *Man and Superman* in a reserved section
for special readers. In 1906 Harry Thaw shot Stanford White, who
for some time had been shocking a good many of his fellow townsmen with the kind of parties he gave in his Madison Square Garden
studio. Also in 1906 Maxim Gorky visited New York, bringing with
him as his traveling companion a woman to whom he was not
married: a fact of which the papers made such a scandal that no
hotel in the city would receive the pair. In the same year George
M. Cohan wrote "You're a Grand Old Flag," and in 1907 Anna
Held captivated the town with a song called "It's Delightful to Be
Married."

Except for a passing reference or two to Cohan in his stories,
and a single reference in a letter to Shaw's *Man and Superman*
(a reference which does not make clear whether or not he had
read the play), Porter's writings do not indicate that he had any
connection with the circles in which such events occurred, and
it is characteristic of his stories that people of wealth or position
are never portrayed otherwise than in terms of comic-strip caricature. Except for a handful of editor-friends, his social life remained
as limited as ever.

In addition to Anne Partlan (of whom he did not see a great deal
apparently, close as their relationship was), one of his few non-
editorial associates was Athol's stepsister, Nettie Roach, whom he
had known in Austin and who was now working in New York.

Porter liked to go out with her, and often had her buy clothing to send to Margaret at school. He would sometimes appear at her place of business at closing time and insist on taking her to an expensive restaurant or to the theater, inappropriately dressed though she was. "I made a hundred dollars in fifteen minutes," he would say. "Let's go and spend it." Once, when Nettie was dressed with plumes and a train, Porter kept walking behind her until she protested. "Miss Vanderbilt," he said, "I didn't know whether you would allow me to walk by your side or not." [1] After Nettie began having dates with the man she later married, she would sometimes return home at night to find Porter waiting on her porch. "Well," he said on one such occasion, "I might as well quit coming, as all I can do is sit on the porch and see you come home." [2]

Once Mrs. Roach came from Pittsburgh to visit Porter and her stepdaughter in New York. Playing the lavish host, Porter paid all of her expenses for the trip, only to find himself caught in one of his characteristic dilemmas. According to Mrs. Roach, he was ready to send to one of his publishers "a paper" (doubtless a request for some quick cash) when he discovered that he did not have even enough change to pay the messenger boy. The boy, who must have known Porter, not only gladly gave him credit but returned in a short time to empty his pockets of dimes and quarters, with which he covered the top of a small table, explaining, "I know you need this little change, and you can pay me back just any time you have it." Before Porter could protest, the boy had rushed out. [3]

There is also his personal-column romance with Ethel Patterson, a correspondence which most appropriately of all illustrates the underground aspect of Porter's life. On September 10, 1905, he inserted in the *New York Herald* the following personal:

Two neighborly "literary fellows," 35 and 30, seek social acquaintance of two intelligent, attractive and unconventional young ladies interested in artistic ideas, with a view to mutual improvement and entertainment. Omar. 116 Herald. [4]

Ethel Patterson, herself living alone in a furnished room, was moved to answer. "Indeed I am awfully lonesome," she wrote. "There's only one of me. Take my word for it that it is not nice to be a girl working all alone in a city where you scarcely know a human soul. I am at a point where I talk to elevator boys and car conductors." Asking for particulars about the identity of Omar, she signed herself "A Woman."

In prompt reply, Porter explained about his friend (who remained unidentified throughout the correspondence) and himself:

Weary of the counterfeit Bohemia into which people who "write" are dragged, we sent forth the "Personal" into space with the hope of winging some wild, free creature of the aerial regions above who might prove congenial company in our quiet excursions in search of the (genuinely) romantic and the (reasonably) adventurous.

I came from the saddle of a Texas broncho four years ago to New York. The conventionalities and the routine of the little circle I have been revolving in have about caused me to stampede. The more "people" I meet, the "lonesomer" I get. I can well sympathize with a woman who is lonely in the Big City.

Porter enclosed a picture of himself as well as his card and his address, an act of candor which prompted his correspondent to reply: "It was decent of you, Mr. Porter, to send me your card and address. . . . I don't know whether or not I should show my appreciation by being equally frank. I'm afraid I can't. I shall have to remain a 'paper sport.' Will you let me be unknown to you a little longer? You can't lose much, you see—you literary fellows. But for me—it's so unfairly different." She said that she too was from Texas and that she would like to meet him but didn't quite know how to manage it. "Shall I wear a red rose? Isn't that the proper thing under such circumstances?"

With her problem Porter dealt at length in his next letter. If she was really from Texas, he pointed out, she should know that one was always safe in approaching a Texan's campfire. Even so, he continued (obviously remembering the awkward visit he had made to Mabel Wagnalls's home):

I would have been disappointed, O mysterious "A Woman," if you had revealed yourself and given me permission to "call." I'm glad you didn't do that. These are but wireless signals through space. Why should they be spoiled by a "call"? Why should I add to the awful tedium of your life by sitting on a slippery couch in your "parlor," hitching up my trousers an inch at the knees to preserve the crease (when you weren't looking) and drinking a cup of English breakfast tea (which is no good—always get uncolored Japan), and asking you whether you like "Man and Superman" or the Hippodrome the better.

In an attempt to explain himself he said that he was tired of the "New York bluff," that he wanted a "pal who hates this sort of conventionality, who will be a 'good fellow'—in the best sense of the term—and would like to go about and enjoy the Arabian Nights that can be found here by the true followers of the Commander of the Faithful. *Unconspicuously unconventional*—these two large words seem to hit off the idea."

Although he could not abide self-conscious writers who sat around and gravely read each other their work, he said, he liked the idea of dining at a stylish restaurant and shaking hands with "well-known artists and hungry writers." The next night, though, he would want to explore the East Side, and the next to stay home and read Clark Russell's sea stories. Again he would want to go first to the theater and then to a dance hall, where he could "entice somebody into a corner and inveigle them into telling me THINGS!—the things that make literature if only the editors should let us write 'em." After which he would want to spend another evening at home like a proper descendant of his "Puritan ancestors," writing letters and reading Macaulay's essays. But following out all his impulses as indicated, he said, would still leave him dissatisfied, "because I haven't got a 'pal' to help me enjoy these things." He expressed satisfaction that his correspondent was a brunette (he had admired blondes all his life, he said, and his "judgment and taste" had proved faulty), and he tried to suggest a suitable method for meeting her:

Of course I could walk up Broadway at 7:45 with one shoe off and a fur boa around my neck screaming "Murder!" every thirty seconds. You could come down the street singing "Hiawatha" in a pink kimono and your hair cut short—and so we would know each other. But that is unconventional; isn't it?

Lemme see! I'll tell you.

(This is all new to me. I'm accustomed to lasso ladies to whom I take a fancy, throw them across my saddle, and gallop away, firing my trusty revolver as the horse's hoofs strike fire from the asphalt pavement on the prairie.)

Let them meet, he suggested at the 125th Street and Lenox Avenue subway station (he had previously described himself as resembling, "more than anything else, a retail butcher who is worried about his bills"). He would bring his friend or not, as the lady preferred. They could have a quiet dinner, discussing Shakespeare or the musical glasses. "I lay my hand on the cigars in my upper left hand pocket and assure you that your lightest wish shall rule all the procedure after we meet."

Perhaps the prospect of an actual meeting frightened Miss Patterson. In any event Porter's last letter went unanswered, and the two of them did not meet until two years later, when a mutual friend unknowingly introduced them at a party. Miss Patterson told Porter who she was, and he—then a married man—called her "Miss Terry" when they met from then on.

Although Porter expressed the need for a "pal," he still avoided people. He hardly ever spoke to the other lodgers at 55 Irving Place, though he observed them all closely and had each one ticketed to his satisfaction. With people of the neighborhood whom he could not avoid meeting in his comings and goings, he was "friendly but distant." [5] Though at this time he reread Murger's Vie de Bohème with real pleasure, he shunned the actual bohemian friends he could have had in Greenwich Village. He confined his Village activities to those of a detached and fun-poking observer.[6] There was not even the outlet of churchgoing, an earlier habit of his which had long since been broken. Clarence Cullen, a journalist-friend, wrote that Porter was not a religious man. "He was on the contrary one of the most complete types of the modern world pagan that I ever knew." [7] Except for the evenings he spent with some editor-friend, Porter occupied his time working or sitting at his big bay window watching the passers-by, or else lounging on a bench in Madison Square or Union Square.

He was still in correspondence with Al Jennings (who was now practicing law in Oklahoma and whose literary ambitions he encouraged), and apparently he was genuinely glad to have Jennings come for a visit to New York in 1905.[8] After a preliminary telephone conversation the two met in a bar, Porter arriving in "a handsome gray suit with a rich blue tie, the everlasting glove and cane in his right hand." They sat at a table together, where, after ordering a drink, they "forgot to drink it and sat there shaking each other's hand and nodding to each other like a pair of mutes."

Jennings had just had his citizenship restored by President Roosevelt (having left prison with a pardon obtained for him by Senator Mark Hanna), and still had with him his friend John Abernathy (United States Marshal in Oklahoma and hunting friend of the President), who had helped to bring his case to Roosevelt's attention. Porter, arriving at eleven the following morning after Jennings and Abernathy had been up waiting since six, took the two of them on a "rubberneck wagon," as he called it. Jennings's account of the visit makes it clear that Porter also showed him some of the city's night life during the three weeks. In particular there was the evening when, according to Jennings, Porter conceived the idea for his story "The Furnished Room." In a cheap bar the two men had picked up two girls, "pretty, shabby, genteel, the stark, piercing glare of hunger in their eyes." They took the girls to Porter's room, where Porter ordered in an ample meal and, with a towel over his arm, acted as waiter while the girls ate and talked about what had brought them to their low ebb. One of them—Sue, Jennings calls her—had come from Vermont with a friend named Sadie, looking for a career in the theater. Finally Sue, unable to stand it any longer, went out "to git some grub." But Sadie would not join her, for Sadie was in love with a farm boy back home who had vowed he would come and get her if she did not make good in the city, a boy she kept expecting to arrive every day. When Sue returned after two weeks, with enough money to pay her friend's fare home, she found that Sadie had finally given up hope. "Took the gas route," Jennings quotes Sue as explaining, "in that very room where we used to stay." [9]

Jennings found Porter subject to violent extremes of mood, gay and full of quips one evening but next day sunk in the depths of despondency, as on the afternoon when he sat at his desk unresponsive to Jennings's arrival. Jennings was about to leave when Porter finally spoke. He was holding a photograph of his daughter, which he said he wanted to give to Jennings. "If anything should happen to me," he said, "I think I'd feel happy if you would look after her." [10]

It was during this visit, presumably, that Jennings asked one day, while Porter was shaving and they were talking of the old days in Columbus, "Bill, what did you fall for?" To which Porter replied, looking at him quizzically: "Colonel, I have been expecting that question, lo, these many years. I borrowed four from the bank on a tip that cotton would go up. It went down and I got five." (Jennings professes, however, to have taken Porter's reply as a mere quip, and to be completely persuaded of his innocence of the embezzlement charge.) [11]

Another event of the year 1905 was Porter's reunion by correspondence with a boyhood sweetheart, Sara Lindsay Coleman, who was still living in North Carolina. On hearing that the well known writer O. Henry was the Will Porter she had known, Sara wrote him: "If you are the boy who once liked a small girl in a green-sprigged muslin dress, and I think you are, when you come to Asheville don't stop there. Ride through the town and keep on riding until you reach a lane to the left. At the end of the lane you'll find a big green pine tree, a white house and me. P. S. I have one of your stories and I love it." [12] The story in question was "Madame Bo-Peep of the Ranches," which had appeared three years before in the *Smart Set*. Porter answered Sara's letter on July 15: [13]

MY DEAR "MISS SALLY":

Just once, if I may—and then I'll try to think of you as Sara.

I was gladder to get your little note than the biggest editor's check I ever saw. Seems to me (after trying very hard) I do remember a small "sassy" girl that used to visit Aunt "Bert". . . . Here is the latest picture of the distinguished Mr. Henry. Does it look anything like the moonstruck little shrimp that used to hang around and bother you so much? I can remember what an awkward, bashful, sentimental, ugly, uninteresting nuisance I was then. No wonder I couldn't make any impression on you! I've improved a good deal since then. In fact, it seems to me that the older I grow, the better looking and more fascinating I become. Of course it doesn't sound just right for me to say so, but if I didn't tell you you mightn't find it out.

In those days I took life mighty seriously and sentimentally. . . . And in after years I learned that life is only a jolly good comedy—for the most part—and I began to enjoy it.

He was sending her, he added, a copy of *Cabbages and Kings*, which she need not feel she must read. "It's just the thing to prop the kitchen door when the wind is in the east."

Sara Coleman, a summer visitor to her aunt's home in Greensboro during Porter's adolescent years, had become something of a writer herself, in addition to teaching school. The *Delineator* had published a series of her local-color stories featuring a mountain boy named Bijie. Her mother, on a visit to Greensboro in 1905, had heard the talk about the local boy who had gone to Texas some twenty-five years ago and had reportedly got into some trouble there and had now turned up as a famous writer. Sara, a spinster of thirty-seven, was interested enough to investigate, and Porter not only replied to her query but continued the correspondence, motivated in part by the same feelings which had led to his correspondence with Mabel Wagnalls and Ethel Patterson and in part by his nostalgia for a past which antedated his trouble in Texas. Evidently he assumed that news of his trial and conviction had not filtered back to North Carolina, and his assumption seems to have been substantially correct.

In reply to Sara's second letter, he dealt with her modesty ("Was it cheeky of you to write to me?" he began) by advising her: "Don't chain up your impulses, dear friend; let 'em skallyhoot around. We don't live more than nine times; and bottles and chains weren't made for people to confine and tie up their good impulses with." He had looked up a recently published story of hers, he said, which was "very sweet and tender." He congratulated her on her work, and advised her to come to New York, where she would be on the ground and could know the editors personally. In conclusion he begged: "Miss Sally, please, please send me that picture of yourself that you mentioned. . . . If your heart hadn't been so hard and cruel you'd have enclosed it before instead of talking about it."

The self-conscious game continued. He addressed her in his next letter, "Dear Lady of the Lavender-Scented Memories," and insisted: "Please send that picture. You have moved to the very last seat in the car and I have picked up my traps and followed you. Will you send it, or are you going to move into the Pullman?" Sara finally submitted to his importunity, but, immediately regretting her decision, insisted in the next mail that he return the picture. In an undated reply Porter said that on his return from a trip (presumably to Pittsburgh) he had found the photograph, which he was not going to return. "What's the matter with it?" he demanded. "It looks all right to me. . . . It has lots of your old expression in it, and although the fool photographer did all he could to spoil it by making you turn your head as if you were looking to see if your dress was buttoned all down the back, it's a ripping nice picture, and you needn't want to be 'any better to look at than the picture.' "

Very clearly Porter's early letters to Sara were those of a man playing the role that he imagined was expected of him. "I need a boss," he wrote. "For the last month I've been so no-account and lazy I haven't turned out a line. I've felt kind of melancholy and dreary and lonesome." He had felt bad enough, in fact, to go again to a doctor (he had told Davis of being under treatment in November or December of the preceding year), and this time he had been advised "to take a trip to Europe or some tablets he had in a box. But none of them knew that what I needed was just somebody to fix a cushion for me on the sofa and tell the gas-bill man I wasn't in." In answer to Sara's question about the prices his stories now commanded, he could not resist telling her, "I get ten, fifteen, sometimes twenty cents a word, and everything engaged long before it's written." He went even further: "Oh, Sally, if you 'knowed' how folks try to get letters from me and can't, you'd appreciate the delightful toil I take in writing to you." But this was an uncharacteristic and momentary lapse from Porter's very real modesty, and is not duplicated in the continuing correspondence.

In April, 1906, Porter's second book was published: *The Four Million,* a collection of stories selected almost entirely from back numbers of the *World.* Approaching the editor for permission to republish the stories, Porter was so diffident that he offered to write the *World* a free story in return for the favor he was asking: an offer which was naturally declined by an editor accustomed to granting such permission as a matter of course. *The Four Million,* containing such favorites as "The Gift of the Magi," "Mammon and the Archer," "An Unfinished Story," and "The Furnished

Room," was well received by the critics, though not so enthu-
siastically as the opinions expressed some years later would lead
one to expect. "These sketches of New York life are among the best
things put together in many a day," the *Critic* said.[14] "The author,"
explained the *Independent,* "thinks that no cold 'Four Hundred'
should limit our interest, as there are at least four million people
in the metropolis who are worth writing about. . . . A bit like
'The Unfinished Story' is of more value than many long and labored
books upon social conditions." [15] The *Bookman,* although preferring
Cabbages and Kings, agreed with the publishers' comparison of
O. Henry with Maupassant: "Beyond this we need say nothing." [16]
The book even attracted the notice of the *Atlantic Monthly,* whose
reviewer wrote:

His stories are pervaded by gentleness. In symbolism and color his
slang need not yield to that of Mr. George Ade; he knows his world as
well, but he sees it with an eye for its beauty as well as its absurdity.
There is imagination as well as vision, and beyond his expert knowledge
of our colloquial tongue he possesses in the background, to be used when
needed, a real style. . . .

[By way of comparison with certain French writers:] Where their tendency is to forget that they are writing stories, to approximate as far as
possible to a literal document, 'O. Henry' does not hesitate to round out,
to fill in, to take advantage of coincidence, in short, to indulge his
reader's weak-minded craving for a little human enjoyment. . . . And
perhaps his picture with its glimmer of arc light and sunshine may be to
the full as true as if it were altogether drawn in India ink and charcoal.[17]

Looking through such reviews with Porter, his friend Hart Mac-
Arthur remarked: "You're a casual cuss. I would feel pretty happy
if any work of mine should ever count for so much." To which
Porter replied, "Train's late for any happiness, colonel." [18]

It was after reviewing *The Four Million* for the Pittsburgh
Gazette that George Seibel heard from one of his associates the
story of the silver dollar which Porter had borrowed when he was
preparing to move from Pittsburgh to New York. Seibel wrote up
the story for the *Gazette,* and three months later, in July, Porter
walked into the newspaper office to introduce himself while on
one of his visits to see Margaret. Delighted at meeting the famous
author, Seibel insisted on taking Porter home to lunch and after-

ward (since he was a member of the Board of Education) out to the auction of a run-down, discarded schoolhouse in one of the suburbs. "I've had a bit of experience in a land office," Porter told him. "I'll be an Eastern capitalist looking for investments, and maybe I can get you a better price by bidding up the property. I always felt I'd like to impersonate a plutocrat, and here's my chance at last." Porter's scheme worked, and the Board of Education was able to sell the property without incurring the loss which the members had feared was inevitable.[19]

During the same summer, back in New York, Porter seems to have been sufficiently struck by a story called "Her That Danced," recently published in *McClure's*, to have expressed a wish to meet the author, a Mrs. Wilson Woodrow. A mutual friend, Archibald Sessions, then editor of *Ainslee's*, arranged a dinner for the three of them at the Café Francis, but Porter when he came was in one of his low moods. Mrs. Woodrow, who had been greatly flattered at the invitation, later wrote that her first impression of him was one of severe disappointment. For fully half of the evening Porter seemed "stolid" and so unresponsive that she "had the miserable feeling that I was a failure as a guest." Then, abruptly and unaccountably, Porter came alive, and in the light of the second half of the evening and of later meetings Mrs. Woodrow wrote: "I am sure that if his table-talk had ever been taken down in shorthand, it would have sounded very much like his written dialogue. . . . His wit was urban, sophisticated, individual. . . . It was packed with world-knowledge, designed to delight the woman of thirty, not of twenty, and yet I never heard him tell a story even faintly risqué. He was the most delightful of companions . . . and his wit never flagged; quite effortless, it bubbled up from an inexhaustible spring." [20]

Porter's humor, Mrs. Woodrow suggested, was—like his formality of manner—a sort of protective armor worn by an extremely sensitive man. Of this hidden self she could only suggest the nature by describing two bare glimpses. At the time of their first meeting, Upton Sinclair's novel *The Jungle* had just been published, and Porter, like herself, was not eating meat after reading the book. On a later occasion they emerged from another restaurant to find rain pouring down to the accompaniment of lightning and thunder. In

the cab that took them home the two of them crouched in appre-
hensive silence, for Porter had not outgrown his terrifying experience at the Halls' ranch in Texas.

Later in the same year or early in 1907 Porter met William
Griffeth, who had succeeded Theodore Dreiser as editor of the
Broadway Magazine and who tried to enlist Porter as a contributor.
This proved a difficult undertaking because of Porter's chronic
indebtedness to a small group of editors who had advanced him
money for future stories. Griffeth, too, later commented on Porter's
initial reserve. But after the ice was broken he found the man more
interesting than his stories—a criticism which suggests what no
one except Porter himself ever put so succinctly: that Porter was
potentially a finer writer than he actually turned out to be, that his
work never really did justice to his talent.

At this stage of his career, as one of his friends later remarked,
if Porter had written twenty-four hours a day with both hands he
could not have turned out a tenth of the work sought by competing
editors. By now, however, his output had already begun to slacken.
During 1907 he published only eleven stories, and writing had become an increasing drudgery. "If I had a prosperous peanut stand
on Broadway," he remarked to Clarence Cullen, "I would never
write another line." [21] As a protective measure against publishers
and readers who tried to seek him out, he moved his lodgings during the summer of 1907. Some time earlier he had left Irving Place
and tried at least two different apartments, one of them being
Gilman Hall's apartment in Waverly Place. He now settled in the
Caledonia Hotel on West Twenty-sixth Street. Here no one could
gain access to him unless known and approved by one of the Negro
bellboys or elevator boys, who formed a sort of bodyguard for him.
"His reluctance to meet strangers," as Cullen put it, "amounted to a
passionate aversion." So well trained was the Caledonia staff in
guarding his privacy that once, soon after his marriage (after which
he kept the Caledonia apartment as a place to do his writing), Mrs.
Porter herself was made to wait until he was consulted and his permission granted.

The correspondence with Sara Coleman had continued into 1907.
"Don't you think you might come up this way sometime?" he wrote

her. "I do so long to see a human, heaven-sent, home-bred, ideal-owning, scrumptious sweet, wholesome woman with a heart." [22] By now Sara seems to have begun to take the courtship quite seriously. "I am sick for a bigger life," her heroine thinks in the fictionalized account she wrote after the death of Porter (who is named Bobby in her story). "Teaching is routine after twelve years. . . . Luxuriously I dive again into the most wonderful box of candy I ever dreamed of; luxuriously I sniff the perfume of the most exquisite flowers I ever saw. Tomorrow when I wear my flowers to church I'll feel like a real princess . . . , your princess, Bobby." [23]

In the late summer of 1907, with the sum of $150 just earned from her writing, Sara decided to make a trip she had long talked about —a visit to see some friends in Boston. On the way back she stopped for several days in New York, where on September 11 (his birthday) she and Porter met for the first time since their childhood romance. Rising to the occasion, Porter played the ardent suitor so vigorously that in the end he convinced himself as well as Sara. He proposed to her. But now he suddenly faced the problem which he would have had to face before now if his earlier intentions had been serious. Sara later told of a conversation which they had on her last night in New York. In a highly distraught condition Porter confessed that he had concealed something from her, something which would make it impossible for her to marry him. Unable to finish what he had begun, he promised to write her the full story as soon as she reached North Carolina. He assumed that this was the end of their engagement.[24]

In such a manner did Porter stumble into the confession which he had longed to make and had once almost made to Robert H. Davis. There was no possibility of backing out of it; he had gone too far for that. So, not in person but on paper and addressing himself to someone hundreds of miles away whom he expected never to see again, he took the plunge. He wrote her the facts of his trial and imprisonment, maintaining of course his innocence of actual wrongdoing. "My husband was not a thief!" Mrs. Porter later replied to a question on the subject. "As long as he lived Will believed he was innocent of the charge that was brought against him. He told me that." [25]

Porter's written confession has been destroyed or lost, as has Sara's reply. It is evident, however, that Sara did not wish to break off their engagement, for in a second letter Porter urged her to think the matter over again from all angles before she committed herself.[26] He assured her of his own love and need for her, but it seems fairly clear that he was motivated less by love than by loneliness augmented by nostalgia for a past which was desirable because he had seemed irrevocably cut off from it. There is, moreover, Anne Partlan's comment, made after Porter's death, that he had loved only one woman in his life—his first wife.[27] Having lived as he had lived since coming to New York, Porter could not realistically have hoped to find—or to give—happiness by marrying any woman, let alone a home-town girl who had reached the age of spinsterhood. The state of his health was enough to deter him, although he seems characteristically not to have faced the fact that by 1907 he was on the verge of a crack-up.

As for Sara, probably an accurate statement of her feelings is contained in her fictionalized version of their courtship (which of course omits all reference to the true nature of her problem at this point): "I have faced it. I love Bobby. . . . Bobby's wife must give. The hands that take into their keeping that precious thing—his genius—what tender, comprehending hands they must be." [28]

The wedding was set for November 27.

CHAPTER TWELVE

· ༺✦༻ ·

Shortly before the wedding, in a letter from Asheville dated merely "Wednesday," Porter asked his best man, Gilman Hall, to help with some of the last-minute arrangements. Sara's mother, he said, was writing to Mrs. Hall, who was to stay at the Coleman home, while Hall and Porter himself would stay at the hotel in town.

(1) Please go to Tiffany's [he continued] and get a wedding ring, size 5⅛. Sara says the bands worn now are quite narrow—and that's the kind she wants.

(2) And bring me a couple of dress collars, size 16½. I have ties.

(3) And go to a florist's—there is one named Mackintosh (or something like that) on Broadway, East side of street five or six doors north of 26th St., where I used to buy a good many times. He told me he could ship flowers in good shape to Asheville. . . . I am told by the mistress of ceremonies that I am to furnish two bouquets—one of lilies of the valley and one of pale pink roses. Get plenty of each—say enough lilies to make a large bunch to be carried in the hand and say three or four dozen of the roses.

I note what you say about hard times and will take heed. I'm not going into any extravagances at all, and I'm going to pitch into hard work just as soon as I get the rice grains out of my ear.

I wired you to-day "MS. mailed to-day, please rush one century by wire."

The story which he was sending, he said, would reduce his overdraft "right smart," but if *Everybody's* was willing he would "mighty well like to run it up to the limit again, because cash is sure scarce, and I'll have to have something like $300 more to see me through."

Would Hall therefore bring along $300 in addition to the $100 to be telegraphed? By way of a honeymoon, Porter explained, he would take Sara to Hot Springs, North Carolina, for a week or ten days. As soon as he got back to New York he would begin to clear up his indebtedness. He was "simply tickled to death that 'you all' are coming," and he added, in response to some further advice which his friend had felt constrained to offer:

I'm right with you on the question of the "home-like" system of having fun. I think we'll all agree beautifully on that. I've had all the cheap bohemia that I want. I can tell you, none of the "climbers" and the cocktail crowd are going to bring their *vaporings* into my house. It's for the clean, merry life, with your best friends in the game and a general concentration of energies and aims. I am having a cedar-wood club cut from the mountains with knots on it, and I am going to stand it in my hallway (when I have one) and edit with it the cards of all callers. You and Mrs. will have latchkeys, of course. . . .
The protoplasm is in Heaven; all's right with the world. Pippa passes.[1]

The wedding seems to have involved all the fanfare and tension of a union of young lovers. When Hall in his role as best man tried to go over the minister's instructions with Porter, he found that he had a traditionally overwrought groom on his hands. "Look here, Gilman," Porter protested, "you and that preacher needn't try to rattle me. I have a ring in every pocket." [2] After the ceremony, which was performed in the Presbyterian church by the Reverend R. F. Campbell, Sara's mother shed the appropriate tears, prompting the ebullient Porter to grasp her by the hand and quip, "I'm so happy to welcome you into the family." This brought an outburst of the sort of laughter which appropriately follows the tears on such occasions; and after being duly made over by the guests, the newlyweds left on their honeymoon.

As is indicated by one of Sara's thank-you notes, dated December 18,[3] the honeymoon was prolonged beyond Porter's estimated week or ten days. The reasons seem to have been less romantic than therapeutic. Sara later told of meeting "a sweet old lady" at the hotel, with whom she once entered the billiard room to find Porter, by himself, idly practicing his shots. The new acquaintance remarked, "It must be very dull for you here," to which Porter replied with quiet sincerity, "These are the happiest days I've had in many years." For a number of years he had never allowed himself the luxury of a real rest, and during the weeks they stayed in the solitude of Hot Springs he kept repeating: "Do you find it too quiet? Would you like to stay another week?" [4] Over and above the tiredness which Sara sensed, Porter had a sick spell at Hot Springs (he was beginning to have these attacks with premonitory frequency). Simultaneously he received from New York an urgent plea to complete a story of which he had characteristically turned in only the beginning. "Despite my pleading," Sara remembered, "he got up and wrote twelve pages." [5]

Probably this call from New York was not the only reminder of the grind from which he was having a temporary escape. His latest collection of stories, *The Heart of the West,* had been published the month before his marriage, and was now being reviewed not too favorably. "We never like O. Henry quite as well anywhere else as when he writes of 'little old New York,' as his characters call it," the *Outlook* reviewer wrote,[6] and the critic for the *Nation* commented in terms even more blunt:

After the intrinsic delicacy and fancy of *The Four Million*, Mr. Porter's new volume of short stories is a distinct disappointment. Clever it is; Mr. Porter can hardly fail to be that, but cheaply clever, mistaking grotesqueness for humor, exaggeration for animal spirits, and too often ending in a trick, a cheap surprise. His vocabulary, so agreeable in *The Four Million* and *Cabbages and Kings,* here seems overstocked. His Texan cow punchers talk like intoxicated dictionaries, old-fashioned negro minstrels, and the advance agents of a wild west show. . . . At a time when such quality as he has shown is rare, Mr. Porter must take that talent a trifle more seriously.[7]

The charge of exaggeration and of unrealistic caricature, so frequently and so justifiably brought against O. Henry, applies less to his Western stories than to most of the others, as has been recently pointed out by a Southwestern scholar.[8] For example, there is Calliope Catesby in "The Reformation of Calliope," who, in his cups, has a way of invading the main street of Quicksand with a "fearful brassy yell . . . reminiscent of the steam piano. . . . Down the street went Calliope, shooting right and left. Glass fell like hail; dogs

vamoosed; chickens flew squawking; feminine voices shrieked con-
cernedly to youngsters at large. . . . All along the main street in
advance of his coming clerks were putting up shutters and closing
doors. Business would languish for a space." [9] It is instructive to
compare Calliope's performance with some of the exploits of Ben
Thompson, Austin's notorious city marshal, who was killed in 1884
but about whom Porter would have heard many detailed accounts
from Lee and Richard Hall. After being defeated in his first campaign for the marshalship, Thompson in his annoyance invaded
Congress Avenue, shooting up the Iron Front Saloon, firing into the
office of the *Statesman*, and even sending a few slugs of lead into police headquarters during his progress through the heart of town. But
Ben Thompson was not the type of person with whom New York
critics could have been expected to be acquainted.

Another O. Henry character, the Cisco Kid (in "The Caballero's
Way"), seems modeled on the Texas desperado-author-teacher John
Wesley Hardin, who by the age of twenty-one had killed forty men.
Hardin is portrayed by his biographer "as killing on slight provocation, and on no provocation at all. He never forgave an injury, and
to incur his displeasure was simply suicide." [10] By way of comparison with a letter composed by the Cisco Kid (the grammatical cor-
rectness of which has been questioned by some readers), a letter
written by Hardin to his wife might be relevant:

Jane, dearest, I think as much of your pa and family as ever and blame
him for nothing, although I have been badly treated. Dear one, on your
account and sister Matt's I forgive your pa. Dear one, your pa wanted to
know if there was a statement I could make that would save Brown. I
told him no, not an honorable, truthful one. [11]

Several other Western characters in the O. Henry stories can
instructively be compared with Texans of the 1870's and 1880's.
Black Bill (in "The Hiding of Black Bill") is clearly suggestive of
Ham White, who was arrested by Lee Hall in 1877; and King James
(in "The Last of the Troubadours") seems to have been modeled
after King Fisher, who was murdered in San Antonio while trying
to mediate between two brawling gamblers. "A Chaparral Christmas
Gift" is a thinly disguised account of an episode in the notorious
Sutton-Taylor feud. In short, in the words of the scholar who has

collected an impressive group of such parallels, O. Henry's Texas badman "is a truthful reflection of a creature who lived in a lawless and uncertain age." [12]

At the end of a month in North Carolina, Porter and his wife returned to New York, to an apartment at the Chelsea, a family hotel on West Twenty-third Street, where they began what Sara was afterward to call "our poor, tragic little life together." One of the first things Sara did was to buy a small kerosene-burning night lamp so that Porter would not continue to burn holes in his handkerchiefs by tying them around the electric light he kept burning all night. Already she was beginning to find him a problem to deal with. Porter's marriage was a futile attempt to re-establish himself as a member of respectable society, to reactivate the roots from which he had tried to cut himself off when he left North Carolina to find a new life in Texas. From the very beginning—and for both of them almost equally—the marriage was a strain and little more than that. For Sara the initial trouble was the decision to live in a hotel, where she—a woman of thirty-nine, with a long-established routine of teaching school and living with her mother in the family home—had nothing at all to occupy her time. As she herself later expressed it:

> I was alone all day. I even breakfasted alone, for my husband was off to the rooms where he worked [the Caledonia] as soon as he could struggle into his clothes and get away. I rarely ever saw him again until evening. I used to try to prolong the time the maid tidied the apartment. . . . I knew very few people. My life indoors . . . and our irregular hours of eating and sleeping . . . wrought havoc with nerves and digestion. . . . Often when my husband wanted amusement and relaxation, a little dinner somewhere, the play—I was too sick to enjoy it. Sometimes I refused to go. My husband used to say I was changed.[13]

Porter himself, having married without considering the problem of adapting his life to that of another, began now to seem moody and restless, "utterly different from the man who had swept me off my feet with his tempestuous wooing." Just when his creative energy had begun to flag, he had taken on a responsibility which required more money than he had ever needed before, and the only way to make money was to produce stories. During the year 1908, by driving himself steadily, he published twenty-nine stories (as compared with eleven in 1907 and eight in 1909), and at the then market value of his name twenty-nine stories possibly netted him as much as $14,000. But that was almost his total income, for he had sold his collected volumes outright for a few hundred dollars each; it was not until Doubleday, Page & Company became his publisher and took over the earlier copyrights in 1909 that, despite the lack of any such contracts, royalties began to be paid him on his books.[14] With a wife to support, not to mention the establishments he maintained in two hotels and his incorrigible habits of spending and giving money away, even $14,000 was not enough to live on, and it soon began to seem impossible for him to keep his head above water. The nervous strain mounted and mounted. Sara decided that her husband regretted his marriage, and no true communication seems to have been possible between them.

The merest trifles caused heartbreaking scenes. One evening Sara was dressing for dinner when Porter came in and noticed some flowers in a vase—roses and an orchid. He inquired about the orchid. Sara explained that the man who had sold her the roses had thrown in the orchid without charging her for it. "And didn't you know better than to take it?" Porter demanded. "Didn't your instinct tell you not to take it?" Sara argued that it would have been rude of her not to accept the flower.

Without another word, but with his face black, my husband left the room. I flung myself on my bed . . . and wept. The washerwoman saved the situation. She brought the clothes home. I heard the gratitude in his voice as he paid her. Somewhat awkwardly he came to me and offered me a five-dollar gold piece. . . . [He] said he always felt as rich as a lord with a five-dollar gold piece. "You don't know this big town, and I do," he said. "I am trying to protect you, to take care of you." [15]

As Sara herself realized, they did not know each other well enough to reach an understanding. One evening Porter came home in an unusually bad humor. When Sara tried to jolly him out of it, he refused to cooperate, asking her to leave him alone. Finally he was goaded into threatening that, if she spoke of the matter again, he would go to bed. Sara accepted the challenge, and off Porter went to bed. But Sara followed him into the bedroom to read him a little lecture on his conduct. This time Porter announced that if she spoke one more word he would walk out. Defiantly Sara spoke the forbidden word, "and he got up, dressed and left. . . . I thought he was lost to me forever." At the end of three months of such scenes Porter suggested that Sara go back to Asheville for a while. She wept, and he tried to put things in reasonable-sounding terms. Not only did she need a change, he said, but he desperately needed to get some extra work done. So Sara went home to her mother. Very soon Porter wrote wretchedly: "I know I have been cross and ugly. . . . I'll be so different you won't know me." Sara took the next train back to New York. "If I could only," she later wrote, "have been more sensible; if he could only have been tenderer." But it was not quite that simple. As one of Porter's friends said to her during the second winter of their marriage, "You've got one of the biggest matrimonial problems in this town, but [as a kindly afterthought] I believe you are going to come out conqueror." [16] The problem was too strenuous for Sara. During a visit her mother made to New York, while Sara sat exhausted in the restaurant where the three of them were dining, Porter turned to her and said, "You know, honey, I wish I liked you as much as I do your mother. Look how she's enjoying this!" To which Sara could only reply plaintively, "But I just can't keep up with you and Mama, Will." [17]

During the early part of the year 1908 Al Jennings made another visit to New York in response to Porter's continued encouragement of his literary ambitions. Porter was so busy with a story that it was a week before he got around to seeing Jennings, who had decided that Porter was ashamed to introduce him to his wife. At last Richard Duffy called for Jennings with the news that they were invited to join Porter for dinner. When they picked him up at the Caledonia, he seemed tired, but he gave them a drink and apologized for having been so tied up with work. The three of them dined not at Porter's home but at Mouquin's, where the old convivial spirit gradually overcame Jennings's annoyance and Porter's tired detachment. After dinner Porter said to Jennings, "I'd like you to meet my wife." It was about ten-thirty when they reached the Porter apartment, where Sara, according to Jennings, "greeted us with great cordiality . . . served us refreshments, and chatted with pleasant ease." When Jennings and Duffy started to leave about midnight, Porter took up his hat to go with them. "Why, you're not going too, are you, Mr. Porter?" Sara asked. Porter stayed behind for a moment, catching up with his friends in the street just as Jennings was remarking to Duffy: "What the hell did Bill want with a wife? It puts an end to his liberty—his wanderings." Porter, who had heard the remark, discussed the matter freely with Jennings after Duffy had left them. "You're dissatisfied with my matrimonial venture?" he inquired. Jennings said bluntly that it was the silliest thing he had ever heard of. "She is a most estimable young lady," Porter replied, not taking his friend's attitude very seriously. But, Jennings persisted, what had he wanted with her?

"I loved her," Porter said dutifully.

"Oh, my God! That covers a multitude of sins," Jennings retorted.

Porter did not pursue the point. Instead he went on to soliloquize as to whether he had acted quite honorably: "I've married a high-bred woman and brought all my troubles upon her. Was it right?" [18]

In his doubts about Porter's marriage Jennings was not alone. William Wash Williams, although regularly invited to dinner whenever Porter ran into him, never could bring himself to accept the invitation. "For some reason or other—I have never been able to explain it to myself satisfactorily—I didn't want to meet Mrs. Porter, though I was told she was a most excellent lady and a charming hostess." [19]

In May, 1908, Porter's new collection of stories, *The Voice of the City,* appeared. It had been preceded by an appreciative critical essay, "O. Henry's Short Stories," by Henry James Forman, in the *North American Review.*

For the first time since the eclipse of Mr. Kipling [Forman wrote] the short story is again beginning to make public appearance between book covers. . . . The stigma of the genre is wearing off, and for the rehabilitation one man is chiefly responsible. Mr. Sidney Porter . . . has breathed new life into the short story. . . . The facility, the light touch of O. Henry, his mastery of the vernacular, his insight into the life of the disinherited, make it needless for him to resort to such inventions as Stevenson's learned Arabian. . . . Yet it is idle to compare O. Henry with anybody. No talent could be more original or delightful. The combination of technical excellence with whimsical, sparkling wit, abundant humor and a fertile invention is so rare that the reader is content without comparisons.[20]

The new book was received much more favorably than *The Heart of the West* had been. A reviewer in the *Outlook,* remarking that "A new book of stories about New York by O. Henry is sure of a welcome," proceeded to comment on the unity of purpose in a collection of stories all growing out of the author's great love for the city and his sure knowledge of its people.[21] A writer in the *Independent,* who considered the new collection to be in O. Henry's best vein, singled out for special praise "A Lickpenny Lover," "The Memento," and "The Plutonian Fire." In conclusion the writer would have warned Mr. Henry against overproduction "were it not for the fear of missing by unhappy chance some rare bit of *genre* cameo, cut from life. Almost anyone would gladly sort over a bushel of oyster shells for a handful of pearls, and the present critic is no exception." [22]

The Voice of the City was Porter's third volume of New York stories. There were to be three more (*Strictly Business* in 1910 and the two posthumous volumes *Whirligigs* and *Sixes and Sevens*), but in *The Voice of the City, The Trimmed Lamp,* and *The Four Million* are to be found all of the various facets of O. Henry's New York. There is the life of the early-twentieth-century working girl, not only the shopgirl but the clothier's model, the waitress, the stenographer, the showgirl, and the would-be artist.[23] There are the New York Irish: the policeman, the saloonkeeper, the boardinghouse keeper, the "sport," and the wife who makes strategic use of the weekly manhandling received from her husband.[24] There is the Jewish community (and even the Jewish-Irish rapprochement suggestive of *Abie's Irish Rose*),[25] and there are the park bums,[26] the gangsters and their girls,[27] the bohemians of Greenwich Village,[28] and the people with more money than they know what to do with.[29] Porter's interest in New York was never, however, that of the naturalist or even the realist. His half-dozen Jewish characters, for example, are superficial types, revealing no serious interest in the impact which New York had on the Jewish immigrant. Nor does he show any interest in one of the crucial issues of his day, the growing fight between capital and labor. Aside from his sentimental and somewhat ambivalent concern for the underpaid shopgirl, Porter's interest in New York was that of the perennial tourist. Porter never became a citizen of his gaudy, teeming Bagdad-on-the-Subway, with a citizen's involvement in its beliefs and mores. He was, of course, a very special tourist, and his collection of pictures brings vibrantly before us the spectacle of life. Porter's portable camera was not an adequate instrument for portraying the drama of a few deeply responsive individuals, but it was admirably efficient for recording the endlessly varied succession of anonymous people in the city of the four million at the beginning of the century of the common man.

Shortly after the publication of *The Voice of the City,* Porter began writing the series of stories later to be collected under the title *The Gentle Grafter.* Of the fourteen stories in the series, three had been published previously; the other eleven appeared in McClure's syndicate during the summer of 1908. Reportedly these stories were based on yarns told him by fellow prisoners in the Ohio Penitentiary ("I remember hearing him recount many of them," Dr. John M. Thomas stated).[30] Porter must have been hard pressed when he went back to his prison years in search of material. In any event, he was working harder now than he had ever worked before, even though he produced only twenty-nine stories in 1908 as compared with fifty-four in 1905 and sixty-six in 1904.

As always, money problems continued to vex him. Margaret had come to live with her father and stepmother after leaving Belmont, and for the summer Porter moved his family to a cottage at Good Ground, Long Island, some forty miles from New York. Even with the additional member of the family and the two servants he kept on Long Island, the trouble was not so much the scale on which he was living as it was his complete lack of money sense. But to this fact he never awakened, even in the midst of his sometimes farcical difficulties. Once, for example, he discovered after inviting an editor-friend to dinner that there was not enough money in the house to buy the necessary groceries. After a sleepless night he got up at six o'clock, worked for several hours to grind out a story, and by noon had succeeded by telephone in selling it.[31] Looking back later, Sara spoke regretfully of the way he drove himself, but said that neither of them realized his true condition at the time.[32] Not long after their marriage Porter had told her that he had diabetes; in fact, he said, "if I have diabetes as bad as the doctors say I have, I'll be dead two years from now." [33] The prophecy proved a sound one, but at the time his living habits did not indicate that he took the idea very seriously.

On Long Island, Porter fixed up a workroom in the loft of an unused stable on the place and attempted, for a time, to become a country gentleman presiding over a well run home. He had what Sara called an aristocratic manner, an illustration being his refusal to come to the table without his coat no matter how hot the weather might be. In most other ways he did not make a very convincing paterfamilias. There was, of course, the very real pleasure which he derived from his relationship with his daughter (now seventeen), who was henceforth to live in his household or with her stepmother in Asheville. "Never did he give a command," Margaret later wrote, "and never did I fail to follow his advice or try to fulfil his expressed wish." [34] Never perhaps except once, but on at least the one occasion even his daughter was no great satisfaction to him. He very much wanted her to go on to college, specifically to Smith College, and when Margaret was unwilling to continue in school any longer, it was a keen disappointment to Porter. He had often declared that he would have given the eyes out of his head for a college education, and now he remarked irritably to his wife that Margaret's lack of ambition did not come from either of her parents.[35]

(It was not a matter of lack of ambition. Margaret wanted to become a writer, like her father, and on New Year's Day, 1909, Porter exhibited to a friend a new scarfpin, explaining with considerable satisfaction, "My daughter wrote a story and sold it, and she bought me this with the proceeds." [36] But Margaret was never to succeed in finding herself, either as a writer or as a person. In 1916 she married the well known cartoonist Oscar Cesare, but she divorced him in the same year, after which she drifted helplessly. Her second husband was Guy Sartain, who befriended her in her last attack of tuberculosis and whom she married three days before her death in 1927 in order to leave him her possessions and her share in the royalties from her father's books. She was buried in Asheville, at her father's feet.)

The discussion of Margaret's education in 1908 was one of the few times Porter ever mentioned his first wife to his second; in fact, Sara did not even know Margaret's mother's name or the cause of her death until Mrs. Roach came to New York to pay them a visit. Porter never took Sara fully into his confidence, and his attempt to live as a family man on Long Island was not a happy experiment. According to Margaret, his gay moods were abruptly followed by "black silences." According to Sara, he soon began to return to New York for several days at a time, and it was not long before he was away as much as he was at home. "Once when he went back to the city [Sara remembered] after two weeks of what seemed endurance of the place and of me, I vowed grimly I would not be decent to him. . . . A week later he came home bringing company. . . . 'I was mad? Sick, then?' 'No, I was not sick.' 'Then you are not glad to see me?' " At last Sara gave in. Flinging her arms around his neck, she promised to stop trying to force him into the mold of home-loving, affectionate husband. "He was queer because he didn't want to be fussed over." In fact, he once told her bluntly, he could not endure marriage if she did not leave the cage door open, but if the cage door stood open he would always come back.[37]

During this trying summer Porter had at least one bout with the unspecified malady which he refused to deal with realistically. On July 10 he wrote to William Griffeth, apropos of the story "Strictly Business," which appeared the following month in *Hampton's* (the magazine for which Griffeth was now working):

> She'll be up in just a day or two—the first of next week at the outside. I've been kind of an invalid lately; but am rejuvenating in this fine cool air. . . .
> Some time when you can, like to have you run down here for a few days.—Nothing much to promise you except plenty of good grub, fine sailing & cold, cold nights under cover.[38]

Despite this alluring picture, it must have been a great relief to Porter to move back to town in the fall. Instead of again spending the winter in a hotel, Porter signed a lease for "the apartment on the first floor East in 88 Washington Place . . . for a term of 7 months beginning on the 15th day of November, 1908 . . . and ending on the 15th day of June, 1909 . . . at the rent of $100 on the 15th day of each and every calendar month." [39] It must have been a luxurious apartment, but this final attempt to maintain a family household was no more successful than the arrangements of the summer or of the preceding winter. After a few months Sara went to Asheville for a protracted visit, Margaret was enrolled in a school in Englewood, New Jersey, and Porter resumed his bachelor life, except for occasional brief visits to Sara in Asheville. Such an arrangement must have simplified many things, among them the problem of Porter's drinking. On Sara's part there had always been a polite refusal to admit that her husband was an alcoholic: it was the kind of attitude which had caused him on one occasion to lean against a lamppost in front of the house, reluctant for his friends to leave him. "I'm ashamed to go in to Sara like this," he said, and probably it did not simplify matters for Sara to refrain from any comment when she saw his condition.[40]

Marriage had not changed Porter's financial ineptitude nor his drinking habits, nor had it altered his shyness. Despite his position in the New York literary world, he still could not bring himself to accept an invitation, extended at Archibald Henderson's suggestion, to address the North Carolina State Literary and Historical Association. There was indeed one gradual change which the years had brought. Clarence Cullen, who came to know him at this time, found him "absolutely one of the most world weary men I have ever known . . . not so pessimistic as he was thoroughly tired."[41] Cullen felt that Porter the zestful looker-on at life was watching a spectacle which had lost its relish. But Porter was never one to wear his heart on his sleeve. Most of the time he wore a mask of raillery, and he gave Cullen the appearance of "a thoroughly content, roly-poly proprietor of a delicatessen establishment." Despite his world-weariness, he still had his pride, of which Cullen witnessed a somewhat youthful exhibition one day when a letter arrived from a magazine which had consistently rejected the early O. Henry stories. The letter contained a check for $1,000 in advance payment for anything which Porter might be willing to write. Such a check must have been a sore temptation, but Porter proceeded without a word to readdress it to the editor in question and, opening the door of his Caledonia apartment, deposited it in the hall mail-drop.

Just before the publication of *The Gentle Grafter* in November, *Current Literature* ran an article entitled "A Yankee Maupassant," which was the most gratifying tribute yet to appear. Based on the thesis that "no one else can write stories like O. Henry's," the article is a compilation of undiscriminating praise from various representative sources. When *The Gentle Grafter* appeared, it was reviewed in equally favorable terms. A typical estimate was that of the *New York Times Book Review:*

His creations are so true to human nature that no matter how strange their dialect or unfamiliar their appearance, neither this unfamiliarity nor this strangeness strikes you as you read—it is the humanity which we all share that comes home. . . . And howsoever vastly their ideas of honor may vary from your own, you can nevertheless extend to them a brother's hand. For there is about each of them something vital, warm, and human that commands your liking.[42]

Surely this is a sentiment which needs reaffirming after the widely publicized and influential attack, led by F. L. Pattee, on the work of O. Henry in general and on *The Gentle Grafter* in particular. Beginning in 1917 in a series of pronouncements extending over the next twenty years, Pattee leveled against O. Henry the charge of immorality on the ground that he wrote without moral standards, even with a grin of sympathy for such lawbreakers as Jeff Peters, the central character in *The Gentle Grafter* and undoubtedly O. Henry's closest approach to a genuine character creation.[43] On this point at least, one of the most extravagant overpraisers (Stephen Leacock, who proceeded to lose his sense of proportion entirely) seems much closer to critical soundness in comparing Jeff Peters to Robin Hood or Alfred Jingle or Scapin "or any of the multifarious characters of the world's literature who reveal the fact that much that is best in humanity may flourish even on the shadowy side of technical iniquity." [44]

In spite of the rising chorus of praise, Porter himself was increasingly dissatisfied with his work. About this time, it is true, he was capable of writing—not entirely flippantly—the following reply to an Asheville acquaintance who had inquired how to go about writing a story:

The first step is to get a kitchen table, a wooden chair, a wad of yellow fool's cap writing paper, one lead pencil and a drinking glass. These are the props. Then you secure a flask of Scotch whiskey and a few oranges, which I will describe as the sustenance. We now come to the plot, frequently styled the inspiration. Combining a little orange juice with a little Scotch, the author drinks the health of all magazine editors, sharpens his pencil and begins to write. When the oranges are empty and the flask is dry, a saleable piece of fiction is ready for mailing.[45]

But Porter began very definitely to feel that he had not taken his work seriously enough. He was extremely proud of the message which Kipling commissioned a friend to give him: "Do you know O. Henry? Well, when you see him tell him hello for me." [46] But to Robert H. Davis he expressed his dissatisfaction even more strongly: "I'm a failure. I always have the feeling that I want to get back somewhere, but I don't know just where it is. My stories? No, they don't satisfy me. . . . It depresses me to have people point me out or introduce me as 'a celebrated author.' It seems such a big label for such picayune goods. Sometimes I feel that I'd like to get into some business; perhaps some clerkship; some place where I could see that I was doing something tangible, something worth while." [47]

In the last years of his life, according to Seth Moyle, a literary agent with whom he had occasional dealings, Porter tried to draw up more ambitious plans than he had had in the past. He outlined a series of stories about the contemporary South, a scheme detailed enough for Moyle to get a contract from *Collier's* for the series. The idea was to show up the professional Southerner who was still trying to blame all of his troubles on the Civil War, as contrasted with the new Southerner who, Porter remarked, "is so busy making good that he has forgotten that there was such a thing as the Spanish-American War." [48] None of the projected stories were ever written, but Porter's interest in the subject—stimulated no doubt by his new associations in North Carolina—is indicated by "The Rose of Dixie" (1908), "Thimble, Thimble" (1908), and "A Municipal Report" (1909), which was voted in a 1914 symposium conducted by the New York *Times* to be the greatest American short story. Porter's own conception of this story is stated in a scenario which he wrote for the editor William Griffeth:

The old negro carriage-driver is a relic of the old South. He is a night-hawk and a ruffian (probably) but his piratical depredations upon travelers & transients are for the sole purpose of supporting an elderly lady (the poetess) who is the last of the family to which he once belonged. All his small earnings are contributed to that end.

Major Caswell, a type of the degraded Southerner, is living off the slender income of his relative (Azalea Adair). He is the rat & utterly despicable. . . .

In the end there is a dramatic and mysterious murder, the victim being Major Caswell. The "snapper" comes in the last paragraph, revealing the slayer by a bare intimation. The whole scheme is to show that an absolutely prosaic and conventional town (such as Nashville) can equal San Francisco, Bagdad or Paris when it comes to a human story.[49]

In addition to the projected series of Southern stories, Porter had plans for a novel, which was never actually begun. The McClure Company had already, during the summer of 1908, advanced him $1,500 on this project, as he now explained to Henry W. Lanier, who was the secretary of Doubleday, Page & Company,[50] his new publishers. Porter's novel was the subject of several letters to Lanier. On February 13, 1909, he wrote to inquire: "If I have enough 'stuff' in your hands in the way of collateral would it fetch a further advance of—say $50 for temporary emergencies?" It was the familiar refrain, but now the financial problem was complicated by the state of Porter's health. As he explained to Lanier in the same letter: "I've been 'ailing' for a month or so—cant sleep, &c; and haven't turned out a piece of work in that time. Consequently there is a temporary hiatus in the small change pocket. . . . I hope to be in shape Monday so that I can go to Atlantic City, immure myself in a quiet hotel and begin to get the 'great novel' in shape." [51] This scheme, for one reason or another, did not work out. On March 16 Porter was still in New York and still reassuring Lanier:

In a short time—say two weeks at the outside—I'll turn in enough of the book for the purposes you require, as per your last letter.

I've been pretty well handicapped for a couple of months and am in the hands of a fine tyrant of a doctor, who makes me come to see him every day, & who has forbidden me to leave the city until he is through with me, & then only under his own auspicis [sic] and direction. It seems that the goddess Hygiene and I have been strangers for years; and now Science must step in and repair the damage. My doctor is a miracle worker and promises that in a few weeks he will *double* my working capacity, which sounds very good both for me and for him, when the payment of the bill is considered.

I'll get you in part of the new work just as soon as I can, with the title, &c. as you suggested.[52]

In the same letter Porter inquired whether Doubleday-Page would send him their own check in exchange for a $500 check from "Harry Askin head of the theatrical trust in Chicago. . . . The check, as you will perceive, is on Chicago, and as I am not maintaining a bank a/c just now, I couldn't get it cashed in the ordinary run of business." The money, he explained, was an advance payment on a musical comedy (based on an O. Henry story) which Franklin P. Adams was writing. All he had to do was to approve the finished script, he said, so that Lanier need not fear that the project would interfere with his novel.

Two weeks later Porter was still feeling "rocky" and had noticed "now and then some suspicious tracks outside the door that closely resembled those made by Lupus Americanus." He wondered if anything had accumulated in the way of royalties which might be sent to him that afternoon.[53] A few days later, on April 9, he wrote again to thank Lanier "for your very kind response to my wireless call. The amt. will tide me over very nicely until prosperity calls again. Am working hard to give you something to start on *in re* the novel." [54]

In two ways Porter was not playing fair with Lanier. First, as far as is known, during all these months of negotiations with Doubleday-Page and previously with McClure, Porter never produced a single word of the novel on which he was "working hard." No doubt his intentions were, as always, the best in the world, but the episode is all too revealing as to the way he failed to face the realities and the ethics of business. Second, the musical comedy, not the novel, was the project to which he was in fact devoting such energies as he could muster. Franklin P. Adams, who had been sounded out by a Chicago producer about a play to be based on O. Henry's story "To Him Who Waits," which had appeared in *Collier's* in January, discussed the idea with Porter in February. As Adams later put it, Porter's "other pseudonym was Barkis. We agreed to collaborate, both of us to work on the dialogue and both on the lyrics. As it happened it was almost a complete collaboration. Hardly any independent line was written." [55]

The two men met nearly every afternoon to talk and make notes of their ideas. Losing sight of the original idea of the story, they ended up with an anthropological expedition to Yucatan to ascertain whether the American Indian was descended from the Aztecs. The title *Lo!*, suggested by Porter, was taken from Alexander Pope's couplet:

> Lo, the poor Indian! whose untutored mind
> Sees God in clouds, or hears him in the wind.

The collaborators wrote and, at the producer's insistence, rewrote. The work went on and on—for some six months, in fact. Adams was afterward quoted as saying that Porter was "fairly lazy," but clearly most of whatever work he did in 1909 went into the play. During the entire year he published only eight short stories, so that his financial difficulties were more acute than ever. At times, now that Margaret was in school again, he did not have enough money to pay her bills, and before the association with Adams came to an end he had borrowed some $1,600 (which, Adams later reported, was duly repaid).[56]

Lo! opened in Aurora, Illinois, on August 25, 1909, and although (according to Adams, who went with the company in order to attend to any necessary revisions in the script) the Aurora audiences "seemed to like it" and he himself "rather enjoyed it," it somehow did not make the grade. After fourteen weeks of performances (in Waukegan, Illinois; Janesville, Wisconsin; St. Joseph, Missouri; and Milwaukee) the play folded on December 5, leaving behind only Adams's copies of most of the lyrics. One of these, incidentally, is the poem entitled "The Crucible," which was found among Porter's papers after his death and erroneously taken to be one of his last writings. Another of the lyrics, "Snap Shots," which Adams identified as being entirely the work of Porter, gives a good idea of the flavor of the show:

> Watch out, lovers, when you promenade;
> When you kiss and coo, in the deep moon shade.
> When you're close together in the grape-vine swing,
> When you are a-courting or philandering.

Mabel, Maud and Ann, Nellie, May and Fan,
Keep your eyes open for the Snap Shot Man! . . .

Watch out, you, Sir, when your wife's away,
When you take your "cousin" to see the play,
With best aisle seats and in the bass drum row,
And holding her hand when all the lights are low.
Billy, Bob and Dan, Smith and Harrigan,
Keep your eyes open for the Snap Shot Man! . . .

When you're swimming in your bathing suit,
And Hubby's in town, slaving like a brute,
And handsome young stranger, "Teach you how to swim?"
It's not my affair, it's up to you and him.
But, Adele and Pearl, in the water's swirl,
Keep your eyes open for the Snap Shot Girl. . . .[57]

During the work on *Lo!* and the postponements of the novel which
Porter was supposed to be writing, Harry Peyton Steger had succeeded Lanier as Porter's taskmaster and paymaster at Doubleday-
Page. Steger (who had grown up in Bonham, Texas, and entered
the University of Texas in 1897 and afterward gone to Oxford as a
Rhodes Scholar) not only occupied an apartment across the hall at
the Caledonia Hotel, but became such a close friend that after Porter's death he acted for a time as a legal guardian for Margaret. In
1909 Steger undertook a campaign to promote the O. Henry books,
past and future, in a bigger way than had been attempted before.
Realizing the potential value of the properties, he authorized further
advance payments to Porter, without too much concern over the
delayed novel. ("We paid him many thousands of dollars," Steger
later said. "At the time of his death his account was deep in the red
on our books.") [58] It was Steger who, after six weeks of maneuver-
ing, arranged the interview which Porter granted in April, 1909, to
George MacAdam of the New York *Times* (the only interview to
which he ever submitted). Ready with a chronology of his life to
conceal his prison years, Porter began with the uneasy question:
"Are you going to draw a pen picture of me? . . . Then let me ask
you to say that I look like a healthy butcher, just that, and no adorn-
ments." He also stated, for what it was worth, that in his novel he
was "going to give particular attention to style, also to character

and plot. These really are the essential things in a novel. Tell the world that this novel will be worth a dollar and a half of any man's money." [59]

Steger furthered his promotion campaign by taking to print himself. In an article entitled "O. Henry, Who He Is and How He Works," published in *World's Work* in June, he wrote:

For the past six or seven years O. Henry has been, perhaps, the most popular short-story writer in America. . . .

Sydney Porter, which happens to be the baptismal name of O. Henry, is a flat-dweller in Manhattan. The reasonable design of Mr. Porter to share none of O. Henry's fame has brought into existence a vast quantity of O. Henry legend. . . .

These bits of romantic gossip have been misleading to the public.[60]

Steger proceeded to summarize Porter's life (as it had been told to MacAdam). He then pointed out that the O. Henry stories commanded the highest prices paid by editors, "and editors pay for breadth and depth of appeal." In conclusion he suggested that the O. Henry stories composed a sort of "Comédie Humaine," and that O. Henry "takes rag-time and gives an effect that challenges the effect of grand opera."

As a final achievement Steger persuaded Porter to be photographed, apparently for the first time since his coming to New York. Years afterward the photographer, W. M. Van der Weyde, remembered the occasion vividly. It had taken, Steger told him, nearly an hour to get Porter dressed and out on the street, and nearly another hour to negotiate the two blocks from the Caledonia to the studio. Having been cautioned to proceed gently, Van der Weyde first made conversation about Porter's Central American stories, trying out the little Spanish he knew. Then, straddling a chair with his arms folded on the back of it, he suggested, "This is a comfy sort of pose for a picture; let's try it." Docilely Porter followed instructions, finally relaxing enough to lean back in a rocking chair and become engrossed in a newspaper while Van der Weyde worked on a series of photographs. A few days later when the proofs were sent to him, Porter was so pleased that he wrote Van der Weyde a note of appreciation, admitting that "photographers are not half so bad as dentists, after all!" [61] Shortly afterward one of the pictures appeared in the *Bookman,* with the comment: ". . . at last we are able to present a portrait of O. Henry that does something like justice to this subject . . . , a portrait that satisfies the imagination. One can study it and fancy him eating of the lotus in company with Johnny Atwood" [62] (a character in *Cabbages and Kings*).

During the summer the new volume *Roads of Destiny* received a somewhat mixed greeting, and the feeling of the reviewers is understandable. All of the O. Henry collections had been assembled somewhat haphazardly, but *Roads of Destiny* lacked even such a unifying element as had held together the three volumes of New York stories. The settings include Texas, New Orleans, North Carolina, and Central America, as well as New York; and all stages of Porter's career are represented, from "Whistling Dick's Christmas Stocking" (1899) to half a dozen stories written in 1907 and 1908. The quality of the stories is equally mixed. With the exception of the title story and two of O. Henry's best-known stories ("A Retrieved Reformation" and "The Halberdier of the Little Rheinschloss"), it is a disappointing collection. By this time it was his New York stories on which O. Henry's chief significance rested, but even of these, *Roads of Destiny* contains only such mediocre examples as "The Discounters of Money" and "The Enchanted Profile."

CHAPTER THIRTEEN

· ༄ ·

That Porter was still serious about his projected novel and continued to work on the idea of working on it is attested by an unfinished letter to Steger found among his papers after his death:

I do not remember ever to have read an autobiography, a biography, or a piece of fiction that told the *truth*. Of course, I have read such stuff as Rousseau and Zola and George Moore; and various memoirs that were supposed to be window panes in their respective breasts; but mostly, all of them were either liars, actors, or poseurs. (Of course, I'm not trying to belittle the greatness of their literary expression.) . . .

The trouble about writing the truth has been that the writers have kept in their minds one or another or all of three thoughts that made a handicap—they were trying either to do a piece of immortal literature, or to shock the public or to please editors. Some of them succeeded in all three, but they did not write the *truth*. . . .

It is well understood that "all the truth" cannot be told in print—but how about "nothing but the truth"? That's what I want to do. . . .

The "hero" of the story will be a man born and "raised" in a somnolent little southern town. His education is about a common school one, but he learns afterward from reading and life. . . . I'm going to take him through all the main phases of life—wild adventure, city, society, something of the "under world". . . . I want him to acquire all the sophistication that experience can give him, and always preserve his individual honest *human* view, and have him tell the *truth* about everything. . . .

I want this man to be a man of natural intelligence, of individual character, absolutely open and broad minded; and show how the Creator of the earth has got him in a rat trap—put him here "willy nilly" (you know the Omar verse): and then I want to show what he does about it. There is always the eternal question from the Primal Source—"What are you going to do about it?" [1]

231

Although the conception sounds somewhat nebulous, the basic idea seems to have been in Porter's mind for a long time. Anne Partlan, of whom he had seen little or nothing since his marriage, knew all about the project. The title he had in mind, she said later, was *The Rat Trap,* and the point of the story was to be the observation that one "must go through destiny before freedom begins." [2] Such an observation—an extension of the theme of "Roads of Destiny"—suggests that Porter was groping toward an awareness of his own artistic dilemma. Although the letter to Steger ends with a disclaimer that the story was to be autobiographical, Porter's harping on the absence of "truth" in the writings of others seems primarily, if unconsciously, a comment on his own work. Freedom, personal and artistic, could have begun for Porter only after he had come to grips with his problems, artistic as well as personal, and his compulsive evasions of them. One example, which needs no further elaboration, is the problem of financial responsibility. Another is his puritanism. The letter to Steger contains the statement: "If you find a word or a suggestive line in any of my copy, you cut it out and deduct the royalties." For all his admiration of Maupassant's technique, Porter disliked being called the American Maupassant. "I never wrote a filthy word in my life," he is quoted as protesting more than once, "and I don't like being compared to a filthy writer." [3] In the matter of sex, as well as money, Porter never faced up to the truth which he professed not to find in the work of others.

As late as the fall of 1909, in spite of the state of his health, it still seemed possible that Porter might find himself and write the kind of novel which he had in mind. In early September, Steger paid him a visit from across the hall in the "noisy Caledonia" to urge that he give up the pretense of carrying on in New York. Steger's proposal was that he join his family in Asheville and submit to a real rest cure, after which he could begin work on the novel. (The word *begin* in the account of the matter suggests that, in one situation at least, the truth had by now been faced and accepted.) "But why," Porter demanded, "go to Asheville to write a novel? You remind me of the man who said he was going to win the long jump in the athletic meet. He felt sure of it because he was going to take a three-mile running start." [4]

After more than a year of fruitless visits to doctors, Porter was ready for Steger's advice. Shortly afterward he gave up his Caledonia apartment and went South, and it was either on his arrival this time or on a previous visit during the summer that Sara remarked on how worn he looked. "Oh, how you have suffered," she said penitently. "I shall not leave you again." And for a while now their reunion seemed to bring Porter happiness. "We came very close in the days that followed," Sara remembered. "Walking through a snow-filled wood one late afternoon, he threw his arms around me and said, 'It is just like the old times, isn't it?' " [5] Instead of writing stories, though, Porter soon placed himself in the hands of a physician, who, according to a letter to Steger on November 5, "says I have absolutely no physical trouble except neurasthenia, and that out door exercise & air will find me as good as new. As for the diagnosis of the N. Y. doctors—they are absolutely without foundation. I Am 20 pounds lighter, & can climb mountains like a goat." [6]

As it turned out, the diagnosis of the New York doctors—assuming that they had diagnosed his trouble as kidney or liver disease, or both—had all too much foundation. But for the time being, after a "slight relapse," Porter allowed himself to believe that he was "improving vastly." The nature of his new course of treatment he was afterward to describe in the story "Let Me Feel Your Pulse," published in July, 1910, the month after his death. No doubt he exercised a certain artistic license, although both he and his agent, Seth Moyle, stated that the account is substantially factual. Written by a man who by the time of writing seems to have understood his true condition, the story is a remarkable display of the triumph of the (comic) spirit over matter. It begins:

So I went to a doctor.

"How long has it been since you took any alcohol into your system?" he asked.

Turning my head sidewise, I answered, "Oh, quite awhile."

He was a young doctor, somewhere between twenty and forty. He wore heliotrope socks, but he looked like Napoleon. I liked him immensely.

"Now," said he, "I am going to show you the effect of alcohol upon your circulation." I think it was "circulation" he said; though it may have been "advertising."

He bared my left arm to the elbow, brought out a bottle of whiskey, and gave me a drink. He began to look more like Napoleon. I began to like him better.

Then he put a tight compress on my upper arm, stopped my pulse with his fingers, and squeezed a rubber bulb connected with an apparatus on a stand that looked like a thermometer. The mercury jumped up and down without seeming to stop anywhere; but the doctor said it registered two hundred and thirty-seven or one hundred and sixty-five or some such number.

"Now," said he, "you see what alcohol does to the blood-pressure?"

"It's marvelous," said I, "but do you think it a sufficient test? Have one on me, and let's try the other arm." [7]

Unlike that of his more fortunate fictional self, Porter's own condition continued to deteriorate, even though he performed the remarkable feat of giving up alcohol entirely. The irregular, scrawling penmanship in the few letters he wrote during his six months in North Carolina gives a graphic idea of his condition. Nevertheless he continued to make futile gestures, not in the direction of his novel but again, irresistibly, in the direction of the theater. For some time before leaving New York he had been the object of a persistent campaign on the part of the producer George Tyler, who was convinced that Porter could write a successful play. There had been, in fact, an understanding that Porter was to dramatize his story "A Retrieved Reformation," but he seems never to have made a start on this project. Instead, he preferred another of his stories, "The World and the Door." Finally Tyler, who was determined to get his play even if someone else had to write it, offered Porter $500 for the dramatic rights to the story, and on October 27, 1909, Porter replied:

I hereby transfer to you the entire dramatic rights etc. of the story you write me about—the title is "A Retrieved Reformation." I am glad to be able to hand over to you anything you might be able to use. . . .

I've been in bad shape for a long time both as to writing and refunding. I'm wrestling with a bad case of neurasthenia (so the doctor says) but I'm getting back into shape again. . . . I eat like a drayman and don't know what booze tastes like. In fact I'll be better than ever in a week or two.[8]

He was beginning to work, he said, on a dramatization of "The World and the Door" ("I got out the scenario . . . some days ago and began to plan out the acts and scenes. I'll surprise you with it as soon as I get down to hard work").

A few days later he wrote Steger that he was ready to discuss the new collection of stories (*Strictly Business*) which Doubleday-Page was planning for February; he asked for a list of titles from which to make a selection. Partly for business reasons and partly out of friendship, Steger had suggested that he might come down for a brief visit, a proposal to which Porter replied: "I am six miles out of town, & although the house is quite large it has been full for quite a while. If we cant arrange it here I'll come into Asheville & we'll put up at the Battery Park Hotel. Would be mighty glad to see you." He added that he expected to "be able to write a novel with each hand simultaneously in a short time." [9]

Of Steger's visit, during which he apparently stayed in the Coleman home, only one detail has survived. Porter had a habit, it seems, of going out at dusk each day to watch the chickens seek safe perches for the night. "See those old sisters fussing and fuming about who is to sit next to the rooster," Steger quotes him as remarking. "Listen at 'em quarrel and watch 'em peck each other. . . . Old Chanticleer is right in the middle of them, with a long row of worshipping sisters on either side. Lots more fun than to watch a bunch of people go to bed." [10]

Possibly during Steger's visit, or at any rate about the same time, an incident occurred which Margaret was to remember vividly— the trivial-seeming sort of incident which remains in the mind more clearly than the crucial occurrences in a relationship. Having been unusually high-spirited during dinner, Porter afterward went on to entertain the group with a series of impersonations staged on the stair landing in the living room. "Buffalo Bill!" he would call out, holding one forefinger across his upper lip, with the other forefinger vertically dividing his chin. He proceeded through a list of such personages until he was momentarily interrupted by someone entering the room. In that moment his mood changed. When the attention of the group returned to the stair landing, Porter was gone. "I found him," Margaret remembered, "sitting in the far corner of the dark porch overlooking the mountains. The night seemed filled with premonition. I felt that he sensed it too. I could not—and knew that he would not have me—speak. I sat on the steps near him. After a long time, still without words, we got up and went into the house together." [11]

The wonder is that Porter bore up as cheerfully as he did through the long, empty weeks and months in the country. "It's as lonesome down here," he wrote Griffeth, "as Broadway when you are broke, but I shall try to stick it out a couple of weeks longer—I hope in time to wet my ears in a crock of Tom and Jerry with you at the glad Yuletide." [12] This was a vain hope. Instead of celebrating the glad Yuletide in his beloved New York, he took walks in the woods, often accompanied by Margaret. Each of them carried a gun, but only for target shooting; Porter had never been willing to kill any living creature for sport. Once, Margaret remembered, he returned home at dusk from a solitary walk carrying in his hand a dead bird. With a "rueful" expression and a "not quite steady laugh," he explained that he had shot it when aiming at a cornstalk. Why he had brought the bird home was not clear, for immediately he squatted to scoop out a hollow and cover the little grave with earth and leaves.

In due course the attempt to believe in his own improvement (aided and abetted by the need for money) led to an attempt to start writing again. Sara found an office for him in the Legal Building in downtown Asheville. Here he made friends with Judge Thomas A. Jones, in whose office he often stopped for a chat. He also spent a great deal of time at his window, according to Sara, staring down into the street with a faraway look in his eyes.[13] But he got no writing done, and the reviewers' reception of his new volume, *Options* (which had appeared in October), was not one to inspire renewed creative effort. The *Nation*, for example, suggested that structural cleverness was O. Henry's "darker angel," and found no new development in the present collection except on one count: "Love is allowed to figure somewhat seriously here and there; but it must still be dealt with brusquely, curtly, and with a touch of ironic disdain befitting the hotel veranda or the smoking car." [14]

In addition to the somewhat unconventional love stories (in which the interest centers less on the inevitable union of the lovers than on the milieu depicted), *Options* is noteworthy for the inclusion of two of O. Henry's best-known stories. "The Rose of Dixie" is a still-valid satire on Southern parochialism, and "Thimble, Thimble"—another Southern story—created something of a sensation with its tantalizing ending, suggestive of Stockton's "The Lady or the Tiger?" The magazine which Porter entitled the *Rose of Dixie* seems to have been modeled after the violently misnamed periodical the *Bohemian*, published in Fort Worth, Texas, from 1899 to 1904, and edited by Mrs. Henrie Clay Gorman. The *Bohemian*, which included a section devoted to Bible stories and temperance pieces, specialized in articles such as "What Emancipation Did for My Old Nurse," by Mrs. B. M. Carter, of Carter's Hill, Virginia. Widely read all over the South, the magazine was one in which the local citizens took considerable pride.[15] After the publication of "Thimble, Thimble," in December, 1908, *Hampton's Magazine* ran a contest for the best solutions to the unsolved problem in the story. The extent of the response to this contest is made clear by the letter which Porter wrote to the editor after he had selected the winning letters:

. . . To me it was an interesting task to read the nearly 3,000 letters that you so cheerfully inflicted upon me and I am quits with you because what you gleefully hoped would be a burden turned out to be a pleasure to me. . . .

And in conclusion, let me say that the other day I saw a cartoon in a newspaper showing a large gentleman (recently elected to a responsible governmental position) chopping heartily away with an axe at a fence labeled "Mason and Dixon's Line." Let us all hope that when the fence is down, across the line will surge northward many things besides the expected votes. Let us hope that some of the old-time Southern chivalry which is a useful leaven, may meet some of the south-coming poise and cool sagacity of the North, and combine into what would make a people superior to any other on the globe at the present writing.[16]

Now, nearly a year after the writing of that letter, Porter in Asheville was turning his own gaze northward and again in the direction of the theater, for George Tyler continued to prod him. After buying the dramatic rights to "A Retrieved Reformation," Tyler had turned the assignment over to a playwright named Paul Armstrong, who reportedly locked himself in a room in the Hotel Algonquin and a week later emerged with a script entitled *Alias Jimmy Valentine*. The next day he and Tyler left for Chicago.

Eleven days later *Alias Jimmy Valentine*, starring H. B. Warner and featuring Laurette Taylor in her first important part, began a run which—in Alexander Woollcott's words—"was to tweak and tantalize playgoers all over America, England, France, Spain, and South Africa; and which was to breed a very epidemic of plays in which no self-respecting protagonist would think of approaching the first act without a neat murder or at least a bank robbery to his credit." [17] The royalties which went to Armstrong were soon running as high as $800 a week,[18] a fact which Tyler—almost cruelly, it seems in perspective—did not allow to be lost on Porter. Each week he mailed to Asheville a copy of the box-office receipts.

By the end of the play's run Armstrong had made over $100,000 from his week's work, but it did not take Porter that long to understand the significance of the figures. In an undated letter to Tyler (which arrived early in January, 1910) he said he had "a little proposition" to make with reference to his proposed dramatization of "The World and the Door": "If you'll advance me $500, I'll come to New York, establish myself in some quiet rural spot known only to yourself and your emissaries and go to work and finish a play. . . . As collateral, I can only make over to you the dramatic rights of all my stories until the work is done. The new play "Alias Jimmy Valentine" inspired me to believe I can do something for both of us." [19] Tyler's response to this proposition seems not to have been entirely satisfactory, for on January 25 Porter wrote again, to explain why he needed the money in a lump sum (the amount had now increased to $750). He was, he said, "about as nervous and reflexactionary as the hind leg of a frog as shown in the magazine section of any Sunday newspaper," but even so he was "almost as strong and tough as a suffragette." As a result of his rest cure he found himself possessed of about as much cash "as was left lying around the box-office at the last performance of 'Lo.' " He continued:

Now suppose we have a few moments' conversation as heart-to-heart as an editorial on chicken salad in the Ladies' Home Journal by Edward Everett Hale.

I owe something in the neighborhood of $500 down here that should and shall be paid before the obsequious porter of the So. Ry. Co. can have the opportunity of brushing the soot off the window-sill of Mr. Pullman's car onto the left knee of my new trousers. I'm not after any money now—it's transportation, and a chance that I want. I can work the proposition out in the short story line; but it's slow, Colonel, slow. I want to get into the real game, and I'll stake my reputation as the best story writer with a radius of Asheville that we can pull it off.

Here's what I need in order to start things going.

I've got to pay up everything here and leave a small bunch of collateral with my long suffering family to enable them to purchase the usual cuisine of persimmons and rabbits for a while.

If Tyler would send the money, he said, he would start for New York at once, placing all of his time at Tyler's disposal until the play was finished. To keep his presence a secret, he would even have his mail continue to go to North Carolina and be forwarded to him. There was one other matter, too.

You know how much "front" counts. I'm not afraid of New York police and editors; but if I arrive there in a linen suit, with helmet and tennis shoes, what would Big Bill Edwards do but shovel me into a cart and dump me into the East River?

So get busy with your telegraph blanks. Send me $750 *by wire* when you get this and I'll strike New York Thursday at the latest. I've got to have some margin, and you'll get my exclusive services thereby. Take another chance. You can't lose.

I am enclosing you as rather poor collateral the rights to my stories.

I hate to make any new dickers with the magazine people and that's why I put the matter so strenuously to you. I know now how much better (financially) the stage business is; thanks to you.

Porter's next communication (toward the end of February) was a telegram:

Like to have funds. Do wire to-day. Will positively be there on time. Have cut out spending and Chianti.

Even this brought only partial compliance. Apparently Tyler sent only $500, to which Porter's response was another telegram:

Wire balance. Am waiting at the depot.

In addition to $500 already advanced during the previous autumn, the present $750 brought to $1,250 the amount which Tyler gambled on the dramatization of "The World and the Door." Perhaps *gambled* is hardly the word, since he now held the dramatic rights to all the O. Henry stories. According to Woollcott's later statement, Porter "had received the money, retained the margin, and started North. But once he found himself at the gates of Bagdad he had stood wide-eyed for a moment and then drifted happily off to the bazaars, stumbled on some old cronies, and given himself over to celebrating his return from exile. Tyler never saw him again." [20] The actual details, however, are less picturesque.

On the night he was to leave for New York, Porter had—or intended to have—a farewell talk with Margaret, who later recalled their leave taking: " 'Bill,' he began—he had always called me 'Bill,' 'Jim,' or 'Pete,' seldom 'Margaret'—'Bill. . . .' It was an attempt to put into words all the unspoken things of the past. In it I sensed his realization of the futility of attempting to express the emotions that crowd the moment of parting. Also I felt, as I believe he did, that this parting was going to be different from all the others." [21] Sara, however, had no sense of the finality of the occasion. She wrote him shortly after he had left:

You shall be segregated when you come and want to work. . . . Never again will I ask you to tear your affection for me out of your body and hand it over to me to look at the roots to see if your love for me is alive. I know it is, because mine is. . . . Sometimes when you have disapproved of wives we know, you have looked at me with that funny, wise, cynical little smile of yours and have said, "You're better than most." I am going to wait ten whole years . . . and I mean to be wonderfully good—then some night when we get home from some place where you haven't approved of the wives' methods of managing their husbands, you're going to say, "You are better than any." See if you don't.[22]

Sara's touching letter went unanswered, although Porter attended to a small matter of business she had requested of him. "He was good," she commented afterward, "at remembering to do the little trifles."

In New York, Porter seems to have ensconced himself in the Hotel Chelsea, on West Twenty-third Street,[23] but he neither kept his whereabouts a secret nor set to work on the play he had come to write. The reason for his breach of agreement is painfully clear. As he remarked to a friend: "New York doesn't seem to agree with me as it used to. . . . Yet New York . . . is all the mountains and

SARA COLEMAN PORTER

PORTER IN NEW YORK THE YEAR BEFORE HIS DEATH

the streams, the hills and purple valleys of mother earth. All the daffodils of spring meadows are blooming here. There's more poetry in a block of New York than in twenty daisied lanes." [24] Even more revealing is the series of notes written to Richard Duffy about a story which he managed to grind out shortly after his arrival. Clearly a full-length play was beyond his strength, since it took him a week, instead of a few hours as in earlier years, to write a 3,500-word story, chronicled as follows:

DEAR BILL: This is for publication; not as a guarantee of good faith. The rest tomorrow if possible—anyhow, a good day's work.

> Yours,
> BILL.

MY DEAR DUFFY:
Here is part of the story I was reasonably sure I could have for you by 4 this afternoon. I think you know that it's better for both sides not to have it spoiled by hurry. I will send in all the rest of it tomorrow afternoon, and I am sure you will like it.

> Yours as ever,
> S. P.

P.S. I always wait for a story to end before I give it a title.

MON CHER DUFE:
Here is some more of the story. I am giving all my attention to the finishing of it. I am rather sanguine of handing you all the rest of it tomorrow. All I can surely promise is that I will put all my time at it until it is completed.

No one could do less—everybody could not do more.

Am pretty sure to-morrow will wind it up. Do the best I can. It will be worth waiting a day longer for, because I think it is a good story.

> Yours as ever,
> S. P.

MY DEAR DUFFY:
Here's all of the story except about 200 words. It will have to be finished tonight. I am so sick that I can't sit up. I'll go home and knock out the rest to-night if I can hold a pencil. I am hugging the radiator with an overcoat on and will be here till about six. You can call me up or come by if you want to.

> Sincerely,
> S. P.[25]

Porter's ailment at the moment (the end of February or the first of March) was apparently nothing more serious than a case of influenza, but his general condition was deteriorating steadily, as he himself seems to have realized. A few days after the death of Anne Partlan's father in March, Porter called on her. "He had learned of my loss and called," she later wrote, "eager to know how it was with the one who had gone. Did he leave debts, or was he free from material obligations? Was he resigned? All this interested him. Then suddenly he almost groaned, 'Oh, I don't want to die; I am swamped with obligations.' Then he quieted and asked how my father felt about a hereafter." [26]

"Did you ever hear the little chickens picking at the shells, trying to get out?" he remarked. "We're like them. We're picking at our shells."

"But outside?" Anne asked. "What happens when we get out?"

Porter shrugged. "Would there be any sense in it? Suppose you and I got another chance, with the experience and knowledge we have now. Wouldn't we boggle up our lives just as badly?" [27]

In the same month *Strictly Business* appeared, the collection of stories which Porter had planned with Steger during the previous autumn in North Carolina. For this volume he had returned to his fund of New York stories, chiefly those which had appeared in the *World*, but by now he was probably not much concerned with the reception of the book (the last to be published in his lifetime). A reviewer in the *Nation* said that *Strictly Business* added twenty-three chapters to O. Henry's "encyclopaedic account of the impudence, the energy, the recklessness, the vulgar loves, the fat and cynical materialism of proletarian America." [28] But the stories were glaringly uneven, said the reviewer, who lamented the author's overhasty production and hoped for the day when O. Henry would have leisure to do his best more consistently.

It was not leisure which Porter lacked now; it was the capacity to write at all. He was trying to write for *Hampton's* a story entitled "The Snow Man," for which he had already received advance payment, but he simply could not finish it. He had to call on a staff member of the magazine to help him out. Harrison Merton Lyons, who wrote the last two-thirds of the story,[29] later reported that Porter had by now lost so much flesh that "his neck stood in his collar like a stick in a pond, his face mercilessly lined, his lisp a broken whisper murmured with an effort. He gave me a curious feminine impression—not effeminate—as he sat in his chair, something grandmotherly." [30] Lyons quotes Porter as confiding that he was tired of writing stories with surprise endings. "There gets to be a sameness about the trick," he said. "It is nothing but a trick. . . . The next stories I write are going to have your serious endings to them."

Another of the few people who saw Porter during these last months of his life was Seth Moyle, with whom he discussed the prospect of death and who quotes him as remarking casually: "We're both up against it financially, Colonel. But when the Big Show comes off, and I suppose they will make a big show of it, just you hire a taxi and you and Jo breeze down Riverside Drive as though you were millionaires. It'll probably be 'In the Good Old Summer Time' and they'll be wearing top hats and frock coats and all that sort of stuff. That will be uncomfortable. Stick to a straw hat and hock your frock for a taxi." [31]

By now Porter was a semi-invalid. As he wrote James P. Crane on April 15: "I thought I was much better and came back to New York about a month ago and have been in bed most of the time. . . . I didn't pick up down there [in North Carolina] as well as I should have done. There was too much scenery and fresh air. What I need is a steam-heated flat with no ventilation or exercise." [32] It was about the same time that a group of friends coaxed him out to dinner. He had become almost a complete recluse, refusing to take telephone messages and leaving his room (he was back in the Caledonia by now) only for a painful daily walk of three blocks over to Madison Square and three blocks back. At the dinner with his friends—his last recorded appearance—he was not able to eat at all, as Will Irwin remembered the occasion, "but he tried pathetically to talk and to summon those glints of cynic wisdom which were the salt at every table where he sat. They noticed then how his face had changed. [He had had] . . . a repressed upper lip which hid his teeth. Now he had lost control of that upper lip; it drew up as he talked, giving a sinister change to the whole aspect of his face." [33]

Since his return to New York, he had turned to whisky again to keep himself going. Presumably soon after his return his Asheville friend Judge Thomas A. Jones visited the city and spent an evening with him. The nature of the evening is indicated by an inscription in the copy of *The Four Million* which Porter presented to his guest before they parted: "To Marsa Tommy Jones in commmmmemmoration of our evening on seeeeeing The Four Million—for he's a joooly good fellow. O. Henry." [34] After his death, his Caledonia apartment yielded some even more graphic evidence. "I know it is true," Robert H. Davis said many years later, "that nine empty whiskey bottles were found under his bed after that last bout that was the death of him." [35]

His death, when at last it came, came quickly. On the evening of Friday, June 3, three months before his forty-eighth birthday, Porter telephoned Anne Partlan, who lived in an apartment not far from the Caledonia. He needed help, and she could tell that he was in the throes of some seizure. Going at once to his assistance, Anne found him semiconscious on the floor, with the telephone receiver dangling as if he had collapsed after speaking to her. She summoned her own physician, Dr. Charles Russell Hancock, who after a hurried examination saw that Porter needed to be in a hospital. Since Porter refused to have an ambulance, a taxi was called, and after helping him on with his clothes, Dr. Hancock tried to brush his hair for him. "You're a poor barber, Doc," Porter said with a smile, taking the brush himself. When the taxi arrived, he was in the midst of a spasm of pain, but as he was helped out to the street he insisted on stopping to shake hands with the manager of the Caledonia, and on the way to the Polyclinic Hospital on East Thirty-fourth Street he made casual conversation about the sights along the streets. On arriving at the hospital he refused to be carried but walked under his own power to the reception desk, where he took out all the cash he had in his pocket—twenty-three cents—and remarked, "I've heard of people being worth thirty cents, and here I am going to die and only worth twenty-three cents." [36]

Knowing his dread of publicity, Anne Partlan had asked him in the taxi what name should be given for the hospital records. "Call me Dennis," he had said. "My name will be Dennis in the morning." [37] Anne had tried to discount this gloomy forboding (phrased in a familiar Texas expression), and Porter had settled for Parker—

Will S. Parker. His identity was therefore unknown in the hospital, unknown even to Dr. Hancock, who later said he knew only that his patient was the most remarkable one he had ever had.

Once he was put to bed, Porter had to be propped up with pillows so that he could breathe. "I kept waiting," Dr. Hancock said, "for the collapse that should have taken place days before . . . but he remained keen up until the very end." [38] He had, in an advanced stage, both cirrhosis of the liver and diabetes, as well as the most dilated heart which Dr. Hancock had ever encountered. At first he was in great pain, and throughout the night and the next day he grew steadily weaker. Except for Anne Partlan, apparently only John O'Hara Cosgrave (editor of *Everybody's*) was allowed to see him before orders were given to admit no visitors. [39]

Dr. Hancock stayed with him until midnight on Saturday, and as he prepared to leave, a nurse dimmed the lights. It was then that Porter spoke the words which have generally been reported as his last. "Turn up the lights," he protested to the nurse, adding in a paraphrase of the popular song of 1907, "I don't want to go home in the dark." Back at the hospital at five-thirty on Sunday morning, Dr. Hancock saw that the end was near. Porter was conscious until almost the moment of death, which Dr. Hancock said occurred at 7:06, after a final murmur: "Send for Mr. Hall." [40] The immediate cause of death, according to the New York *Herald* on Monday morning, was cirrhosis of the liver. [41]

According to Dr. Hancock, Porter had made no disposition of property. "He had no property, or keepsakes or anything, he told me." Apparently he had made no plans of any kind, and his wife did not arrive until five o'clock Sunday afternoon, when she was met by Gilman Hall and William Griffeth, who broke the news to her. Previously Hall, Griffeth, and Steger had met in Porter's Caledonia apartment to make arrangements for the funeral, which they decided should be held in the Little Church Around the Corner, because of its reputation for welcoming all comers and its proximity to Porter's beloved Madison Square. On Sara's arrival, Hall and Griffeth took her to view her husband's body at the undertaking establishment to which it had been removed. According to Hall, the body had been carelessly dealt with in the hospital morgue (where Porter's identity was not known), and the undertaker was having trouble. At any rate, Sara found her husband's body almost unrecognizable. After a long look she turned away, saying: "I think that is he. I'm sure those are his hands." [42]

The O. Henry touch at the funeral is a familiar story. Through some error a wedding had been scheduled for the same hour (eleven o'clock on Tuesday, June 7). The groom's brother, his best man, arrived early to find preparations being made for a funeral. In an attempt to keep from the bride this inauspicious omen, he met the bridal party at the curb and told them that another wedding had been slipped in ahead of theirs and that he had arranged for a twelve o'clock ceremony. So the wedding group adjourned to a nearby hotel while the burial service was read for Porter.

In a letter dated June 7, Walter Hines Page wrote Alphonso Smith:

We had the sad experience of attending poor Porter's funeral today. . . . The truth, I suspect, is that he had been dying for a long time. He led a life for many years that was as far removed as possible from the scientific care of himself. He ate and drank what he pleased, and took no exercise. . . . He ought to have lived, of course, very many years more, and it is a great shame and pity that he didn't.

At the Little Church . . . there was quite a large gathering of the story-writing people and the publishers, and the literary folk of the town, and others whom I didn't know. It was all very simple and sad. [43]

In addition to Page himself, the pallbearers were Richard Harding Davis, Dr. John H. Finley, Will Irwin, Don Seitz, and John O'Hara Cosgrave. The Reverend George Clark Houghton read the service, adding to the ritual a reading of the poem "Crossing the Bar." As it had been with Porter in life, so it was in death. Most of those who attended the funeral had not known him personally, but only through his stories. As Mabel Wagnalls was later to remark, he seemed as always "not quite at home, just a little out of place," [44] for there was a sense of haste at the funeral on account of the wedding guests waiting outside, their voices audible through the open windows.

Immediately after the service the body was taken to Pennsylvania Station to be returned to Asheville, where a graveside service was conducted by the Reverend R. F. Campbell, the minister who had married him in 1907. His grave was marked by a small granite block inscribed:

WILLIAM SYDNEY PORTER
1862   1910

Perhaps his best epitaph is the poem he attributed to the ill-fated shepherd-poet in his own favorite among his stories: [45]

> I go to seek on many roads
>   What is to be.
> True heart and strong, with love to light—
> Will they not bear me in the fight
> To order, shun or wield or mould
>   My Destiny?

APPENDIX

· ⟨∾⟩ ·

NOTES AND REFERENCES

APPENDIX: The *Rolling Stone*

• ᴄᴡᴀᴏ •

Except for syndicated material (mainly Bill Nye's column), which never occupied more than a fourth of the contents, Porter himself wrote and drew practically everything in his paper: part of the time a five-column 13 x 20 sheet, then 10 x 12 size with four columns, containing eight or twelve pages respectively. For the mechanical and business sides of the undertaking he had a succession of some six assistants. Having begun operations with James P. Crane (and with his father-in-law and his wife as production helpers), he announced in the fifth issue (May 12, 1894) the addition of S. W. Teagarden as manager and J. E. McGillivray as city circulator. By July 14 Teagarden's name was dropped, to be replaced on August 11 with that of Dixie Daniels (who later said, however, that he had been acting as printer from very early in the venture). The following two issues announced the addition of Guy McLaughlin, first as subscription agent and second as advertising agent as well, but McLaughlin did not last long. On October 13, after his place had been vacant for two issues, J. T. Tyler joined the staff for an indeterminate period. As if in preparation for the expansion that was in the making, Dixie Daniels's name was dropped on December 21 (though presumably he continued with the paper), and on January 26, 1895, came the addition which Daniels had opposed: that of Henry Ryder-Taylor as co-editor. Finally, on March 30, Ryder-Taylor was demoted to "Manager of the San Antonio Department," and H. A. McEachin was added as "associate in the business and management of this paper." Four weeks later the *Rolling Stone* expired.

In spite of repeated self-ads (not to mention, first, a two-week offer of a six-months' subscription for seventy-five cents instead of the usual dollar rate, and, second, an offer of "*The Rolling Stone* one year and a half dozen of Hill's best Cabinet Photographs for $2.00"), the paper rolled for only about a year "and then," as Porter later put the matter,

251

"showed unmistakable signs of getting mossy. Moss and I were never friends, and so I said good-by to *The Rolling Stone*." During the fifty-five weeks of its publication, only forty-eight issues appeared (if the masthead numbering can be trusted). Of the thirty-six extant issues in the only known file of the paper (now in the Rare Books Collections of the University of Texas), Harry P. Steger, who began the file, found twenty-four issues among the papers of Major Brackenridge (president of the First National Bank in Austin) and five more issues elsewhere in the city. Since Steger's time, seven more issues have been added to the file.

In a careful study of the financial side of the enterprise, Paul Tracy ("A Closer Look at O. Henry's *Rolling Stone*," Master's thesis, University of Texas, 1949) has estimated that on the basis of 1,500 subscriptions at $1.50 each, Porter might have made as much as $2,250 from subscriptions, but that since he probably never averaged over 1,000 subscribers (many of whom were in arrears or had subscribed for six months or less), he may easily have made as little as $1,000 from subscriptions. The matter of advertising revenue is even more difficult to pin down with any exactness. At a glance there seem to have been a great many advertisers, ranging all the way from "C. A. Graves, Dentist, Painless Extraction Guaranteed," to the Blue Front Store with its "Elegant Black Hose, 25c. You can't match them for 40c anywhere else in Austin." The same store also advertised "H. & S. Corsets. We sell the H. & S. $1.25 Corset for 85c. [And somewhat disconcertingly:] We sell the H. & S. $1.15 Corset for $1.65." Incidentally, the meretricious devices employed by some of Porter's advertisers aroused the ire of one merchant, who used his space to announce:

An Advertisement. There are many ways to advertise, many dodges to catch the eye. This is not one. This is a straight, clean cut, paid for advertisement of a legitimate business. W. H. Richardson, hardware and dry goods. [September 29, 1894, p. 8.]

The only available figures on advertising rates are, first, a notice of a charge of $1.00 per inch for one insertion, and later (on January 26, 1895) a special offer of half that rate, with a monthly rate of $1.00 (for four issues). Assuming that the regular monthly rate had been $2.00 per inch (or fifty cents per issue), Tracy has estimated that up to January 26, 1895, Porter cleared perhaps a matter of $55 a week (based on an average of 110 inches of advertising at fifty cents per inch). This would make a total of slightly over $2,000 for the thirty-seven issues involved. At half of the former rate, the eleven remaining issues would have netted some $300, bringing the total advertising revenue to something like $2,300.

Contrary to Dixie Daniels's statement that one cause of the failure of the *Rolling Stone* was the involvement in the Elmendorf-Callaghan mayoralty race in San Antonio, it is possible to surmise that Porter's incentive in the matter was the chance to collect a share of the campaign funds. It is entirely possible that instead of wrecking his paper, participation in the San Antonio campaign furnished him the money to keep publishing through the spring of 1895. But such possible revenue cannot be estimated, and on the basis of the $3,300 which can be accounted for during the year of publication, Porter would have grossed somewhat less than $300 a month. With printing costs and staff salaries to be paid, Tracy guesses at a net income of as little as $50 a month. At any rate, it was not enough for a family of three to live on, and some four months after losing his bank job Porter gave up the attempt to live on his editorial earnings.

While the *Rolling Stone* lasted, though, its high-spirited gaiety camouflaged completely the editor's financial worries, as well as his difficulties at home and in the bank. It dealt only lightly, too, with such national perplexities as free silver, the Populist party, the tariff argument, labor relations, and the six-months' jail sentence of Eugene V. Debs in connection with the Pullman strike. Without a consistent political attitude, Porter seemed at times to have a liberal slant on affairs, as in an editorial he ran on the subject of Coxey's Army:

General Coxey has made a great blunder. He and his fellows should have gone to Washington clad in broadcloth and fine garments, and backed by a big bank roll, as the iron, steel, sugar, and other lobbyist delegations do. He should have taken apartments at the Arlington, and given receptions and dinners. That's the way to get legislation at the hands of the American congress.

This thing of leading a few half clothed and worse fed working men to the capitol grounds to indulge in the vulgar and old-fashioned peaceable assemblage to petition for redress of grievances, with not a dollar of boodle in sight for the oppressed and overworked members of congress, was of course an outrage, and so the perpetrators were promptly squelched by the strong hand of the "law." [May 12, 1894, p. 4.]

In the next breath, however, Porter was condoning a lynching which had occurred the week before in Corsicana:

Of course, northern papers will teem with misrepresentations of the affair and will indulge in abusing the South generally and the State of Texas in particular. But what do we care for their strictures? Southern manhood has a method of dealing with this class of crime that is at least satisfactory to those who mete out justice. . . . Our people will pursue the even tenor of their way until it again becomes necessary to make an example of some brute of northern proclivities, and they will then prove themselves equal to the emergency. [April 27, 1895, p. 4.]

In the governor's race Porter first supported Reagan, then Culberson, but he was not consistent in his attitudes toward either of them. And as for the Populist candidate, Porter informed his readers: "A great State like Texas, which bathes her feet regularly, can have nothing in common with the average populist" (May 5, 1894, p. 5). He went on to make fun of the Populists in cartoon and in verse, as well as in a detective story featuring the discovery of a pair of socks in the luggage of Congressional candidate "Sockless" Simpson (*Works*, p. 1015).

It was not politics, however, but the spectacle of life in and around Austin which received most of Porter's attention, and although the quality of his humor varies considerably, the occasions for it seem to have been endless. There was, for example, his feud with the local Germans, carried on by way of cartoon as well as text. (Incidentally, Dixie Daniels's statement attributing the failure of the paper partly to the offense given to the German subscribers is balanced by the fact that E. Von Boeckmann's advertisement ran from the first issue straight through to the last. Surely the long-continued and thoroughly good-natured thrusts at the Germans would have ceased if business had been seriously affected.) It all began with a write-up of the state *Saengerfest* in Houston, headlined: "Full Report of the Twentieth Meeting Held at Houston—Between Drinks." The story began: "Houston, Texas, May 8—The city is filling up with alarming quickness. Visitors are rapidly pouring in. Pouring in beer more than anything else." A continuation of the story, dated May 9, begins: "Yesterday was the first day of the Saengerfest, and today is universally acknowledged to be the second. Tomorrow, if the beer holds out, will be the third" (May 12, 1894, p. 1).

There were, as had no doubt been expected, letters of protest from readers who supposed "that *The Rolling Stone* has been endeavoring to pour insult upon their particular nationality and are accordingly in great wrath." In reply to such readers Porter stated that his *Saengerfest* story had been "conceived in a spirit of pure fun and printed without a wish or thought that it would possibly give serious offense to anyone" (May 19, 1894, p. 4). But the occasions for further space fillers on the subject were irresistible. Next came an "explanation" from the imaginary Houston correspondent, Gottlieb Kremhauser:

Editor *Rolling Stone*

Your letter asking me vy I write apout dot saengerfest in de vay I didt lies pefore me on a peer parrel. I haf peen mit der subrise gefilled ven you say dot dose Cherman citizens in Austin haf peen apout my little letter mad.

I am a Cherman, but I the English language write and gespeak so petter as anybody, vich you gan see ven you reat mine letter.

I sent you a little schreibenbrief apout dot music und dot commers, but I not de half of it you told. . . . It vas de krandest wunderschon, most peautiful, high-doned und boetical dime efer seen in dis country. We trink tree hundert kegs peer. De music vas schveet und knocked most all der blastering from der walls in de opera house.

I don't dink I was sober but dree hours in dree days, und den I write you mein ledeer von die saengerfest. . . . [June 2, 1894, p. 1.]

Still not content to drop the matter, Porter wrote a farcical story about a German detective, Hans Von Pretzel, whose attempt to follow up a tip that a diamond thief was hiding in a schooner led him not to the waterfront but to a beer garden (August 18, 1894, p. 1). And since the letters to the editor had apparently ceased by now, Porter was reduced to inventing one for a final thrust:

Meinheer Rolling Stone:

I vant to keek. Last Sunday I invite mein friends in mein garten to gome and see me a vile. Der vas Kreger mit his vlute, Baumhauser mit his pase trum, Vilhelm von Toodleberg mit der drombone, Schnitzer und his pig viddle, and me dot blays der violin. Vell I haf drei keg peer in mein garten, and we all go dere und a ferry goot kviet dime ve haf. Ve shust haf ein salamander, und hit dot dable mit our mugs, und den ve blay dot obening chorus from Tannhauser. Den hav more peer, und Schnitzer he sing "Die Wacht am Rhein," und Kruger giv us a goot imidation ohf a pig vast mit a gate unter. Yoost den a tall man in a plack coat raise his head das vence over und say:

"Hwew! you tam Tuchmen, if you ton'd stop blaying dose infernal tunes I vill gall a boliceman und haf de whole gang of you arrested. . . ." [October 13, 1894, p. 5.]

Another of Porter's favorite targets was the "new woman," as opposed to the old-fashioned girl with whom Porter said he used to go on picnics ("and we fished and pulled flowers and made lemonade, and played 'drop the handkerchief,' and then when we drove home we wreathed our hats with green leaves and flowers, and all hands sang the 'Suwanee River,' and that was our idea of a good time").

Nowadays, when a fellow wants a picnic he hires a horse and buggy, and gets his girl, and they drive up and down the Avenue. He smokes cigarettes and she chews gum.

Her conversation is embellished with such expressions as "You bet your life," "You ain't in it," "I should smile," "Rats," and "Come off." She chews gum.

She wears shirts and ties, and either cuts her hair short or blondines it.

She will not refuse a glass of beer, if insisted upon and not more than fifteen persons are looking. She chews gum.

She says "hello" and catches young men by the sleeve on the street when she talks to them, which is every time she meets them.

She rides a bicycle if her figure justifies it, and sometimes whether or no. She chews gum.

She goes on excursions to other towns and up the river with young men whose reputations and intentions are well known.

She is losing that delicacy and spotlessness that a man may not look for in a companion for a boat ride, but demands in a wife. With her own hands she is brushing that bloom from the grape, that morning dew from the rosebud, that is her most precious possession. She is cheapening her charms by advertising them, and the day will come when she will be "marked down" in price. [June 2, 1894, p. 2.]

So exercised did Porter become over the subject of the new woman's clothing that he resorted to verse:

> She was a new woman,
>   In a mild kind of way,
> Wore coat, vest, and collar
>   And—don't give it away.
>
> One day this girl wandered
>   With Jack by her side,
> They were awfully spoony
>   Like bridegroom and bride.
>
> But she was uneasy,
>   For she had her care,
> She wanted to tell him
>   And yet didn't dare.
>
> But she mustered up courage,
>   And said, oh so tender,
> "Say, Jack, what do you do
>   When you burst a suspender?"   [April 27, 1895, p. 8.]

One of the popular features in the *Rolling Stone* was a page made up in imitation of a backwoods newspaper entitled *The Plunkville Patriot*. Beginning as a single item called "Special Correspondence—Pflugerville" (Pflugerville being a small German settlement fifteen miles from Austin), the *Patriot* developed into a running account of the career of its fictitious editor, Colonel Aristotle Jordan, who, among his other activities, ran for mayor on a platform whose main plank was his promise to get rid of the smelly hogpen of his opponent, Judge Perkins. Colonel Jordan became mayor, perhaps partly as a result of offering a year's subscription to his paper for each vote, but as an editor he continued to have his troubles. He was reduced, first, to accepting merchandise in payment for subscriptions, but merchandise of such random and dubious sort that finally he requested "anyone desiring to exchange a good pair of blankets for ½ bottle of sasparilla and a souvenir litter of pups will do well to call at this office" (October 27, 1894, p. 6). Then, too, there was the problem of getting and holding advertisers, a problem which became so acute that the colonel resorted to direct retaliation: "Adams & Co. have ordered out their $2.25 add with us that has been running about two months. No less than three children have been poisoned by eating their canned vegetables, and J. O. ɣdams, the senior member of the firm, was run out of Kansas City for adulterating cod fish balls it pays to advertise" (March 2, 1895, p. 7).

The colonel's most chronic problem, of course, was that of typography: the mixing of different sizes and kinds of type, the way letters had of appearing upside-down and sideways, the juxtaposition of lines from advertisements with lines from news items:

> Miss Mattie Lungweiler a charming
> brunette of Hog Prairie is on a visit to
> The Elite Saloon, open
> day & Night
> her friend, Miss Gussie Shaw. [October 13, 1894, p. 3.]

Or even more regrettable:

> Miss Rena Baldy, a talented and
> accomplished young lady from Corn
> Shuck Crossing, called at our office
> yesterday, and informed us that
> When she was a child she cried for
> Castoria. . . . [December 7, 1894, p. 5.]

At this time Porter was equally facile in prose and verse. Most of his better efforts in verse were parodies—for example, one called "The Bridge of Ryes," directed at Thomas Hood's "The Bridge of Sighs":

> One more unfortunate
> Weary of breath,
> Chewing cloves hastily,
> Scared half to death.

O, it was pitiful,
  He left the city full
Quarter past one.

Prop him up tenderly
  By the hall stair,
On a big bender, he
  Needs some fresh air.
Now run! His wife's got her
  Hands in his hair.   [September 8, 1894, p. 4.]

Longfellow's poem "The Bridge" furnished Porter an occasion to reveal his somewhat shocking acquaintance with the mysteries of poker:

I stood on the straight at midnight,
  As the clocks were striking the hour,
And some man raised me the limit
  Behind a hand of power.

I saw the long procession
  Of chips pass to and fro,
The young heart hot and restless,
  The pat hand soft and slow.

But now it has fallen from me,
  And the pot has gone, I see,
For a king full held by another,
  Cast it's shadow over me.   [August 18, 1894, p. 5.]

There is an impressive quantity of verse in the *Rolling Stone*, including a fair number of serious poems. The more serious and ambitious they are, however, the more mediocre and even banal. Despite his facility and cleverness, Porter had no genuine talent for poetry.

The same thing might be said of his art work in the *Rolling Stone*, of which there is an equally impressive quantity. In fairness it should be pointed out, as the Houston *Post* explained in an editorial at the time of Porter's death, that both for the *Rolling Stone* and later for the *Post* "he did most of the work on chalk, in which the drawing was made, a cast of lead being afterward made with more or less general results of reproducing the drawings in the shape of printing. The generality of the result was at times disheartening to the artist." It seems an exaggeration, however, to go on to say, as the *Post* did: "As a cartoonist Porter would have made a mark equal to that he attained as a writer had he developed his genius" (see *The Caliph of Bagdad*, p. 79).

NOTES AND REFERENCES

· ᏩᏊᎤ ·

Of the manuscript materials used in this book, the following collections are most noteworthy.

The large O. Henry Collection in the public library of Greensboro, North Carolina, actually consists of two collections, here referred to as *Smith papers* and *Greensboro papers*. The Smith papers are the notes on interviews, letters from various friends and acquaintances of Porter, and other documentary materials collected by C. Alphonso Smith in preparation for writing his authorized biography in 1916. In addition to Smith's own collection, the library has over the years assembled a very large collection of clippings as well as various manuscript materials pertaining to O. Henry.

A small but invaluable body of material, here referred to as *Rollins papers*, consists of letters from and interviews with Porter's friends and acquaintances in Austin, who in 1914 supplied information (pertaining chiefly to the embezzlement charge and trial) to Dr. Hyder E. Rollins, retired professor of English at Harvard University. These papers are in the Houghton Library at Harvard.

As indicated in the notes, other significant collections are to be found in the Library of the University of Virginia, in the records of the United States District Court in Austin, and in the files of the Department of Justice in Washington.

In the interest of brevity, the following abbreviations are used in the notes:

The *O. Henry Biography*, by C. Alphonso Smith (New York, 1916), is here referred to as "Smith, *Biography*."

The Caliph of Bagdad, by Robert H. Davis and Arthur B. Maurice (New York, 1931), is here referred to as "*Caliph*."

O. Henry, The Man and His Work, by E. Hudson Long (Philadelphia, 1949), is here referred to as "Long, *O. Henry*."

The references to O. Henry's stories are to *The Complete Works of O. Henry* (2 vols.) (New York, 1953), here referred to as "*Works*."

*　*　*　*　*

FOREWORD

[1] "Recalling O. Henry," *New Yorker*, July 12, 1930, p. 22.

[2] "The Plutonian Fire," *Works*, p. 1303.

[3] Smith, *Biography*, p. 3.

[4] "The Duel," *Works*, p. 1623.

[5] "O. Henry," *Texas Review*, Jan., 1917, p. 248.

[6] F. L. Pattee in *The Cambridge History of American Literature* (New York, 1933; originally published in 1918), II, 394.

[7] Smith papers: the exact figure furnished by Russell Doubleday was 4,721,000.

[8] Smith, *Biography*, p. 9.

[9] F. L. Pattee, "The Journalization of American Literature," *Unpopular Review*, April–June, 1917, p. 394.

[10] C. Alphonso Smith, "O. Henry—the Man and His Work," *Mentor*, Feb., 1923, p. 3.

[11] *Literary Digest*, Aug. 19, 1922, p. 30.

[12] Albert Parry, "O. Henry Invades Russia," *Mentor*, May, 1927, p. 38.

[13] "Soviet Finds Modernity in American Authors," *Library Journal*, Jan. 1, 1945, p. 12.

[14] Deming Brown, "O. Henry in Russia," *Russian Review*, Oct., 1953, p. 253.

[15] Information furnished to the present writer by Doubleday & Company, Inc.

[16] *Prejudices: Second Series* (New York, 1920), p. 43.

[17] *New York Times Book Review*, June 7, 1931, p. 5.

[18] *Expression in America* (New York, 1932), pp. 326 ff.

[19] *American Fiction* (New York, 1936), pp. 545 ff.

[20] E. Hudson Long, *O. Henry, The Man and His Work* (Philadelphia, 1949).

[21] Luther W. Courtney, "O. Henry's Case Reconsidered," *American Literature*, Jan., 1943, p. 361.

[22] *Understanding Fiction* (New York, 1943), p. 118.

[23] "The Amazing Genius of O. Henry," reprinted in *Waifs and Strays* (New York, 1917), p. 189.

[24] *The Confident Years* (New York, 1952), pp. 276 ff.

[25] Caroline Gordon and Allen Tate, *The House of Fiction* (New York, 1950), p. 228.

CHAPTER 1 (pages 1–17)

[1] Porter was christened William Sidney, but in 1898 dropped the first name and changed the spelling of the middle name to "Sydney." Properly, therefore, he should be called either Sydney Porter or William Sidney Porter.

[2] "Let Me Feel Your Pulse," *Works*, p. 860.

[3] The quoted phrases are those of William Laurie Hill: Smith, *Biography*, p. 32.

[4] Compilation of the list of owners of the property at 426 West Market Street: Greensboro papers.

[5] Smith, *Biography*, p. 40.

[6] David Scott: quoted by Smith, *Biography*, p. 42.

[7] Joe Reece: quoted by Smith, *Biography*, p. 42.

[8] Smith, *Biography*, p. 26.

[9] Letter from John H. Dillard: Smith papers.

[10] Shirley Worth Porter, "O. Henry as His Brother Knew Him," Greensboro *Daily News*, May 12, 1929: clipping in Greensboro papers.

[11] Letter from Charles J. Brockmann: Smith papers.

[12] Interview with Anne Partlan: Smith papers.

[13] Shirley Worth Porter: Greensboro papers.

[14] Tom Tate: Smith papers.

[15] Letter from John H. Dillard: Smith papers.

[16] Letter from Charles J. Brockmann: Smith papers.

[17] John H. Dillard: quoted by Smith, *Biography*, p. 44.

[18] Letter from John H. Dillard: Smith papers.

[19] "The Voice of the City," *Works*, p. 1253.

[20] Interview with Mrs. Thomas Crabtree, Greensboro *Daily News*, Oct. 4, 1925: clipping in Greensboro papers.

[21] Smith, *Biography*, p. 76.

[22] Interview with Tom Tate, *Literary Digest*, March 10, 1928, p. 52.

[23] Smith, *Biography*, p. 90.

[24] Interview with Bettie D. Caldwell: Smith papers. Also the *New North State*, March 11, 1874 (clipping in Greensboro papers), which states that W. C. Porter (Will's uncle) had begun building both a house for himself and one next door for his mother.

[25] Mrs. Thomas Crabtree: see Note 20.

[26] Long, *O. Henry*, p. 15.

[27] John H. Dillard: Smith papers.

[28] Smith, *Biography*, p. 26.

[29] Letter from Mrs. G. B. Bush: Smith papers.

[30] Interview with Mrs. Richard Hall: Smith papers.

[31] Letter from Col. R. Bingham: Smith papers.

[32] Letter from William M. Smith: Smith papers.

[33] "The Love Philtre of Ikey Schoenstein," *Works*, p. 50.

[34] Rufus W. Weaver: quoted by Smith, *Biography*, p. 66.

[35] Letter from James T. Morehead: Smith papers.

[36] *A Fool's Errand* (together with Part II, *The Invisible Empire*) (New York, 1880), p. 147.

[37] Smith, *Biography*, p. 67.

[38] Tom Tate: quoted by Smith, *Biography*, p. 67.

[39] Sara Lindsay Coleman, *Wind of Destiny* (New York, 1916), p. 29.

[40] See Mary S. Harrell, *O. Henry Encore* (New York, 1939), p. 119.

[41] Cathleen Pike, "O. Henry in North Carolina," *N.C. State*, Aug. 17, 1946: clipping in Greensboro papers.

[42] Arthur W. Page, "Little Pictures of O. Henry," *Bookman*, June, 1913, p. 385.

[43] Letter from John S. Michaux: Smith papers.

[44] Mrs. Richard Hall: Smith papers.

[45] In a letter to Smith, Bettie D. Caldwell spoke also of the "kind-hearted Aunt Lina," whose "kindness was the only pleasant feature" of her stay in the Porter home that year (along with another orphan girl, a cousin of Will's named May Lou). Miss Lina, said the writer, "loved and was very proud of" her nephew Will. If Miss Lina could afford to give free board to two orphan girls, however, one wonders why the nephew of whom she was so proud could not be equipped with the uniform and books which would have allowed him to go to the Bingham School. Perhaps the explanation is that some other relative was paying Miss Lina for the girls' keep.

[46] Page, *op. cit.*, p. 386.

[47] Letter from A. W. McAlister: Smith papers.

[48] Smith, *Biography*, p. 41.

CHAPTER 2 (pages 18–34)

[1] Dora Neill Raymond, *Captain Lee Hall of Texas* (Norman, Okla., 1940), p. 14.

[2] In *The Great South* (New York, 1874) Edmund King included an account of one of "Red" Hall's daring encounters with desperadoes.

[3] Letter dated March 13, 1884: Long, *O. Henry*, pp. 22–23.

[4] Lollie Cave Wilson, *Hard to Forget* (Los Angeles, Calif., 1939), pp. 1 ff.

[5] "Madame Bo-Peep of the Ranches," *Works*, pp. 1242–1244. The Lee Halls had originally occupied the 12 x 8 frame house where Will

lived with the Richard Halls. Afterward they had built a 12 x 35 log house. Hyder Rollins ("O. Henry's Texas Days," *Bookman*, Oct., 1914, p. 155) speaks of a "fine brick house" in which they lived during Will Porter's time.

[6] Corpus Christi *Caller*, April, 1883: quoted by Raymond, p. 206.

[7] Letter from Mrs. Lee Hall: Smith papers.

[8] See, e.g., "The Caballero's Way" and "An Afternoon Miracle."

[9] "The Last of the Troubadours," *Works*, p. 815.

[10] "The Hiding of Black Bill," *Works*, p. 704.

[11] "Madame Bo-Peep of the Ranches," *Works*, 1247.

[12] Letter to Mrs. J. K. Hall, March 13, 1884: Smith, *Biography*, p. 113.

[13] Rollins, *op. cit.*, p. 154.

[14] *Ibid.*, p. 156.

[15] Letter from Mrs. Lee Hall: Smith papers.

[16] Letter to Mrs. J. K. Hall, Jan. 20, 1883: Smith, *Biography*, p. 110.

[17] "The Higher Abdication," *Works*, p. 187.

[18] Letter to Dr. Beall, Feb. 27, 1884: *Works*, p. 1074.

[19] Rollins, *op. cit.*, p. 158.

[20] Letter dated Nov. 31 [*sic*], 1883.

[21] Interview with Mrs. Richard Hall: Smith papers.

[22] Letter from Mrs. Wilson Woodrow: Smith papers.

[23] Letter from Mrs. Clarence Crozier Stuckert: quoted by Mary S. Harrell, "O. Henry's Texas Contacts," (Univ. of Texas Master's thesis, June, 1935), p. 18.

[24] "The Pimienta Pancakes," *Works*, p. 138.

[25] Florence Stratton and Vincent Burke, *The White Plume* (Beaumont, Tex., 1931), p. 11.

[26] "The Pimienta Pancakes," *Works*, p. 139.

[27] Stratton and Burke, *op. cit.*, p. 13.

[28] *Ibid.*, p. 19.

[29] *Ibid.*, p. 30.

[30] Letter to Dr. Beall, Feb. 27, 1884.

[31] Letter dated Jan. 20, 1883.

[32] Harrell thesis, p. 15.

[33] *Ibid.*, p. 40.

[34] "The Princess and the Puma," *Works*, p. 233.

[35] "Hearts and Crosses," *Works*, p. 117.

[36] "The Higher Abdication," *Works*, p. 178.

[37] "The Missing Chord," *Works*, p. 223.

[38] Interview with Mrs. Richard Hall: Smith papers.

[39] Letter dated Feb. 27, 1884: Long, *O. Henry*, p. 38.

[40] Letter to Mrs. J. K. Hall, May 5, 1883: Long, *O. Henry*, p. 35.

[41] Letter to Mrs. J. K. Hall, March 13, 1884.

[42] *Works,* p. 1049.

[43] Letter to Dr. Beall, Dec. 8, 1883: *Works,* p. 1072.

[44] Letter to Dr. Beall, Jan. 13, 1884: *Works,* p. 1074.

[45] Letter to Vesper Reading Club: Smith, *Biography,* p. 108. The letter is undated, but Beall said it was probably written in 1884.

[46] Arthur W. Page, "Little Pictures of O. Henry," *Bookman,* July, 1913, pp. 498–499.

[47] Interview with Mrs. Richard Hall: Smith papers.

[48] *Caliph,* p. 205.

CHAPTER 3 (pages 35–53)

[1] Dan Hollis, "The Persecution of O. Henry," Austin *American-Statesman Magazine,* Aug. 30, 1925, p. 10. (The series is in 8 installments: Aug. 16 to Oct. 4, 1925.) According to W. A. Kerr, a cousin of Clarence Crozier (quoted in Harrell thesis, p. 44), the Kerrs had moved from Fort Ewell to Cotulla by the time Porter left La Salle County, and he visited in their home for several days before leaving for Austin.

[2] *Works,* p. 1043.

[3] Hollis, *op. cit.,* Aug. 30, p. 10.

[4] *Ibid.,* p. 10.

[5] Letter dated May 26, 1884: *Independent,* Sept. 5, 1912, p. 543.

[6] Edmunds Travis, "O. Henry's Austin Years," *Bunker's Monthly,* June, 1928, p. 495. Since Will's departure his uncle had taken in a partner.

[7] Hollis, *op. cit.,* Aug. 30, p. 14.

[8] Lollie Cave Wilson, *Hard to Forget,* p. 11.

[9] *Ibid.,* p. 95.

[10] Arthur W. Page, "Little Pictures of O. Henry," *Bookman,* July 1913, p. 503.

[11] *Ibid.,* p. 502.

[12] Wilson, *op. cit.,* p. 35. Her autograph album was signed on Aug. 1, 1885, by the four original members: C. E. Hillyer, 1st Tenor; R. H. Edmondson, Jr., 1st Tenor; Howard H. Long, 1st Bass; H. C. Searcy, 2nd Bass. "When Clay Searcy went away Bill Porter took his place."

[13] Page, *op. cit.,* p. 502.

[14] Harrell thesis, p. 58.

[15] Wilson, *op. cit.,* p. 32.

[16] Letter dated May 10, 1885: *Works,* p. 1078.

[17] Wilson, *op. cit.*, p. 99.

[18] *Ibid.*, p. 112.

[19] *Ibid.*, p. 124.

[20] *Works*, p. 1077.

[21] *Letters to Lithopolis, from O. Henry to Mabel Wagnalls* (New York, 1922), p. 26.

[22] Harrell thesis, p. 56.

[23] "When O. Henry Edited *The Rolling Stone*," Dallas *Morning News*, Feb. 25, 1912, Part III, p. 2.

[24] C. E. Hillyer, quoted in Harrell thesis, p. 56.

[25] Smith, *Biography*, p. 118.

[26] Page, *op. cit.*, p. 502.

[27] Frances G. Maltby, *The Dimity Sweetheart* (Richmond, Va., 1930), p. 17.

[28] *Ibid.*, pp. 45 and 11.

[29] *Ibid.*, p. 18.

[30] Undated letter, Univ. of Texas Rare Books Collection.

[31] Maltby, *op. cit.*, p. 20.

[32] *Ibid.*, p. 24.

[33] *Ibid.*, p. 25.

[34] *Ibid.*, p. 23.

[35] Interview with Mrs. Roach: Smith papers.

[36] Cited by Maltby, *op. cit.*, p. 25.

[37] *Ibid.*, p. 29.

[38] *Ibid.*, p. 30.

[39] Interview with Mrs. Richard Hall: Smith papers.

[40] The city directory at this time (as noted by Robinson, Elmquist, and Clark, "O. Henry's Austin," *Southwest Review*, July, 1939) listed Porter's residence as a rooming house at 110 E. 9th St. Perhaps this was one of the temporary rooms where he kept "bachelor hall." At any rate he seems definitely to have boarded with the Andersons and to have considered their home his headquarters.

[41] Maltby, *op. cit.*, p. 31.

[42] *Ibid.*, p. 34.

[43] Statement by Lawrence Smoot: Harrell thesis, p. 71.

[44] *Ibid.*, p. 73.

[45] Maltby, *op. cit.*, p. 32.

[46] Interview with Charles E. Anderson: Smith papers.

[47] Maltby, *op. cit.*, p. 34.

[48] Harrell thesis, p. 74.

CHAPTER 4 (pages 54–81)

[1] "Sisters of the Golden Veil," *Works,* pp. 81–83.

[2] Smith, *Biography,* p. 121.

[3] Long, *O. Henry,* p. 61.

[4] *Caliph,* pp. 348–351.

[5] Maltby, *The Dimity Sweetheart,* p. 72.

[6] *Ibid.,* p. 40.

[7] Letter from Anne Partlan: Smith papers.

[8] Smith, *Biography,* p. 123.

[9] *Ibid.,* p. 123.

[10] *Ibid.,* p. 123.

[11] Maltby, *op. cit.,* p. 40.

[12] Wilson, *Hard to Forget,* p. 33.

[13] Maltby, *op. cit.,* p. 40.

[14] Interview with Betty Hall: Smith papers.

[15] Maltby, *op. cit.,* p. 39.

[16] Interview with Mrs. Roach: Smith papers.

[17] *Works,* p. 1051.

[18] *Ibid.,* p. 1216.

[19] Shirley Worth Porter, "O. Henry as His Brother Knew Him," Raleigh *News and Observer,* May 19, 1929: clipping in Greensboro papers.

[20] *Works,* p. 735. For Porter's own expedition, see Paul Adams, "O. Henry and Texas," *Bellman,* Sept. 22, 1917, p. 321.

[21] "Valentines That O. Henry Made," Dallas *Morning News,* Feb. 12, 1933, Feature Section, p. 2.

[22] Margaret Porter Cesare, "My O. Henry," *Mentor,* Feb., 1923, p. 17.

[23] Maltby, *op. cit.,* p. 43.

[24] "The Hand of Fate," *Rolling Stone,* April 27, 1895, p. 6.

[25] See Note 19 above.

[26] Harrell thesis, p. 81.

[27] Interview with Charles E. Anderson: Smith papers.

[28] *Works,* p. 460.

[29] Letter from Ernest Kippenheimer: Smith papers.

[30] Interview with W. B. Wortham: Smith papers.

[31] Interview with Mrs. Roach: Smith papers. If Porter did actually pay off such a sum, he surely was helped by his father-in-law.

[32] Harrell thesis, p. 83.

[33] Maltby, *op. cit.,* p. 58.

[34] Letter to the present writer from William F. Price, Nov. 7, 1955.

[35] Interview with Ed R. Smith: Smith papers.

[36] "The Enchanted Kiss," *Works,* p. 479.

[37] Interview with Ed McLean: Smith papers.

[38] Interview with Mrs. Roach: Smith papers.

[39] *Ibid.*

[40] Interview with Mrs. Richard Hall: Smith papers.

[41] Margaret Porter Cesare, *op. cit.,* p. 17.

[42] Ed Smith: quoted in Harrell thesis, p. 95.

[43] *Ibid.,* p. 93.

[44] Maltby, *op. cit.,* p. 46.

[45] Letter from Mrs. Elnora McLary: Rollins papers.

[46] Interview with Mrs. Richard Hall: Rollins papers.

[47] Maltby, *op. cit.,* p. 48.

[48] *Ibid.,* p. 42.

[49] Letter from James P. Crane: Smith papers.

[50] Letter from Ernest Kippenheimer: Smith papers.

[51] Rollins, "O. Henry's Texas Days," *Bookman,* Oct., 1914, p. 163.

[52] Paul Tracy, "A Closer Look at O. Henry's *Rolling Stone,*" Master's thesis, Univ. of Texas, Aug., 1949, p. 49.

[53] *Rolling Stone,* April 28, 1894.

[54] Paul Adams, p. 321 (see Note 20 above), says that Crane did much of the writing for the early issues. Even if this is true (there is no other mention of any writing by Crane), the association soon ended. By Dec., 1894, Crane had for some time been living in Chicago.

[55] Arthur W. Page, "Little Pictures of O. Henry," *Bookman,* July, 1913, p. 506.

[56] Letter from Crane: Smith papers.

[57] "When O. Henry Edited *The Rolling Stone,*" Dallas *Morning News,* Feb. 25, 1912, Pt. III, p. 2.

[58] Rollins papers.

[59] Interview with Mrs. Richard Hall: Rollins papers.

[60] Rollins papers.

[61] Rollins, *op. cit.,* p. 164.

[62] "Valentines That O. Henry Made," Dallas *Morning News,* Feb. 12, 1933, Feature Section, p. 2.

[63] Wilson, *op. cit.,* p. 142.

[64] Statement by W. H. Stacy: Smith papers.

[65] Interview with Mrs. Richard Hall: Smith papers.

[66] Smith, *Biography,* p. 126.

[67] Austin *American,* Dec. 20, 1937, p. 1.

[68] Letter from F. B. Gray to the Comptroller of the Currency, July 13, 1895: Files of the Dept. of Justice (No. 10547, 1895; File No. 7243, 1891).

[69] Maltby, *op. cit.*, p. 60.
[70] Harrell thesis, p. 105.
[71] Smith, *Biography*, p. 126.
[72] *Rolling Stone*, Jan. 26, 1895, p. 4.
[73] Arthur W. Page, *op. cit.*, p. 507.
[74] Matthew Paxton, "An O. Henry Story That Was Not Written," London *Bookman*, July, 1929, p. 204.
[75] *Ibid.*, p. 205.
[76] *Works*, p. 480.
[77] *Ibid.*, p. 483.
[78] Paxton, *op. cit.*, p. 205.
[79] *Works*, p. 253.
[80] *Rolling Stone*, June 9, 1894, p. 4.
[81] Sept. 15, 1894, p. 5.
[82] June 9, 1894, p. 1.
[83] Aug. 25, 1894, p. 6.
[84] July 14, 1894, p. 5.
[85] *Works*, p. 1051.
[86] See, e.g., *Works*, pp. 1015, 1021.
[87] Oct. 20, 1894, p. 2.
[88] Ed R. Smith: Smith notes.
[89] Edmunds Travis, "O. Henry Enters the Shadows," *Bunker's Monthly*, May, 1928, p. 672.
[90] Vic Daniels, "O. Henry on a Treasure Hunt," Dallas *Morning News*, Aug. 9, 1931, Feature Section, p. 2.
[91] March 30, 1895, p. 4.

CHAPTER 5 (pages 82–98)

[1] Austin *American*, Dec. 20, 1937, p. 1.
[2] Letter dated July 13, 1895: Dept. of Justice files: No. 10547, 1895; File No. 7243, 1891.
[3] Dept. of Justice files: A. G. 7243, 1891.
[4] Dept. of Justice files: 11,156, 1895.
[5] Dept. of Justice files: A. G. 7243–91.
[6] "Friends in San Rosario," *Works*, p. 451.
[7] Maltby, *The Dimity Sweetheart*, p. 51.
[8] Harrell thesis, p. 115. The blackboard inscription was found by W. A. Roberts, husband of the Artie Slaughter whose invitation preserved a written record of the New Year's Ball attended by Porter.
[9] According to Paul Adams ("O. Henry and Texas," *Bellman*, Sept. 22, 1917, p. 322), during the summer Porter held briefly a $15 a week

reporting job on the San Antonio *Express,* but a San Antonio news-paper man who has studied Porter's connections in the city (Gerald Ashford of the *Express*) has been unable to find any evidence of such work.

[10] Florence Stratton, *Postscripts* (New York, 1923), p. x.

[11] Edmunds Travis, "O. Henry Enters the Shadows," *Bunker's Monthly,* May, 1928, p. 673.

[12] Harrell thesis, p. 122.

[13] Interview with Ed McLean: Smith papers.

[14] Adams, *op. cit.,* p. 321.

[15] Stratton, *op. cit.,* p. xi.

[16] "O. Henry Once Houston Writer," Houston *Post-Dispatch,* Oct. 26, 1930, Magazine Section, p. 10; and Stratton, *op. cit.,* p. xiii.

[17] Stratton, *op. cit.,* p. xi.

[18] *Ibid.,* p. 31.

[19] "O. Henry Once Houston Writer" (see Note 16), p. 10.

[20] Stratton, *op. cit.,* p. 178.

[21] *Ibid.,* p. 74.

[22] Harrell thesis, p. 124.

[23] Wilson, *Hard to Forget,* p. 146.

[24] Austin *American,* Dec. 20, 1937, p. 1.

[25] Rollins papers.

[26] Austin Court Records.

[27] Harrell thesis, p. 124.

[28] Interview with Ed McLean: Smith papers.

[29] Adams, *op. cit.,* p. 322. A letter from Porter to Hill in 1904 substantiates Adams's statement.

[30] Austin Court Records.

[31] Interview with Anna Porter Boyers: Smith papers.

[32] Wilson, *op. cit.,* p. 194.

[33] Two graduate students at the Univ. of Texas, working independently, made the identification at about the same time. Grace Miller Watson, in a Master's thesis entitled "O. Henry on the Houston *Post*" (August, 1934), collected 50 of these longer items, of which she proceeded to make a careful study. Mary Sunlocks Harrell published her collection (substantially the same group) in a book entitled *O. Henry Encore* (New York, 1939).

[34] Watson thesis, p. lii.

[35] *Ibid.,* p. 325.

[36] *O. Henry Encore,* pp. 81–82.

[37] *Ibid.,* p. 93.

[38] *Works*, p. 486.
[39] *O. Henry Encore*, p. 1.
[40] *Ibid.*, p. 11.
[41] *Ibid.*, p. 149.
[42] Watson thesis, p. 279.
[43] *O. Henry Encore*, p. 132.
[44] *Ibid.*, p. 61.
[45] *Ibid.*, p. 203.
[46] Watson thesis, p. 344.
[47] Mrs. Maltby's dating of the event in September is a clear error, of course, since the trial was scheduled for July.
[48] Travis, *op. cit.*, p. 675.
[49] Harrell thesis, p. 127.
[50] Hyder Rollins's review of *The Caliph of Bagdad* in *Sat. Review of Lit.*, June 27, 1931, p. 923.
[51] Maltby, *op. cit.*, p. 64.
[52] Rollins, *op. cit.*, p. 923.
[53] Interview with Herman Pressler: Smith papers.
[54] Interview with Louis Kreisle: Smith papers.
[55] Wilson, *op. cit.*, pp. 192–196.

CHAPTER 6 (pages 99–111)

[1] Smith, *Biography*, p. 145.
[2] Wilson, *Hard to Forget*, p. 197.
[3] Letter from Joe Monget: Smith papers.
[4] "Blind Man's Holiday," *Works*, pp. 1223–1226.
[5] "Hostages to Momus," *Works*, p. 338.
[6] "Blind Man's Holiday," *Works*, p. 1225.
[7] "Cherchez la Femme," *Works*, p. 450.
[8] "The Renaissance at Charleroi," *Works*, p. 496.
[9] "Helping the Other Fellow," *Works*, p. 973.
[10] Wilson, *op. cit.*, pp. 197–198.
[11] Al Jennings, *Through the Shadows with O. Henry* (New York, 1921), pp. 71 ff.
[12] *Ibid.*, p. 94.
[13] Harrell thesis, p. 136.
[14] Maltby, *The Dimity Sweetheart*, p. 65.
[15] Interview with L. H. Kreisle: Smith papers.
[16] Interview with Anne Partlan: Smith papers.
[17] Letter from Mrs. Kreisle: Smith papers.
[18] "Fox-in-the-Morning," *Works*, pp. 554–559.

[19] "The Lotus and the Bottle," *Works,* p. 563.

[20] Interview with Anne Partlan: Smith papers.

[21] Hollis, "The Persecution of O. Henry," Austin *American-Statesman Magazine,* Sept. 13, 1925, p. 6.

[22] *Ibid.,* p. 7.

[23] Wilson, *op. cit.,* p. 198.

[24] Interview with Mrs. Richard Hall: Rollins papers.

[25] Hyder Rollins's review of *The Caliph of Bagdad* in *Sat. Review of Lit.,* June 27, 1931, p. 923.

[26] *Caliph,* p. 115.

[27] *Transcript of Record. W. S. PORTER, Plaintiff in Error versus UNITED STATES, Defendants in Error. Error to U. S. Circuit Court, Western District of Texas. E. S. Upton, 631 Poydras St., New Orleans. Printed Copy of Record FILED May 24, 1898,* p. 6.

[28] Interview with Herman Pressler: Smith papers. Also Rollins papers.

[29] Maltby, *op. cit.,* p. 69.

[30] Letter from Mrs. Kreisle: Smith papers.

[31] Hollis, *op. cit.,* Sept. 13, 1925, p. 7.

[32] Interview with Mrs. Roach: Smith papers.

[33] "The Last Leaf," *Works,* p. 1458.

[34] Maltby, *op. cit.,* p. 73.

[35] *Ibid.,* p. 73.

[36] *Statesman,* July 27, 1897: quoted by Maltby, *op. cit.,* p. 71.

[37] Interview with Mrs. Roach: Smith papers.

[38] *Caliph,* p. 110.

[39] Interview with P. G. Roach: Smith papers. "Old and hard of hearing," Smith noted, "but good-looking, sweet and fine-fibred. . . . Thinks O. H. poorest financier in world."

[40] Smith, *Biography,* p. 124.

[41] *Ibid.,* p. 124.

[42] Paul S. Clarkson, *A Bibliography of William Sydney Porter* (Caldwell, Idaho, 1938), p. 137.

[43] Interview with Charles Anderson: Smith papers.

CHAPTER 7 (pages 112–130)

[1] Dept. of Justice files: No. 1469, 1898. Culberson had written a similar request on June 7, 1897, in preparation for the July term of court, but presumably the case was postponed because of the continuing illness of Porter's wife.

[2] Trueman O'Quinn, "O. Henry in Austin," *Southwestern Historical Quarterly,* Oct., 1939, p. 155.

[3] *Transcript of Record*, p. 5. Although Porter had appeared in court on Feb. 1, no official cognizance of his return was taken, it seems, until the opening date of the court term.

[4] One story is that a publisher later offered Charles Pickle, court reporter, $10,000 for the notebooks containing his shorthand transcript of testimony, but that the notebooks had been lost and Pickle's search was in vain. On the other hand, Luther W. Courtney ("O. Henry's Case Reconsidered," *American Literature*, Jan., 1943, p. 361) reports that in 1935 Pickle told him that it was not customary in 1898 to make complete records in all trials and that he did not make a stenographic record of the testimony or the pleadings.

[5] Charles Pickle, quoted by Courtney, *op. cit.*, p. 369.

[6] Mark Patterson, quoted in Harrell thesis, p. 163.

[7] Smith, *Biography*, p. 146.

[8] *Ibid.*, p. 144.

[9] Wilson, *Hard to Forget*, p. 202.

[10] Harrell thesis, p. 176.

[11] *Ibid.*, p. 164.

[12] *Sat. Review of Lit.*, June 27, 1931, p. 923.

[13] Although a credit slip was sent to Waco on Nov. 12, 1894, two months later (Jan. 16, 1895) J. K. Rose of the Waco bank wrote, "You do not credit $299.60." In reply Dr. R. J. Brackenridge acknowledged an error in the balance of the Waco bank and said a correction was being made.

[14] Dan McAllister, "Negligently, Perhaps; Criminally, Never," *South Atlantic Quarterly*, Oct., 1952, p. 568.

[15] *Transcript of Record*, p. 10.

[16] *Ibid.*, p. 14.

[17] *Ibid.*, pp. 18–19.

[18] Interview with L. B. Mallet: Rollins papers.

[19] Harrell thesis, p. 164.

[20] Interview with Louis Kreisle: Smith papers.

[21] Harrell thesis, p. 166.

[22] *Transcript of Record*, p. 23.

[23] Copied in Rollins papers.

[24] Smith papers.

[25] McAllister, *op. cit.*, p. 562.

[26] Smith papers.

[27] Letter from Dr. John M. Thomas: Smith papers.

[28] Smith, *Biography*, p. 146.

[29] McAllister, *op. cit.*, pp. 566–567.

[30] Harrell thesis, p. 179.
[31] Smith papers.
[32] *Ibid.*
[33] *Caliph,* p. 114.
[34] Smith, *Biography,* p. 144.
[35] *Caliph,* p. 114.
[36] Interview with Judge R. H. Ward: Smith papers.
[37] Harrell thesis, p. 176.
[38] *Ibid.,* p. 177.
[39] Courtney, *op. cit.,* pp. 370–371. According to Courtney, "one of the last circulation managers of *The Rolling Stone*" (the man is unnamed) said he had computed that the subscription and advertising revenue could not have kept the paper going, after the deduction of salaries. This computation indicated that the amount of the insufficiency was almost exactly the amount for which Porter was indicted ($854.08). But Gray's original charges involved the sum of $5,654.20 (before the selection of two charges around which the strongest case could be built), so that the circulation manager's computation seems of dubious value.
[40] Interviews in Rollins papers.
[41] Smith papers. According to A. B. MacDonald (Buffalo *Evening News,* July 16, 1935: clipping in Greensboro papers), D. H. Hart remarked: "Innocent or guilty, what good would it have done him [to testify]? Had he testified, the judge would have instructed the jury that in considering his testimony they must take into account that the accused would probably color and withhold the truth. Porter knew he was going to be convicted. The fact that he ran away . . . was the big thing against him."
[42] *Works,* p. 229.
[43] *Ibid.,* pp. 452, 454.
[44] Letter to the present writer from William F. Price, Nov. 7, 1955.
[45] *Caliph,* p. 114.
[46] *Statesman,* Feb. 18, 1898.
[47] *Ibid.,* Feb. 19, 1898.
[48] Fact noted in Smith papers.
[49] *Transcript of Record,* pp. 26 and 28.
[50] Smith, *Biography,* p. 146.
[51] *Transcript of Record,* p. 30.
[52] Austin Court Records.
[53] Smith papers.
[54] Smith, *Biography,* p. 158.

[55] Smith papers.

[56] "Hearts and Hands," *Works*, p. 1667.

CHAPTER 8 (pages 131–151)

[1] Warden P. E. Thomas, quoted in Rollins papers.

[2] Jennings, *Through the Shadows with O. Henry*, p. 100.

[3] *Ibid.*, p. 102.

[4] Letter dated May 18, 1898: Smith, *Biography*, p. 154.

[5] *Ibid.*, p. 148.

[6] *Ibid.*, p. 157.

[7] *Ibid.*, p. 158.

[8] *Ibid.*, p. 148.

[9] Statement by J. Clarence Sullivan: Smith papers.

[10] Jennings, *op. cit.*, p. 106.

[11] *Ibid.*, p. 234.

[12] Smith, *Biography*, p. 155.

[13] Letter dated July 8, 1898: Smith, *Biography*, p. 157.

[14] Jennings, *op. cit.*, p. 114.

[15] *Ibid.*, p. 112.

[16] *Ibid.*, p. 238.

[17] Smith, *Biography*, p. 153.

[18] The letter was copied by Rollins from Mrs. Roach's original in 1915: Rollins papers.

[19] "Georgia's Ruling," according to Smith (*Biography*, p. 162), "was so intimately related to Dick Hall and so closely connected with the Austin land office that O. Henry forbade its publication in book form. It may be found in *Whirligigs*, published after O. Henry's death." Porter also wrote poetry (very poor poetry) in prison and at the beginning of his New York career. *Ainslee's* published three of his poems (signed John Arbuthnott) before he left prison: one in May, 1899; one in March, 1901; and one in June, 1901.

[20] Smith, *Biography*, p. 158.

[21] Rollins papers. See Note 18 above.

[22] John A. Lomax, "Henry Steger and O. Henry," *Southwest Review*, April, 1939, p. 158.

[23] Undated letter: Smith, *Biography*, p. 158.

[24] July 8, 1898: *ibid.*, p. 158.

[25] *Ibid.*, p. 160.

[26] *Ibid.*, p. 161.

[27] Oct. 1, 1900: *ibid.*, p. 161.

[28] Undated letter: *ibid.*, p. 164.

[29] Undated letter: *ibid.*, p. 165.

[30] Undated letter: *ibid.*, p. 166.

[31] Undated letter: *ibid.*, p. 166.

[32] Rollins papers: see Note 18 above.

[33] Trueman O'Quinn, *O. Henry's Own Trial* (Brief for W. S. Porter in the Appeal of His Case, Filed by His Attorneys August 30, 1898) (Austin, Texas, 1940). See Foreword, inside front cover.

[34] Rollins papers: see Note 18 above.

[35] Smith, *Biography*, p. 160.

[36] *Ibid.*, p. 150.

[37] *Ibid.*, p. 154.

[38] Smith, *Biography*, p. 163.

[39] Jennings, *op. cit.*, p. 128.

[40] *Ibid.*, p. 133.

[41] *Ibid.*, p. 134.

[42] *Ibid.*, pp. 226–227.

[43] *Ibid.*, p. 222.

[44] *Ibid.*, pp. 253–255.

[45] The letter is quoted in Smith, *Biography*, p. 162.

[46] Jennings, *op. cit.*, pp. 145–147 and 159.

[47] The notebook is among the items in the C. Alphonso Smith Papers held by the Library of the University of Virginia. The notebook includes the following later-published titles: "An Afternoon Miracle," "A Medley of Moods" (or "Blind Man's Holiday"), "Money Maze," "No Story," "A Fog in Santone," "A Blackjack Bargainer," "The Duplicity of Hargraves," "The Marionettes." The two stories "Whistling Dick's Christmas Stocking" and "Georgia's Ruling" antedate the notebook.

[48] "A Blackjack Bargainer" (*Munsey's*, Aug., 1901), "Hearts and Hands" (*Everybody's*, Dec., 1902), "The Pumpkin" (*Brandur*, Oct. 11, 1902), "One Dollar's Worth" (*Munsey's*, March, 1903), "Jimmy Hayes and Muriel" (*Munsey's*, July, 1903), "A Call Loan" (*Everybody's*, July, 1903), "The Reformation of Calliope" (*Assoc. Sunday Mag.*, Feb. 28, 1904). Two other stories were signed *Sidney Porter:* "The Cactus" (*Everybody's*, Oct. 1902) and "Round the Circle" (*Everybody's*, Oct., 1902). Theoretically these two stories should have been written before 1898, when Porter changed the spelling of his name, but the likelihood is greater that *Everybody's* simply made a typographical error that month.

[49] The full list of poems is: "Promptings" (May, 1899), "Uncaptured Joy" (March, 1901), "Sunset in the Far North" (June, 1901), "The

Captive" (Sept., 1901): all signed John Arbuthnott; "Auto Bugle Song" (signed Howard Clark, March, 1903), "April" (signed John Arbuthnott, April, 1903), "Two Chapters" (signed T. B. Dowd, May, 1903), "Spring in the City" (signed John Arbuthnott, June, 1903), "June" (signed T. B. Dowd, June, 1903), "Remorse" (signed S. H. Peters, July, 1903), "The Reporter's Private Lexicon" (signed T. B. Dowd, Nov., 1903), and "To a Gibson Girl" (signed John Arbuthnott, Dec., 1903).

50 He also signed a few later stories with other names to avoid seeming to monopolize the contents of *Ainslee's*, in which he once had three stories in the same issue. The stories signed with other names are: "Cherchez la Femme" (James L. Bliss, March, 1903), "Sound and Fury" (S. H. Peters, March, 1903), "The Robe of Peace" (S. H. Peters, April, 1903), "While the Auto Waits" (James L. Bliss, May, 1903), "October and June" (S. H. Peters, June, 1903), and "At Arms with Morpheus" (S. H. Peters, Oct., 1903): all in *Ainslee's*.

51 Stephen Leacock, "The Amazing Genius of O. Henry," *Waifs and Strays* (New York, 1917), p. 174.

52 George MacAdam, "O. Henry's Only Autobiographia," *O. Henry Papers, Containing Some Sketches of His Life Together with an Alphabetical Index to His Complete Works* (New York, 1924), p. 5.

53 Harrell thesis, p. 35.

54 *Ibid.*, p. 84.

55 Letter to the editor from Paul Adams, *Bookman*, Oct., 1925, p. 229.

56 Carl Goerch, "O. Henry's Brother Lives in Ayden," *N.C. State*, Nov. 24, 1934, p. 1.

57 Letter from Dan W. Williams, chairman of the Ohio Board of Clemency: quoted by William Wash Williams, *The Quiet Lodger of Irving Place* (New York, 1936), p. 201.

58 C. A. Smith, "O. Henry," *Nation*, May 11, 1918, p. 567.

59 Williams, *op. cit.*, p. 200.

60 *Works*, p. 1226.

CHAPTER 9 (pages 152–169)

1 Margaret Porter Cesare, "My O. Henry," *Mentor*, Feb., 1923, p. 17.

2 "A Blackjack Bargainer" (*Munsey's*, Aug.), "Rough et Noir" (*Ainslee's*, Dec.), "The Flag Paramount" (*Munsey's*, Jan.), "The Lotus and the Bottle" (*Smart Set*, Jan.), "The Duplicity of Hargraves" (*Junior Munsey*, Feb.), "The Passing of Black Eagle" (*Ainslee's*, March), "Friends in San Rosario" (*Ainslee's*, April), "The Marionettes" (*Black Cat*, April), and "By Courier" (*Smart Set*, May).

[3] *Works*, p. 1411.

[4] Jennings, *Through the Shadows with O. Henry*, pp. 257, 261.

[5] According to the volume *Rolling Stones*, in which this letter and the following one appear (*Works*, pp. 1090–93), the year was "probably 1902." The second letter is dated "Pittsburg October 24th," however, and Jennings's own account of the negotiations indicates that the acceptance letter from *Everybody's* arrived while he was hoping to be pardoned by President McKinley, who was assassinated in September, 1901.

[6] The article (entitled "Holding Up a Train") was published not in *Everybody's* but in *McClure's*, a fact which might help explain the delay between an acceptance in 1901 and a publication date of April, 1904. *Everybody's* evidently changed its mind, and the article had to be peddled further before finding a buyer.

[7] *Caliph*, p. 169.

[8] Also Porter is quoted as saying in 1909, "I now get $750 for a story that I would have been glad to get $75 for in my Pittsburgh days": *O. Henry Papers*, p. 20.

[9] Letter from H. P. Rhoades: Smith papers.

[10] George Seibel, "O. Henry and the Silver Dollar," *Bookman*, Aug., 1931, p. 593. Porter later told an interviewer (*O. Henry Papers*, p. 17) that there was an "infernal newspaper over in Pittsburgh that printed the story that when I first began to write I blew into its office, looking like a tramp, offered manuscripts for sale, and before blowing out again borrowed a dollar. The story is an embroidered fib. Why, I was the best-dressed man in the office unless it was the editor, whose shoes were a little more pointed than mine."

[11] *Caliph*, p. 263.

[12] Sara Lindsay Coleman, *Wind of Destiny* (New York, 1916), p. 30.

[13] This letter is owned by John S. Mayfield, of Bethesda, Md.

[14] Hall's letter and that of the graphologist (Willis B. Willard), together with Hall's written account of the proceedings, are also owned by Mr. Mayfield.

[15] Arthur W. Page, "Little Pictures of O. Henry," *Bookman*, October, 1913, p. 169.

[16] William Griffeth, "O. Henry at Work and Play," Dearborn *Independent*, Nov. 14, 1925, p. 4.

[17] Page, *op. cit.*, p. 171.

[18] *Biography*, p. 173.

[19] *Caliph*, p. 201.

[20] *Ibid.*, p. 206.

[21] Interview with Gilman Hall: Smith papers.

[22] Jennings, *op. cit.*, p. 297; *Works*, p. 1092.

[23] Seth Moyle, *My Friend O. Henry* (New York, 1914), p. 17.

[24] Smith papers.

[25] *Caliph*, p. 274.

[26] *Ibid.*, p. 265.

[27] "The Pretended O. Henry," *Bookman*, Oct. 1915, p. 123.

[28] Page, *op. cit.*, p. 174.

[29] *Ibid.*, p. 174.

[30] A review of *Sixes and Sevens* in the *Independent*, Oct. 19, 1911, p. 874.

[31] Mabel Wagnalls, *Letters to Lithopolis* (New York, 1922), p. 1.

[32] Dated June 25, 1903: *ibid.*, p. 6.

[33] Dated July 23, 1903: *ibid.*, p. 23.

[34] Dated Sept. 7, 1903: *ibid.*, p. 36.

[35] Oct. 13 [1903], *ibid.*, p. 57.

[36] *Ibid.*, p. xxiii.

[37] *Caliph*, p. 202.

[38] *Ibid.*, p. 204.

[39] William Wash Williams, *The Quiet Lodger of Irving Place*, p. 11.

[40] *Ibid.*, p. 29.

[41] Frank Wilson Nye, *Bill Nye: His Own Life Story* (New York, 1926), p. 174.

[42] According to Williams, it was after living in Irving Place that Porter moved to East Twenty-fourth Street, but Duffy's account of Porter's various residences makes this seem unlikely.

[43] Wagnalls, *op. cit.*, p. 36.

[44] Interview with Anna Porter Boyers: Smith papers.

[45] Moyle, *op. cit.*, p. 16.

[46] *Ibid.*, p. 18.

[47] "A New Page About O. Henry," *Bookman*, Jan., 1920, p. 474.

[48] Letter from H. C. Greening: Smith papers.

[49] Page, *op. cit.*, p. 175.

[50] Williams, *op. cit.*, p. 49.

[51] *Works*, p. 1493.

[52] Williams, *op. cit.*, p. 56.

[53] *Caliph*, p. 260.

CHAPTER 10 (pages 170–195)

[1] *Critic*, Feb., 1904, p. 109.

[2] Paul Adams, "O. Henry and Texas," *Bellman*, Sept. 22, 1917, p. 322.

[3] John D. Barry, "O. Henry," Greensboro *News*, April 12, 1915: clipping in Greensboro papers.

[4] *Caliph*, p. 363.

[5] Arthur W. Page, "Little Pictures of O. Henry," *Bookman*, October, 1913, p. 169.

[6] *Caliph*, p. 286.

[7] *O. Henry Papers*, pp. 17–20.

[8] Smith, *Biography*, p. 14.

[9] *Ibid.*, p. 10.

[10] *Mentor*, Feb., 1923, p. *d*.

[11] William Lyon Phelps, *The Advance of the English Novel* (New York, 1916), p. 128.

[12] Williams, *The Quiet Lodger of Irving Place*, p. 83.

[13] *Ibid.*, p. 163.

[14] *Ibid.*, p. 169.

[15] *Ibid.*, p. 159.

[16] Letter from H. C. Greening: Smith papers.

[17] Alexander Black, *American Husbands and Other Alternatives* (Indianapolis, Ind., 1923), p. 171.

[18] Letter from W. J. Ghent to Richard Duffy: Greensboro papers.

[19] William Griffeth, "O. Henry at Work and Play," Dearborn *Independent*, Nov, 14, 1925, p. 4.

[20] William Johnston, "Disciplining O. Henry," *Bookman*, Feb., 1921, p. 536.

[21] *O. Henry Papers*, p. 13.

[22] Art Young, "Recalling O. Henry," *New Yorker*, July 12, 1930, p. 22.

[23] *O. Henry Papers*, p. 20.

[24] Williams, *op. cit.*, p. 137.

[25] *Ibid.*, p. 148.

[26] *Works*, pp. 1360, 1363.

[27] Williams, *op. cit.*, p. 106. See also, e.g., Smith's interview with Gilman Hall.

[28] Roy Norton, quoted in *Caliph*, pp. 299–302.

[29] Interview with Roach: Smith papers.

[30] Jennings, *Through the Shadows with O. Henry*, p. 305.

[31] Williams, *op. cit.*, p. 211.

[32] *Ibid.*, p. 208.

[33] *Ibid.*, p. 223.

[34] *Works*, p. 1508.

[35] Williams, *op. cit.*, p. 217.

[36] Smith papers.

[37] *Works*, p. 76.

[38] Lindsey Denison, quoted in *Caliph*, p. 309.

[39] Smith papers.

[40] Jennings, *op. cit.*, pp. 312, 294.

[41] James Forman, "The Mystery of O. Henry," *Reader's Digest*, Aug., 1947, p. 94.

[42] "The Furnished Room," *Works*, p. 100.

[43] Williams, *op. cit.*, p. 176.

[44] Letter from Sara Coleman Porter to the *North Carolina Review*, Aug., 1912, p. 4.

[45] Smith papers.

[46] *Works*, pp. 1099–1104.

[47] "Past One at Rooney's," *Works*, pp. 1607, 1613.

[48] *Ibid.*, p. 63.

[49] O. W. Firkins, "O. Henry," in *Modern Essays*, ed. by Christopher Morley (New York, 1921), p. 102.

[50] Isaac F. Marcosson, *Adventures in Interviewing* (London, 1920), p. 269.

[51] The three notes are quoted in *Caliph*, p. 258.

[52] *Ibid.*, p. 221.

[53] *Ibid.*, p. 233.

[54] *Ibid.*, p. 235.

[55] *Ibid.*, p. 238.

[56] *Ibid.*, p. 248.

[57] Jennings, *op. cit.*, pp. 313–314.

[58] *Biography*, p. 180.

[59] Interview with Anna Porter Boyers: Smith papers.

[60] Nettie Roach Daily: quoted by Margetta Jung, "O. Henry in Manhattan," *Southwest Review*, July, 1939, p. 411.

[61] Hart MacArthur, *Graphic*, April 15, 1911: clipping in Greensboro papers.

[62] Smith, *Biography*, pp. 214, 237. The notebook is among the C. Alphonso Smith Papers in the Library of the University of Virginia.

[63] *Caliph*, p. 325.

[64] *Ibid.*, p. 331. Williams, *op. cit.*, (pp. 189–191), gives a slightly different account of the writing of the story.

[65] Williams, *op. cit.*, p. 176.

[66] Smith papers.

[67] See, e.g., Smith, *Biography*, p. 198, and *Caliph*, p. 267.

[68] See Paul S. Clarkson, "A Decomposition of *Cabbages and Kings*," *American Literature*, May, 1935, p. 195. Clarkson analyzes the book as follows: The Proem and half of Chapter 1 ("Fox-in-the-Morning," of which the second half is new) are from the story "Money Maze," as it appeared in *Ainslee's*, May, 1901. Chapter 2 ("The Lotus and the Bottle") is practically identical with the story of the same name

in *Smart Set*, Jan., 1902. Chapters 3 and 4 ("Smith" and "Caught") are again from "Money Maze." Chapter 5 ("Cupid's Exile Number Two") is half new (the latter half) and half from the story "The Lotus and the Cockleburrs," *Everybody's*, Oct., 1903. Chapter 6 ("The Phonograph and the Graft") is identical with the story of the same name which appeared in *McClure's*, Feb., 1903. Chapter 7 ("Money Maze") is entirely new. Chapters 8 and 9 ("The Admiral" and "The Flag Paramount") are both from the story "The Flag Paramount," *Ainslee's*, Jan., 1902. Chapter 10 ("The Shamrock and the Palm") is identical with the story of the same name which appeared in *Ainslee's*, March, 1903. Chapter 11 ("The Remnants of the Code") is entirely new. Chapters 12 and 13 ("Shoes" and "Ships") are from the story "The Lotus and the Cockleburrs," *Everybody's*, Oct., 1903. Chapter 14 ("Masters of Arts") is the story of the same name which appeared in *Everybody's*, Aug., 1903. Chapters 15 and 16 ("Dicky" and "Rouge et Noir") are from the story "Rouge et Noir," *Ainslee's*, Dec., 1901. Chapter 17 ("Two Recalls") again comes from the story "Money Maze," and Chapter 18 ("The Vitagraphoscope") is entirely new.

[69] Clarkson, *op. cit.*, p. 202.

[70] *Critic*, Feb., 1905, p. 189.

[71] *Independent*, Feb. 9, 1905, p. 328.

[72] *Bookman*, Feb., 1905, p. 561.

CHAPTER 11 (pages 196–209)

[1] Margetta Jung, "O. Henry in Manhattan," *Southwest Review*, July, 1939, p. 411.

[2] Margetta Jung, clipping from Raleigh *News and Observer*, June 3, 1934: Greensboro papers.

[3] Dan Hollis, "The Persecution of O. Henry," Austin *American-Statesman Magazine*, Oct. 4, 1925, p. 7.

[4] Ethel Patterson, "O. Henry and Me," *Everybody's Magazine*, Feb. 1914, p. 206. The following letters are from the same source, pp. 206–210.

[5] Arthur W. Page, "Little Pictures of O. Henry," *Bookman*, Oct., 1913, p. 175.

[6] See, e.g., such a story as "Extradited from Bohemia," in the volume *The Voice of the City*.

[7] Clipping from New York *Sun*, Jan. 10, 1915: Greensboro papers.

[8] Jennings indicates (*Through the Shadows with O. Henry*, p. 269) that the year was 1905, although he confuses the matter by saying he found Porter living in the Caledonia (where Porter did not live until the summer of 1907). Jennings was in New York again in 1908, however,

and probably remembered Porter's address only from his second visit. This guess is strengthened by Porter's story "From Each According to His Ability" (1905), which seems to be based on an evening he spent with Jennings, whose own account (pp. 295 ff.) dates the evening as during his first visit.

9 Jennings, *op. cit.*, pp. 284–289.

10 *Ibid.*, p. 303.

11 *Ibid.*, p. 107.

12 Sara Coleman Porter, "O. Henry Himself," unidentified clipping in Greensboro papers.

13 In Sara Lindsay Coleman's *Wind of Destiny* (p. 26) the letter is dated September 25, but in the article above (Note 12), where none of the names of people or places are changed, the date given is July 15. The text of the letters quoted here may be found in both sources.

14 *Critic*, July, 1906, p. 93.

15 *Independent*, July 19, 1906, p. 161.

16 *Bookman*, June, 1906, p. 365.

17 *Atlantic Monthly*, Jan., 1907, p. 126.

18 *Graphic*, April 15, 1911: clipping in Greensboro papers.

19 George Seibel, "O. Henry and the Silver Dollar," *Bookman*, Aug., 1931, p. 593.

20 Letter from Mrs. Wilson Woodrow: Smith papers.

21 New York *Sun*, Jan. 10, 1915: clipping in Greensboro papers.

22 *Wind of Destiny*, p. 59.

23 *Ibid.*, p. 42.

24 Letter from Sara Coleman Porter: Smith papers.

25 Walter Carroll, "An Afternoon with O. Henry's Widow," *Prairie Schooner*, Summer, 1952, p. 141.

26 Smith's copy of the letter is to be found in the Smith papers.

27 Letter from Anne Partlan: Smith papers.

28 *Wind of Destiny*, p. 85.

CHAPTER 12 (pages 210–230)

1 Undated letter in "Rolling Stones," *Works*, p. 1085.

2 Letter from the Rev. R. F. Campbell: Smith papers.

3 Sara Coleman Porter to Mr. and Mrs. C. A. Smith: C. Alphonso Smith Papers in the Library of the University of Virginia.

4 Sara Coleman Porter, letter to *North Carolina Review*, Aug., 1912, p. 4.

5 Ida Briggs Henderson, "How O. Henry Began His Writing Career," *N.C. State*, Feb. 9, 1935, p. 8.

6 *Outlook,* Nov. 2, 1907, p. 497.

7 *Nation,* Nov. 28, 1907, p. 496.

8 J. S. Gallegly, "Background and Patterns of O. Henry's Texas Bad-man Stories, *Rice Institute Pamphlet,* Oct., 1955, pp. 1–31.

9 *Works,* p. 261.

10 N. A. Jennings, *A Texas Ranger* (Dallas, Tex., 1930), p. 113: quoted by Gallegly, *op. cit.,* p. 19.

11 Gallegly, *op. cit.,* p. 22.

12 *Ibid.,* p. 29.

13 Sara Coleman Porter, "The Gift," *Delineator,* May, 1912, p. 376.

14 Seth Moyle, *My Friend O. Henry,* p. 30.

15 Sara Coleman Porter, *Delineator,* p. 376.

16 *Ibid.,* p. 376.

17 Walter Carroll, "An Afternoon with O. Henry's Widow," *Prairie Schooner,* Summer, 1952, p. 139.

18 Jennings, *Through the Shadows with O. Henry,* pp. 309–313.

19 Williams, *The Quiet Lodger of Irving Place,* p. 274.

20 Henry James Forman, "O. Henry's Short Stories, *North American Review,* May, 1908, p. 781.

21 *Outlook,* July 4, 1908, p. 532.

22 *Independent,* Sept. 3, 1908, p. 552.

23 See "The Buyer from Cactus City," "The Brief Debut of Tildy," "The Brief Romance of a Busy Broker," "The Memento," and "The Last Leaf."

24 See "The Badge of Policeman O'Roon," "The Lost Blend," "The Furnished Room," "Dougherty's Eye-Opener," and "A Harlem Tragedy."

25 See "The Love-Philtre of Ikey's Schoenstein."

26 See "Shocks of Doom" and "The Cop and the Anthem."

27 See "Vanity and Some Sables" and "The Guilty Party."

28 See "A Philistine in Bohemia" and "The Last Leaf."

29 See "Mammon and the Archer," "While the Auto Waits," and "A Madison Square Arabian Night."

30 Smith, *Biography,* p. 149.

31 Carroll, *op. cit.,* p. 140.

32 Letter from Sara Coleman Porter: Smith papers.

33 Carroll, *op. cit.,* p. 138.

34 Margaret Porter Cesare, "My O. Henry," *Mentor,* Feb., 1923, p. 19.

35 Letter from Sara Coleman Porter: Smith papers.

36 Hart MacArthur, *Graphic,* April 15, 1914: clipping in Greensboro papers.

37 Sara Coleman Porter, *Delineator,* p. 376.

[38] William Griffeth, "O. Henry at Work and Play," Dearborn *Independent*, Nov. 14, 1925, p. 24.

[39] The lease, signed on Nov. 13, is in the possession of John S. Mayfield, Bethesda, Md.

[40] Carroll, *op. cit.*, p. 140.

[41] New York *Sun*, Jan. 10, 1915: clipping in Greensboro papers.

[42] Hildegarde Hawthorne, "The Picturing of New York Life," *New York Times Book Review*, Nov. 21, 1908, p. 685.

[43] See F. L. Pattee, "The Journalization of American Literature," *Unpopular Review*, April–June, 1917, p. 374.

[44] Stephen Leacock, "The Amazing Genius of O. Henry," *Waifs and Strays*, p. 184.

[45] *Caliph*, p. 361.

[46] Interview with Anne Partlan: Smith papers.

[47] *Mentor*, Feb., 1923, p. 45.

[48] Seth Moyle, *op. cit.*, p. 30.

[49] Dearborn *Independent*, Nov. 14, 1925, p. 24. Griffeth says the letter was written "sometime in 1908," but since the story was not published until Dec., 1909, his memory evidently played him false in the dating.

[50] Letter dated Jan. 1, 1909: *South Atlantic Quarterly*, Jan., 1939, p. 34.

[51] Letter dated Feb. 13: *ibid.*, p. 34.

[52] Letter dated March 16: *ibid.*, p. 35.

[53] Letter dated April 6: *ibid.*, p. 37.

[54] Letter dated April 9: *ibid.*, p. 37.

[55] "The Misadventures in Musical Comedy of O. Henry and Franklin P. Adams," *Waifs and Strays*, p. 205.

[56] Letter from Arthur W. Page: Smith papers.

[57] *Waifs and Strays*, p. 209.

[58] John A. Lomax, "Harry Steger and O. Henry," *Southwest Review*, April, 1939, p. 299.

[59] *O. Henry Papers*, p. 21.

[60] *World's Work*, June, 1909, p. 11724.

[61] W. M. Van der Weyde, "Photographing O. Henry," *Mentor*, Feb., 1923, p. 40.

[62] *Bookman*, Aug., 1909, p. 579.

CHAPTER 13 (pages 231–247)

[1] Undated letter to Steger: "Rolling Stones," *Works*, p. 1089.

[2] Interview with Anne Partlan: Smith papers.

[3] Smith, *Biography*, p. 83.

[4] Harry P. Steger, "Some O. Henry Letters and the Plunkville Patriot," *Independent*, Sept. 5, 1912, p. 543.

[5] Sara Coleman Porter, "The Gift," *Delineator*, May, 1912, p. 376.

[6] *South Atlantic Quarterly*, Jan., 1939, p. 38.

[7] *Works*, p. 881.

[8] *Caliph*, p. 387.

[9] *South Atlantic Quarterly*, Jan., 1939, p. 38, Note 4.

[10] John A. Lomax, "Harry Steger and O. Henry," *Southwest Review*, April, 1939, p. 316.

[11] Margaret Porter Cesare, "My O. Henry," *Mentor*, Feb., 1923, p. 19.

[12] Dearborn *Independent*, Nov. 28, 1925, p. 27.

[13] Interview with Sara Coleman Porter: Raleigh *News and Observer*, Nov. 25, 1934, Section X, p. 2: clipping in Greensboro papers.

[14] *Nation*, Dec. 2, 1909, p. 540.

[15] Albert Parry, *Garrets and Pretenders* (New York, 1933), p. 172.

[16] Paul S. Clarkson, *A Bibliography of William Sydney Porter*, p. 143.

[17] Alexander Woollcott, "O. Henry Playwright," *Bookman*, Oct., 1922, p. 155.

[18] Statement of Judge Thomas A. Jones: *Caliph*, p. 369.

[19] This letter and the others quoted from those written to Tyler are from *Bookman*, Oct., 1922, pp. 155–157.

[20] Woollcott, *op. cit.*, p. 157.

[21] Margaret Porter Cesare, *op. cit.*, p. 20.

[22] *Delineator*, May, 1912, p. 446.

[23] William Griffeth, Dearborn *Independent*, Nov. 28, 1925, p. 3.

[24] Flo Field in New York *Daily Tribune*, July 24, 1910: clipping in Greensboro papers.

[25] Arthur W. Page, "Little Pictures of O. Henry," *Bookman*, Oct., 1913, pp. 176–177.

[26] Seth Moyle, *My Friend O. Henry*, p. 18.

[27] Will Irwin, "O. Henry, Man and Writer," *Cosmopolitan*, Sept., 1910, p. 447.

[28] *Nation*, April 7, 1910, p. 348.

[29] See headnote to "The Snow Man," *Works*, p. 1680.

[30] "A Talk with O. Henry," undated clipping from the *Mirror:* Greensboro papers.

[31] Seth Moyle, *op. cit.*, p. 31.

[32] Greensboro papers.

[33] Irwin, *op. cit.*, p. 447.

[34] *Caliph*, p. 370. Judge Jones dated the evening in 1909, on the evening

he and Porter attended a performance of *The Four Million*. Apparently Jones did not come to know Porter, however, until they occupied neighboring offices in Asheville in the late fall of 1909, and Porter was not in New York again until the spring of 1910. As to the performance of *The Four Million*, there is no record of such a dramatization. Perhaps Jones confused the title of the inscribed book with the play *Alias Jimmy Valentine*, and perhaps Porter was sufficiently deep in his cups to do likewise, or else the reference to *The Four Million* is merely to an evening of sightseeing.

[35] "Bob Davis Talks on *The Caliph of Bagdad*," *New York Times Book Review*, Jan. 5, 1941, p. 2.

[36] Interview with Dr. Hancock by Peggy Mitchell, Atlanta *Journal*, Jan. 3, 1926: clipping in Greensboro papers.

[37] Smith, *Biography*, p. 250.

[38] See Note 36.

[39] According to George MacAdam ("Crossways of 'Roads of Destiny,'" *New York Times Book Review*, June 3, 1923, p. 1). Cosgrave was telephoned and admitted to see Porter before Dr. Hancock ordered no visitors, after which Hall arrived and was refused admittance. Dr. Hancock, however, seemed to think it was Hall who had been admitted (Greensboro *Telegraph*, June 9, 1910: clipping in Greensboro papers).

[40] Statement of Dr. Hancock, Greensboro *Telegraph*, June 9, 1910: Greensboro papers.

[41] New York *Tribune*, June 6, 1910: clipping in Greensboro papers.

[42] George MacAdam (see Note 39), p. 1.

[43] The letter is quoted in an undated clipping in Greensboro *Daily News*: Greensboro papers.

[44] *Letters to Lithopolis*, p. xxv.

[45] "Roads of Destiny," *Works*, p. 355.

INDEX

• ᨄᨆᨇ •